God the Son

God the Son

What John's Portrait of Jesus Means and Why it Matters

RANDY RHEAUME

Foreword by Michael L. Brown

WIPF & STOCK · Eugene, Oregon

GOD THE SON
What John's Portrait of Jesus Means and Why it Matters

Wipf & Stock
An Imprint of Wipf and Stock Publishers
199 W. 8th Ave., Suite 3
Eugene, OR 97401

www.wipfandstock.com

PAPERBACK ISBN: 978-1-5326-3039-2
HARDCOVER ISBN: 978-1-5326-3041-5
EBOOK ISBN: 978-1-5326-3040-8

Manufactured in the U.S.A.   08/07/20

To my church family at
Stony Creek Church, Utica, Michigan

Contents

Illustrations and Diagrams

Permissions

Foreword

Have you often meditated on the mysteries of the Godhead but been unable to wrap your mind around exactly who our God is? Have you found yourself struggling to find adequate words to explain how God can be three and yet one? Have you spent time studying the prologue of John's Gospel (John 1:1–18), only to say, "This is too deep for me?"

Well, be encouraged. The book you are now reading is a godsend. You are about to find profound answers to these deep and difficult questions. Prepare to be enlightened and enriched.

Pastor Randy's doctoral dissertation was devoted to this very subject—John's portrait of God the Son—but dissertations are written for scholars, not average readers. And dissertations tend to be so specialized and focused that they make it all but impossible for the uninitiated to follow the (hopefully) brilliant points the authors are making. Unfortunately, many scholars are unable to make their work accessible to the masses, so others have to study their work, digest it, and then translate it into accessible form.

Thankfully, Randy is both an academic and a pastor, which means that every single week, he is breaking the bread of life for his congregation, making the difficult clear, and making the obscure practical. That's exactly what he has done in his book, even adding study questions at the end of each chapter along with a Scripture to memorize and an assignment to carry out. Talk about practical!

He has also made this study engaging, with topic headings like "The Frankenstein Jesus," to illustrate some wrong understandings of who exactly Jesus was, and with a chapter entitled, "God's Junior Partner," to illustrate a more correct understanding of who Jesus was and is. You will not easily forget illustrations like these.

What I also appreciate is that Randy tells you where he is going at the outset of the book, giving you a clear and readable map to help you navigate the chapters that follow. As I read through the chapter overview, I found myself saying, "Perfect! Those are some of the questions I have asked for years. So glad to see you tackling them!" And tackle them he does, with sound exegetical skills and solid theological foundations. He also does well to move from the Old Testament to the New, then to read the New Testament in light of relevant, ancient Jewish literature. As a Jewish believer in Jesus, I found this methodology refreshing.

And without being polemical or argumentative, Randy demolishes the positions of those who deny the deity of Jesus on the one side, and those who deny God's triunity on the other side. The scriptural evidence he adduces is overwhelming, and his logic is compelling.

From the first page to the last, I found Randy's study to be illuminating, engaging, and, in the end, satisfying. The pieces come together seamlessly, the verses make sense, without being forced, and Jesus is wonderfully glorified as God's unique Son. Your appreciation for him will be greatly enhanced by this practical and important book.

—Michael L. Brown, PhD
author, *Answering Jewish Objections to Jesus*, Vols. 1–5

Preface

It's been said, "If Jesus had never lived, we would not have been able to invent him."[1] That's especially the case for Jesus' portrait in John's Gospel. The Jesus we discover within its pages is as puzzling as he is profound. In the opening sentences, he's pegged as the eternal God who spoke the universe into existence, and yet we're told later that he cannot say or do a thing without the nod of his Father. How does one comprehend such a person?

I wrote most of this book during a sabbatical from my senior pastor duties at Stony Creek Church in Utica, Michigan. I am ultra grateful to the leaders and congregation for their enthusiastic support and gracious encouragement in granting me that time of refreshment and reflection to work on this project. On the other hand, this book has been on the drawing board most of my life—since my early days as a teenage Christ follower pondering the wonders of John's Jesus shortly after my conversion. Struck by his lightning back then, I have yet to recover. Jesus kindled a fire within me and has tended it throughout the decades I've known him.

I was born to write this book. My published PhD dissertation was my scholarly contribution to the topic. But the book you are reading is for people wanting to know who John's Jesus is and why it matters to us. I've kept the technical terminology to a bare minimum; the footnotes provide some additional explanations and resources. If you wish to dig into the scholarly details, I refer you to my technical book on the subject: *An Exegetical and Theological Analysis of the Son's Relationship to the Father in John's Gospel: God's Equal and Subordinate.*

The goal of this book is to show how the contrasts in John's portrait of Jesus (especially his deity and his sonship) fit together and are meaningful for the Christian life. This is not a study on everything John has to say about Jesus or God. That would require a much longer book. My focus here

---

1. Yancey, *Jesus I Never Knew*, 23, attributed in paraphrase to Wink, *Engaging Powers*, 129.

is much narrower. I'm seeking to answer questions such as, is Jesus really God? If so, what difference does it make? How can he be God and yet be in submission to God? Why didn't he ever say, "I am God! Worship me!"? How does the Son's role differ from the Father's? If God is more than one person, how do prayer and worship work? How can I know God better? What will make eternity with God so fun that we'll never get bored? Is the Trinity truly biblical? And where does the Holy Spirit come into the picture? I'm convinced John's Gospel provides profound insight into these and related matters.

Many people deserve my heartfelt gratitude for their encouragement, assistance, and thoughtful insight as I've written this book. First on the list is my loving and supportive wife, Debbie—whose inspiration means so much to me—and also my natural family and church family that show me Christ-like kindness light years beyond my merits. Special thanks to my dear friend and co-worker, Chris Bourdeau, Executive Pastor at Stony Creek Church, for creating the artwork illustrations for this book. Also, sincere thanks to Dr. Michael Brown for taking time from his demanding ministry schedule to read a draft of the manuscript and write the foreword. Thanks as well to those in my church who read the manuscript and offered helpful suggestions and encouragement. I'm also grateful to the many dialogue partners (both advocates and critics!) I've had over the years (far too numerous to list!) who've sharpened my thinking on this topic. God bless you all!

Acknowledgments

Many thanks to Wm B. Eerdmans Publishing Company in Grand Rapids, Michigan, for permission to use the chart on page 141 of Gary M. Burge, *The Anointed Community: The Holy Spirit in the Johannine Tradition*, 1987.

Abbreviations

Ant.	Josephus, *Jewish Antiquities*
Apoc. Ab.	*Apocalypse of Abraham* (OT Pseudepigrapha)
AT	Author's Translation
1–2 Bar.	*1–2 Baruch* (OT Pseudepigrapha)
BD	Beloved Disciple (John)
BDAG	*Bauer, Danker, Arndt, and Gingrich. A Greek-English Lexicon of the New Testament and Other Early Christian Literature*
BDF	Blass, F., A. Debrunner, and R. W. Funk. *A Greek Grammar of the New Testament and Other Early Christian Literature*
Bel	Bel and the Dragon (OT Apocrypha)
Ber.	*Berakhot (Mishnah)*
BU(s)	Biblical Unitarian(s)
CEB	Common English Bible
CEV	Contemporary English Version
Cherubim	Philo, *On the Cherubim* (*De cherubim*)
1–2 Chr	1–2 Chronicles
chs.	chapters
Creation	Philo, *On the Creation* (*De Opificio Mundi*)
CSB	Christian Standard Bible
Decal.	Philo, *The Decalogue* (*De Decalogo*)
Dom.	Suetonius, *Twelve Caesars, Domitian*
1 En.	*1 Enoch* (*Ethiopic Apocalypse*, OT Pseudepigrapha)
2 En.	*2 Enoch* (*Slavonic Apocalypse*, OT Pseudepigrapha)
Eph	Ephesians

esp.	especially
ESV	English Standard Version
Exod	Exodus
Ezek	Ezekiel
FA	Farewell Address
FST	Father/Son Talk (John 5:16–46)
Gal	Galatians
Gen	Genesis
GNT	Good News Translation
GOD'S WORD	God's Word Translation
HALOT	*The Hebrew and Aramaic Lexicon of the Old Testament*
Heb	Hebrews
Hos	Hosea
Isa	Isaiah
Jas	James
Jdt	*Judith* (OT Apocrypha)
Jer	Jeremiah
Jn	John
Jos. Asen.	*Joseph and Aseneth* (OT Pseudepigrapha)
JSNTSS	Journal for the Study of the New Testament Supplement Series
Judg	Judges
JW(s)	Jehovah's Witness(es)
Ker.	*Kerithot (Mishnah)*
1–4 Kgdms	1–4 Kingdoms (LXX)
1–2 Kgs	1–2 Kings
LEB	Lexham English Bible
Lk	Luke
LXX	Septuagint
m.	*The Mishnah*
1–2 Macc	1–2 Maccabees (OT Apocrypha)
3–4 Macc	3–4 Maccabees (OT Pseudepigrapha)
Mal	Malachi
Matt	Matthew
Mk	Mark

NAB	New American Bible
NASB	New American Standard Bible
NEB	New English Bible
Neh	Nehemiah
NET	New English Translation
NETS	*A New English Translation of the Septuagint*
NIRV	New International Readers Version
NIV	New International Version
NLT	New Living Translation
NRSV	New Revised Standard Version
NKJV	New King James Version
NT	New Testament
NWT	New World Translation
OT	Old Testament
1–2 Pet	1–2 Peter
Phil	Philippians
Prov	Proverbs
Ps(s)	Psalm(s)
Pss. Sol	Psalms of Solomon (OT Pseudepigrapha)
REB	Revised English Bible
Rev	Revelation
Rom	Romans
1–2 Sam	1–2 Samuel
Sanh.	*Sanhedrin (Mishnah)*
Sib. Or.	*Sibylline Oracles* (OT Pseudepigrapha)
Sir	Sirach/Ecclesiasticus (OT Apocrypha)
SNTSMS	Society for New Testament Studies Monograph Series
1–2 Thess	1–2 Thessalonians
1–2 Tim	1–2 Timothy
Tob	Tobit (OT Apocrypha)
WBC	Word Biblical Commentary
Wis	Wisdom (OT Apocrypha)
WUNT	Wissenschaftliche Untersuchungen zum Neuen Testament
Zech	Zechariah
Zeph	Zephaniah

CHAPTER 1

Entering John's World

The Gospel of John a weird and confusing book? When I first heard John characterized this way, it was like a punch in the gut. The description came from an unchurched coworker named Mike. I met and became friends with Mike while I was working a summer job before I entered college. In an attempt to share with Mike about Jesus, I had given him a New Testament (NT for short) and suggested he start by reading John's Gospel. I did so because I had always heard John was the best ice-breaker Bible book for an unbeliever. John is the clearest and most direct at explaining Jesus' identity and God's plan of salvation. In fact, it was written for the express purpose of convincing people to believe Jesus is the Christ, the Son of God (20:31).

All true! But Mike had no experience reading the Bible and knew next to nothing about Jesus and Christianity. To my surprise the opening sentences of John sounded otherworldly, philosophical, and mystical to Mike. John begins by saying,

> In the beginning was the Word, and the Word was with God, and the Word was God. He was with God in the beginning. Through him all things were made; without him nothing was made that has been made. In him was life, and that life was the light of all mankind. The light shines in the darkness, and the darkness has not overcome it. (Jn 1:1–5)

"I don't get it," he said frankly. "The author is talking in circles. And what or who is this 'Word'? What's this all supposed to mean?" I was a newbie Jesus follower back then, and yet I had already faced numerous objections to my faith—from skeptics, Jehovah's Witnesses, and many others. But Mike was not objecting as much as sincerely questioning the meaning of words that were so familiar to and cherished by me. I assumed their face-value meaning could be easily understood by anyone who would simply read them. This was a wake-up call, reminding me that a gap of two thousand years and half the globe's distance separates our world from John's.

Since that conversation with Mike decades ago, John's Gospel has become an intense object of study for me. I have immersed myself in John's world. In my earliest days as a Christ-follower, I was thunderstruck by the awesomeness of John's Jesus, and I've never recovered. He both alarms and dazzles me. He freshens my faith and whets my appetite for worship. He also puzzles me with his enigmatic and elusive sayings. Just when I think I've figured him out in one place, he baffles me in another. John's Jesus simply refuses to be tamed.

As a senior pastor for decades, I've taught John's Gospel in countless Bible studies, sermons, and courses. With sheer delight I've used Jesus' words in John to lead many to embrace Jesus as Lord and Savior and have counseled many a troubled person. As a scholar of the NT, I have read through John (and the entire NT) numerous times in its original Greek and have earned a PhD studying John's unique view of Jesus in relation to God the Father. To me every book of the Bible is precious, like a cherished mentor and friend, but as far as I'm concerned, nothing in Scripture compares to the four NT Gospels—Matthew, Mark, Luke, and John. They reveal to us God's personal visit to this planet as one of us, along with his matchless teachings, his atoning sacrifice for our sins, and his triumph over death. How could anything top that? For me, John is the first among equals. If the books of the Bible were mountain ranges, the Gospels would be the Himalayas, and John would be Mount Everest. And yet even after decades of basking in John's awesomeness and studying it at the highest level, I still think back to Mike's perplexity nearly every time I launch afresh into John 1. The "Word" we meet there is distinct from God and yet somehow the same. What does this mean and why does it matter to us? Addressing that question is what this book is about.

IS THIS BOOK FOR YOU?

Does knowing God in a profound and personal way interest you? If so, do you desire God enough to think long and hard about him? If not, this book will not appeal to you. Don't bother reading any further. Does digging into Scripture deeply to discover the author's original meaning interest you? If not, don't bother reading any further.

Many Christian books about Jesus on the market today are devotional in style. They explain scriptural concepts with interesting stories and clever analogies but little interaction with the nuts and bolts of the biblical text. Other books are focused more on biblical study or theological concerns without much application to your everyday walk with the Lord. Books of both sorts can be extremely useful.

In this book, however, my target is both your intellect as well as your daily relationship with God—to look carefully at the biblical text of John to discover its original meaning and then to draw out its practical implications for your life. Prepare to stretch your mind by diving into the culture and history of John's Jesus. Our understanding and application of Scripture must be grounded in a firm grasp of the author's meaning (i.e., his original intent)—not our cultural biases or traditions that have accrued over the centuries. John's Gospel is all about revealing God to us through his Son, Jesus. Prepare to expand your mind and enlarge your soul by encountering John's challenge to know the Father as Jesus knows him.

You can read this book as either a novice or an advanced student of Scripture. For those of you who are new to biblical studies, I've tried to keep the technical jargon to a bare minimum, and when I use more specialized terms, I explain them as simply as I can. If you're a seasoned Bible researcher, you'll find further explanations and documentation in the footnotes, which I've also tried to keep to a minimum.[1]

For full disclosure, I am an evangelical, Trinitarian follower of Jesus. Like everyone else, I have my own biases. All of us come with a background of experiences (both good and bad) and beliefs (whether true or false). One of my working assumptions is that the Christian faith, rightly understood, can withstand the toughest scrutiny. I have devoted my adult life to examining and testing the foundations of my worldview. I have embraced the Bible as God's written revelation—his fully trustworthy and authoritative word. I begin from a Christian worldview in which Jesus' full deity (i.e., his "godness") is believed as a central truth revealed in sacred Scripture. Regarding the topic of this book, I have made it my goal, especially in this lifelong study, to check my biases and consider contrary viewpoints as fairly and objectively as I can. My aim is to go where the evidence leads, even if it takes me where I would not prefer to go. My sincere desire is to learn from those who disagree with me as we dialogue as friends. Whether you agree or disagree with me, I welcome your company in this conversation.

1. To probe the topic of this book in greater depth and with much fuller documentation, see my revised and published PhD dissertation, Rheaume, An *Exegetical and Theological Analysis of the Son's Relationship to the Father in John's Gospel: God's Equal and Subordinate*.

WHO'S THE WORD?

The opening eighteen verses of John's Gospel (often called the Prologue) inform us that Jesus is the key that unlocks the door to knowing God genuinely and deeply. Again verse 1 says, "In the beginning was the Word, and the Word was with God, and the Word was God" (Jn 1:1).

Picture John's Gospel as a play. When the curtain opens for the first scene, only two characters are present on an otherwise empty stage—the Word and God. Nothing else exists because the universe has yet to be created. The Word and God are together, two distinct entities. But then comes the explosive third clause of the narrator's first line: "and the Word was God." This five-word statement has puzzled many a brilliant mind. Are the Word and God two distinct characters or somehow the same? In verse 3 we're told that "all things" were made "through" the Word. Emphatically, John insists that nothing has ever been created apart from this Word. Somehow the Word participated in making all creation. Apparently, the Word is not a created thing, but exists with God outside of the realm of creation. But what or who is this Word?

If you're familiar with the biblical story of creation found in Genesis 1, you can hear a conspicuous echo of it here in John 1. John's Gospel is written within a first-century Jewish framework and is heavily indebted to the Hebrew Bible (what Christians call the Old Testament—or OT for short). Genesis (the first book of the OT) opens with the famous words, "In the beginning God created. . ." (Gen 1:1). John opens the same way, but in the place where our ears expect to hear "God," we instead hear "the Word." Has John smuggled something new into the creation story? Not really. Interestingly, when we look closely at Genesis 1, we find God creates by using words. He speaks and creation happens! When he says, "Let there be light," light instantly appears. Throughout Genesis 1, God creates merely by speaking words that bring creation into being.

As the Hebrew songwriter put it in the Book of Psalms,

> By the word of the LORD
>   the heavens were made,
>   their starry host by the
>   breath of his mouth. . .
> For he spoke, and it came to be;
>   he commanded, and it stood firm. (Psalm 33:6, 9)

Like Genesis 1, this psalm says God's "word" brought creation into being. But when we come to John 1:1, John speaks of this Word (with a capital

W in most English translations) as an entity apparently who is distinct from God, and yet in the last clause of the sentence is somehow "God" as well.

As we will discover later in this book, the Word is God's authorized speaker, the one who talks and acts for God. We might say he's God's voice.[2] Think for a moment about your voice. It's a genuine feature that is distinctly and uniquely yours. On the other hand, your voice is certainly not all there is to you. You can speak of your voice as distinct from you, and yet it's a real part of what makes you who and what you are. Likewise, God's voice is a genuine property of God himself, and yet there's more to God than his voice. As far as John is concerned, God's voice is the primary means humans have of hearing directly from God. When God speaks, he invariably uses his voice. Whenever God speaks or interacts personally with the world, his voice (i.e., the Word) does the talking. But what or who is this Word?

If we keep reading down to the fourteenth verse, the mystery is solved: "The Word became flesh and made his dwelling among us. We have seen his glory, the glory of the one and only Son, who came from the Father." Here we discover two more crucial facts about the Word: 1) the "Word" is a term used to describe Jesus before he became human (i.e., before he became the man, Jesus), and 2) the Word is the only Son of the Father; his human name is Jesus. Back in verse 1 the Word (or Son) is directly called "God," as he is in two other places in John (1:18; 20:28).

The Son is actually no less than God himself! He is God's voice—truly God and yet not all there is to God. In fact, most of the time in John (and the rest of the NT) it is the Father who is called God. The word "God" in the singular (Greek *theos*) is used over 80 times in John's Gospel, and in nearly every case it refers to the Father, not the Son. Jesus is directly called God only three times (1:1, 18; 20:28). Why would this be? If the Son is God right alongside God the Father, why is he so infrequently addressed as God?

HOW CAN HE BE GOD?

Even more puzzling, if Jesus is God, why is he also called "the Son of God?" How can he be both God and God's Son? The traditional Christian answer is that the one true God is a Trinity of persons[3]—the Father, the Son, and the

---

2. The idea to refer to the Word as God's voice was inspired by *The Voice Bible*.

3. When I use the word "person" in reference to the members of the Trinity, I mean a mind without a body—or unembodied mind—similar to what we think of when we refer to the "soul" or "spirit" of a human being. It's the nonphysical part of you. A person in the Trinitarian sense possesses intellect, emotion, and free choice, but no body. Jesus taught that God is spirit (Jn 4:24), that is, God is a nonphysical being. The teaching of the Trinity is that the one true God exists eternally in three distinct persons. Of course,

Holy Spirit. But if this is the case (and I believe it is), why doesn't John or any biblical writer ever use the word "trinity" to describe God? Many who reject the teaching of the Trinity ask, "Where in the Bible does Jesus ever say, 'I am God. Worship me!'?" He never does.

Actually, these are excellent questions; we can't afford to dodge them. If the Bible is God's written word and our supreme authority about all matters it addresses (and I believe it is), we must let it speak for itself. Why, if John's Jesus is truly God, does he say he can do nothing by himself (5:30) apart from what he sees the Father doing (5:19)? Christians often point to John's Gospel as the Bible book that most clearly and forcefully affirms that Jesus is truly God. I agree. But if it is, why does John's Jesus say he cannot perform a single task or even utter a syllable unless his Father tells him to do so?[4] How can God be totally dependent on God? Repeatedly throughout John, Jesus insists that he's completely submitted to his Father.[5] But how can God be in submission to anyone? John's Jesus famously says, "[T]he Father is greater than I" (14:28). But how can anyone be greater than God? Perhaps strangest of all, the resurrected Jesus declares that the Father is *his* God (20:17). But how can the one true God have a God who is over him? When John calls Jesus "God," does he mean God in the full sense or something less? Or might John believe in more than one God?

The Frankenstein Jesus

These questions have puzzled readers of John for centuries, and they have attempted to solve the difficulties in various ways. For example, some biblical scholars have argued that the writer of John's Gospel clumsily edited together various contradictory strands of teaching about Jesus which were current in the late first century AD. The texts supporting Jesus' complete dependence on God represent early teaching that understood Jesus as a mere human whom God used in extraordinary ways—a great prophet or ideal man—but by no means God's equal. (Scholars often refer to views of Jesus like this in the early church as *low Christology*.) But the passages that make Jesus out to be God, says this theory, represent more developed thinking, decades later, as some Christians had come to regard Jesus as coequal

---

the Trinity doctrine also asserts that one of these three persons, namely the Son, joined himself with genuine humanity when he became a flesh-and-blood man in Jesus Christ and therefore also possesses a human body and soul. But his case is unique. The Father and the Holy Spirit remain unembodied.

4. Jn 8:28; 12:49–50.

5. See Jn 5:19, 30; 6:38; 7:16, 28; 10:32; 14:48, 31; 17:4; 20:17.

with God the Father. (Scholars often call this view of Jesus *high Christology*.) Thus, according to this viewpoint, John's Jesus is like the Frankenstein monster—a mishmash of makeshift parts. He's a jumbled hodge-podge of low and high Christology with many built-in contradictions.

But this theory has major problems. John's Gospel is a cohesive literary unit.[6] It is unwarranted speculation to carve it up into a collection of mismatched scraps, as if the author—a literary genius by all accounts—sutured them together into a hybrid monstrosity. But if so, why then do we find John's Jesus described in both lofty and lowly terms?

"The Word was a god"

Others throughout the centuries have approached the issue by insisting that only the Father is truly God. After all, God, as revealed in the OT Scriptures, is one and only one. The most frequently quoted OT text among Jesus' people—the Jews—in his day was Deuteronomy 6:4, which reads, "Hear, O Israel: The Lord our God, the Lord is one." This view says that texts such as John 1:1, 18, and 20:28 have been misunderstood as identifying Jesus as God in the full sense. The Jehovah's Witnesses (JWs for short), for example, claim that John 1:1c should be properly translated, "the Word was a god" (NWT). Thus the Word is a secondary god, whom the JWs claim is a created deity, not *the* Almighty God who alone is uncreated.[7]

But this view has to contend with the fact that Jesus, his early followers, and the writers of the NT strongly adhered to the Jewish belief in only one true God. (We'll discuss this belief in more detail in chapter 2.) John's Jesus himself calls his Father "the only true God" (17:3). If Jesus is another god, is he a false god? Or is he perhaps not *as truly* God as the Father is God? But if that is so, what are we to make of the bold declarations of Jesus' deity in John? We'll probe this question later in the book.

6. See the scholarly work of Anderson, *Christology of the Fourth Gospel.*

7. The ancient name for this position is Arianism. Others who defend this view include Dixon, "Arian View," 65–83, and former Jehovah's Witness Stafford, *Jehovah's Witnesses Defended to Scholars.*

God's Photograph

Others deny Jesus' deity using a different approach. Some claim that the Word in John 1:1 is not a person but God's impersonal self-expression. Prior to Jesus' earthly life, says this theory, the Word was not a "he" but an "it." In other words, this view claims the Word was not a personal entity prior to the earthly life of Jesus of Nazareth; it was God's plan and activity, not a conscious person. But when the Word was made flesh (John 1:14), the man Jesus (a separate entity) was endowed with the Word (perhaps at Jesus' birth or baptism) and became the embodiment of God's self-revelation. Thus, according to this view, Jesus is perfect humanity as God intended it—the unmarred image of God (Gen 1:26). He so perfectly represents God that we might say he is God's human face. He represents God but is not God himself.

In this view (often called Biblical Unitarianism or Socinianism[8]), we might say the Son is like God's photograph. If I show you an iPhone photo of my wife and say, "This is Debbie, my wife," you don't assume I'm married to a digital image on a smartphone. Everyone knows a photo is not the person but only a picture of the person. Likewise, Biblical Unitarians and some well-known NT scholars maintain that Jesus is the perfect representation of God, but not God himself. As such, the Jesus we find in John is a human being, endowed with God's Spirit, who talks like God, acts like God, and should even, to a large degree, be treated as God. Just as the photo of Debbie can be called "my wife," Jesus can be called by Thomas, "My Lord and my God" (Jn 20:28), because to see Jesus is to see the Father (Jn 14:9), and thus to address Jesus is to address the Father. But when push comes to shove, Jesus is not *truly* God; he's only God's perfect representative. As God's Son, Jesus is the "spitting image" of his Father—his "selfie." He is the ideal agent of God. This viewpoint claims to balance monotheism (belief in only one God) with the many texts that state or imply Jesus' deity.

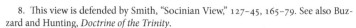

But this view has some major problems. For one, it has to deal with Jesus' statements in John that strongly indicate he existed as a genuine person with the Father *before* his earthly life and was then sent into the world by the Father.[9] This couldn't be so if the Word was merely God's self-expression (i.e., not an actual person) before

---

8. This view is defended by Smith, "Socinian View," 127–45, 165–79. See also Buzzard and Hunting, *Doctrine of the Trinity.*

9. See, for example, Jn 3:13; 6:33, 38, 46, 51, 58; 8:23, 38, 42; 9:39; 10:36; 12:46; 16:28.

Jesus' earthly life. We also find evidence that the Son is called "God" in the full sense. Another problem is that John's Jesus says and does things that the OT Scriptures claim only God himself can say and do. Nonetheless, this view of Jesus has some formidable defenders. But can it stand up to close scrutiny? We'll examine it further in subsequent chapters.

God's Three Faces

Another viewpoint claims that Jesus the Son is the same person as the Father rather than a distinct person. It is only in respect to his mission to save humanity as a man that he is the Son of God. Some people get this view confused with Trinitarianism, even some untaught Christians who say they believe in the Trinity, as did I as a newbie Christian. But this viewpoint rejects the Trinitarian understanding of God in favor of what is often called the "Oneness" perspective.[10] God is one person who manifests himself sometimes as the Father and sometimes as the Son. Father and Son, in this view, are two different roles God plays, just as I am a son (to my parents) and a father (to my two daughters and son). Yet I'm just one person. God, we might say, is one person with two faces (or three if we include the Holy Spirit). Scholars often refer to this perspective (which has taken various forms from ancient times) by the terms "modalism" or "Sabellianism." God is one person who, we might say, wears three different hats—Father, Son, and Holy Spirit.

But this view has major difficulty explaining texts that clearly indicate the Father and the Son are two distinct persons. (We'll address the Holy Spirit later in this book.) For example, Jesus says to the Jewish religious leaders, "In your own Law it is written that the testimony of two witnesses is true. I am one who testifies for myself; my other witness is the Father, who sent me" (Jn 8:17–18). If Jesus and the Father were really only one person,  this statement would be misleading at best. True, Jesus says that he and the Father are "one" (Jn 10:30), but he also prays that his followers may all be "one," as well (17:11). This surely doesn't mean they're one and the same person. Whatever else we might say about the Father and the Son, it's hard to deny they are two distinct persons.

10. The most detailed modern-day defense of this viewpoint known to me is by David Norris in *I AM: A Oneness Pentecostal Theology*. On a more popular level are the works of David Bernard, including *Essentials of Oneness Theology*.

God at the Round Table

Worlds away from the views discussed so far are those who see Jesus, God's Son, as fully equal in every sense with God the Father. Some evangelical Christians see the Father, Son, and Holy Spirit not only as fully God but also with no first among equals—i.e., no permanent leader of the Trinity.[11] In other words, the Trinity has no eternal chairperson at the head of the table who directs the other two members. Instead, we might picture the arrangement as a group of three coequal persons seated at a round table among whom there is no particular leader. The group works as a team of rankless equals. The Round Table perspective is sometimes called the *egalitarian* view of the Trinity. The one God exists as a council of three distinct and coequal members with no one assuming the lead among them. They are ever and always coequals.

The only exception to this eternal arrangement, according to this view, is in regard to Jesus' earthly mission. In his role as Messiah and Savior of the world, Jesus humbled himself and became an obedient servant to his heavenly Father. But after this, he resumed his glorious status of full equality with the Father in every respect. Note the apostle Paul's words in his letter to the Philippians:

> Have this mind among yourselves, which is yours in Christ Jesus, who, though he was in the form of God, did not count equality with God a thing to be grasped, but emptied himself, by taking the form of a servant, being born in the likeness of men. And being found in human form, he humbled himself by becoming obedient to the point of death, even death on a cross. Therefore God has highly exalted him and bestowed on him the name that is above every name, so that at the name of Jesus every knee should bow, in heaven and on earth and under the earth, and every tongue confess that Jesus Christ is Lord, to the glory of God the Father. (Phil 2:5–11 ESV)

Unfortunately, we can't linger here to discuss the fascinating details of this amazing passage.[12] But in brief, like John 1:1, this text speaks of Christ's preexistence (i.e., before he became a man) when he existed with the Father

---

11. Scholars who defend this view include Millard Erickson in *Who's Tampering with the Trinity?*; Kevin Giles in *Jesus and the Father*; and Royce Gruenler, *Trinity in the Gospel.*

12. See Hill, *Paul and the Trinity*, 77–110.

as an unembodied person "in the form of God" (v. 6). This is often referred
to as Christ's *preincarnate state*—i.e., his status as an unembodied person
before he became the man Jesus. But notice this text goes on to say that
instead of grasping equality with God, Christ took the form of a servant and
became human—ultimately lowering himself to the point of a criminal's
death on a cross. After lowering himself to such an extent in obedience to
God, his Father exalted him to the very highest place, even giving him the
highest name of all.

Many Christians point to this text to solve the dilemma of the lofty
and the lowly texts about Jesus. God's Son was God's equal in his preincarnate state, but then when he became human, he voluntarily surrendered
his heavenly lifestyle and rights and took the role of a servant. His role
changed, but he was still the same person. Picture a king who takes off his
royal clothes, puts on cheap, worn-out clothing, and leaves his palace to live
among his subjects as a homeless person. He's still the king, of course, but
let's say he chooses not to use any of his rights as king. He would not look
like or be treated as a king, even though he truly is. Similarly, we might say
this passage indicates Christ took off his heavenly robes of glory to live as
a man in order to serve God and us—ultimately by giving his life on the
cross. But then God restored Christ to his preincarnate glory. This text in
Philippians is hugely helpful in understanding how Jesus could be God and
yet get tired, thirsty, hungry, be tempted, and die. As a true man, he could
experience the limitations of humanity. He had to grow in wisdom (Lk 2:52)
and even experienced lack of knowledge (Mk 13:32). The Son voluntarily
and temporarily restricted himself in order to serve his Father and save us.
It's an awesome demonstration of love and humility for us to follow.

But does this insight solve the question of the Son's subordination to
the Father? Those who take the Round Table approach say that in eternity
(i.e., outside of time), God the Father and his Son exist as fully equal. It is
only in regard to Christ's earthly mission that he is subordinate to God the
Father. Thus when Jesus says, "[T]he Father is greater than I" (John 14:28),
for example, he speaks from his role as an obedient, human servant—not
from his preincarnate status of total equality with the Father. Some advocates of the Round Table view have suggested that the Father, Son, and
Spirit mutually decided on this course of action in eternity past. In what
we might call a heavenly council meeting, it was mutually decided that the
Son—the second member of the Trinity—would become a true man, live on
earth in full dependence on the Father, and obtain redemption for the world
through his death and resurrection. In regard to his human nature and his
role as humanity's Savior, he would be submissive to the Father. But as God
the eternal Son, he is, always has been, and always will be the Father's and

the Spirit's full equal. In time and space, the Son submits to the Father, but in eternity they are coequals in every sense.

This view has some considerable strengths. For one, it affirms that the Son is fully God, not simply God's representative or an inferior, created god. As we will see, the biblical evidence in and outside of John strongly affirms the Son's full deity. The Round Table view also seems to avoid the trap of making the Father and the Son the same person. The Father and Son are two distinct persons, not simply one person with multiple personalities or roles.

But the Round Table view also has some weighty weaknesses. As we will see, relegating all the subordination texts to Jesus' earthly mission is no easy task. Even in John 1:1, for instance, the Word occupies the secondary role of the spokesperson (the voice), rather than the person who initiates the speaking (i.e., God, later identified as the Father). Notice that this is *before* his earthly mission. Like this text, many biblical passages seem to portray the Son in submission to the Father in their eternal relations, not just during Jesus' earthly mission. John's Gospel accentuates this portrayal. Can the Round Table view answer these objections or is there a better approach that avoids all the weaknesses noted so far?

First among Equals

Have you ever seen the famous Norman Rockwell painting known as "Freedom from Want"? It pictures a happy gathering of family and friends seated for Thanksgiving dinner. An aging and kindly father stands at the head of the table with his wife next to him about to place a large, delicious-looking cooked turkey onto the table before the eager onlookers. Rockwell's painting depicts an ideal portrayal of what many would call a traditional family. Though the idea of the father as the head of the household is vanishing in much of our culture, it was once thought to be the norm. This patriarchal view of the family was universally accepted in biblical times.

The First among Equals view understands the Father as the head of the Trinity family. The Father, the Son, and the Spirit are coequal in nature (i.e., in what they are), but God the Father is the first among equals—not just during Jesus' earthly mission, but throughout eternity. He's the head of the family—the leader of the Trinity.

Critics of this view believe there can be no true equality if one person is forever the leader while the others remain permanent subordinates. Some argue this view of God paves the way for oppression from abuses of power. Nevertheless, I believe the biblical evidence fully supports this view of God. In this book, I contend the Son is fully equal to his Father in his deity (his godness) and yet subordinate in his sonship role.[13] Unlike many abusive fathers and authority figures in our world, God the Father is the perfect model of loving leadership.

JOHN WHO?

The Gospel of John itself does not name its author. Most NT scholars believe the title ("Gospel According to John") was tacked on quite a while after the book was written and is not a reliable guide to the actual author's identity. Several suggestions have been offered by scholars—many of whom believe the book went through various editions in which a number of writers, in a close-knit, likeminded Christian community, contributed to it along the way.

My own view is that the traditional answer—long discarded by most NT scholars—is more plausible than any of the alternative suggestions that have been offered.[14] Until modern times the early testimony of the church was accepted by virtually all scholars—that the Gospel of John was written by the once-fisherman apostle John, the son of Zebedee, one of Jesus' original twelve apostles (cf. Mk 1:19–20). Most biblical scholars today, however, have concluded otherwise. Could an unschooled fisherman (cf. Acts 4:13) who spoke Aramaic as his first language have composed such a literary masterpiece, especially in Greek? Fair question.

Taking statements in the book at face value, the author claims to be an eyewitness to the events he reports and a close follower of Jesus.[15] This close

---

13. I have argued for this view at length in my technical monograph, *Exegetical and Theological Analysis*. Though my work concentrates on the biblical data—primarily in John—I also believe my position reflects the historic Trinitarian view. See also the excellent volume by Michael Ovey, *Your Will be Done*. A good treatment of the subject in general (not just in John) is the Dennis Jowers and H. Wayne House book *New Evangelical Subordinationism?*, which features essays from evangelical scholars on both sides of the debate, discussing the topic from biblical, theological, and historical perspectives. For a discussion of John's view of Jesus from an egalitarian viewpoint, see Akala, "Sonship, Sending, and Subordination in the Gospel of John."

14. NT scholars have debated the question of John's authorship at great length. If you're interested in learning more about the nontraditional theories that have been offered, I suggest Brown, *Introduction to the Gospel*, esp. 189–219; Culpepper, *John, the Son of Zebedee*, 56–88; Bauckham, *Jesus and the Eyewitnesses*, 550–89. For a defense of the traditional position, which I embrace, see Carson and Moo, *Introduction to the New Testament*, 229–54.

15. Jn 1:14; 19:35; 20:2, 8; esp. 21:20–25

follower refers to himself obliquely as "the disciple whom Jesus loved."[16]
As we will see in a later chapter, the mystery that surrounds this intimate
nickname plays a strategic role in shedding light on Jesus' relationship to his
Father and our relationship to Jesus. Another intriguing detail is that this
disciple is associated closely with the apostle Peter in the book. This would
fit John the Son of Zebedee nicely because he is a close companion of Peter
in other NT writings.[17] Also, according to findings in recent decades, it's
likely that the author of John was deeply rooted in Jewish ideas that were
common in first-century Israel.[18] This is precisely what we would expect
if an eyewitness such as the apostle John wrote the book. As for his lack
of education, John could have received help with the mechanics of writing from educated and highly-skilled friends. Finally, some scholars have
argued in recent years that the titles of the NT Gospels go back much earlier
(i.e., closer in time to the composition of the books) and are more reliable
than generally assumed.[19] If so, this would bolster the case that the title of
John's Gospel is spot on, rather than just the pious guess of an ignorant edi-
tor. Overall, although the case for the apostle John's authorship is not a slam
dunk, it's quite credible and often dismissed without due consideration.

Church tradition places the apostle John in the city of Ephesus in Asia
Minor in his later years. Most scholars believe the book reached its final
form in the 90s AD—some 60 years after the events narrated in the book.
Throughout his long adult life, John undoubtedly communicated his deeply
pondered account of Jesus' story to numerous congregations of Christ-followers on countless occasions. The book may have been a longtime project
that he carefully honed over the years and then finally completed shortly
before his death as a very old man.

John's Backstory

What was going on in John's world that might have prompted him to write
what we call the Gospel of John? Scholarly theories abound! In recent decades one popular approach is to envision a tight-knit community of Jewish
Christians who were recently ousted from their local synagogues for their
faith in Jesus as God's Son. According to this viewpoint, the harsh encounters
between Jesus and the Jewish leaders we see in John reflect the bitter conflict

---

16. As found in the NIV at Jn 13:23; 21:7, 20 and with slightly different wording in
19:26; 20:2; 21:17, 20.

17. Mark 5:37; 9:2; 14:33; Luke 22:8; Acts 3:1, 11; 4:1,3, 7, 13, 19, 23; 8:14, 17, 25.

18. See, for example, Charlesworth, "Johannine Community," 46–51.

19. See Hengel, *Four Gospels*, 96–106, and more recently Pitre, *Case for Jesus*, 12–38.

many decades later between the Christian Jews in John's community and the wider non-Christian Jewish community. John's account, then, is actually a two-level drama that tells the story of Jesus on the surface level in order to speak pointedly to these dejected believers on another level.[20] Because this community of Jewish Jesus followers was so cloistered and separated from other Christians, John's Gospel employs lots of insider language that outsiders miss. But in order for John to make his two-level drama work, several elements from his later life setting have been awkwardly retrofitted back into the book's story of Jesus.

I do not embrace this approach.[21] But I think certain elements of it are correct. Most importantly, John and his circle of Jewish and non-Jewish Jesus followers had likely clashed with non-Christian Jews about Jesus' identity, especially the claim that Jesus is not only the Messiah but also God. Virtually all first-century Jews strongly embraced the belief that there is only one true God, a doctrine known as *monotheism*. But Christian Jews, who confessed and worshiped Jesus as God, would seem to non-Christian Jews to be blasphemous traitors of their most cherished and foundational beliefs.

This would explain John's strong emphasis on Jesus' deity as well as his insistence that the Son fully submits to the Father. Contrary to the claims of the non-Christian Jews, the Jesus Christians worship is no rival deity to the one true God. He's actually God's unique Son who, like a natural son, possesses the same nature and attributes as his Father. Yes, God is indeed one. No argument there. But John maintains, in accordance with OT precedent and other NT teaching, that one must understand God's oneness as a perfect unity of persons rather than as a mathematical singularity. While there is only one God, there is more to God than just the Father. In other words, John's view of God *expands* monotheism from within to include a plurality of persons in God. According to John, the one God is not simply one person.

Furthermore, John would insist this teaching is not some new invention of the Christians. The OT Scriptures anticipate it in numerous ways. Jesus is not only thoroughly kosher; he's the very embodiment of the God of the OT! John is showing that believers and worshipers of Jesus are genuinely

20. Two well-known scholars who embrace this approach are Martyn, *History and Theology* and Brown, *Community of the Beloved Disciple*.

21. The evidence suggests John aimed at a wide readership which included Christians (both Jewish and non-Jewish) as well as non-Christians. See Bauckham, *Testimony of the Beloved Disciple*, 113–23, and Klink, *Sheep of the Fold*. John's main goal was to demonstrate that Jesus is indeed the Messiah, God's Son (Jn 20:30–31), and to unpack the implications of what it means to believe, worship, and live for him.

embracing Yahweh,[22] the one true God of Israel. From John's perspective, the Jews who reject Jesus' deity are unwittingly spurning the very God they claim to serve.

What's John Up to?

But again, did John really mean for us to think of Jesus as truly God? What does John actually mean when he says "the Word was God"? The classic Trinitarian answer appeals to biblical evidence of a multi-person God—one God in three distinct members. But is this concept conceivable in the context of first-century Jewish culture which, we are told, conceived of God as one and only one? Some argue the idea of a multiperson God (a Trinity) is foreign to John and the other NT writers and is the creation of theologians who lived centuries later. Some claim that the Trinity teaching simply doesn't make any logical sense. Does John really present us with one God who is somehow more than one person? If so, can one of those persons be subordinate to another? Considering the portraits of Jesus presented earlier in this chapter, what's the true picture?

This book will explore these questions. I am convinced that no biblical writer is more helpful in finding the answers than the author of John's Gospel. John's Jesus brings together the lofty and the lowly texts in a way that supplies the key to unlocking the mystery.

WHAT'S THIS BOOK UP TO?

Allow me to sum up this book in a few pages. In chapter 2 ("The World Behind John's World"), we'll ask: What does the Bible mean when it speaks of God as *one*? How was this understood among Jews and Christians in the first century when John wrote his Gospel? If there is really only one God, then why are there others—even in the OT—who seem to act like him and are even addressed by his titles and name? Also, why are we sometimes told, on the one hand, God can never be seen by humans, but then, on the other hand, some people in the OT actually did see him? Is the Bible contradicting itself or is there something deeper going on here? We'll learn that God really wants to fellowship personally and directly with us, but he must first deal with the obstacles between us.

---

22. Yahweh (usually translated into English as "LORD" in all upper case letters) is the Hebrew personal name of the one true God as revealed in the OT. In later chapters, we will explore the importance of this divine name in relation to John's portrait of Jesus.

In chapter 3 ("God's Feature Film"), we'll discover God's answer to the visibility problem. In Jesus Christ, God's Son, we see God as never before. Not only is Jesus the perfect representative of the Father, he is also quite properly called "God the Son." We'll probe the question of appearances of Yahweh in the OT. Could these appearances have been Jesus before his earthly life? Does John give us any clues?

In chapter 4 ("God's Equal"), we'll take an in-depth look at the opening verse of John's Gospel where the Word is called "God." What precisely does John mean by this? Is it possible to take this text differently than Trinitarians take it? Might the Son be "God" only in that he represents, talks, and acts just like the Father? Or is Jesus *actually* God? Or might the JWs be right when they claim the Word was "a god?" This chapter demonstrates that the ascription of deity to the Word/Son goes beyond a representational or functional sense to declare that he is *indeed* God, not only in what he *does* but in what he *is*.

In chapter 5 ("God's Junior Partner"), we'll take a close look at the accusation that Jesus made "himself equal to God" (Jn 5:18). Jesus responds to his critics by painting a word picture of him serving as his Father's apprentice. In doing so, John's Jesus steers a narrow course which affirms both his deity and his full submission to his Father. The Son watches the Father at work and follows his lead (5:19). Jesus' dependence on the Father serves as a model of how the Christ-follower should depend on him.

In chapter 6 ("The Son Before the Sun"), we'll dig deeply into what John means when he calls Jesus "God's Son." Must Jesus' sonship entail some sort of subordination to his Father? If so, could his role as the Son have started when he became the man Jesus? Was he the Son before he came into the world, or was he the Word before he became the Son? Is his sonship eternal or is it confined to his earthly mission? Can a person be permanently subordinate in role to another and still be equal in every other way? We'll explore John's view of Jesus in search of answers.

Chapter 7 is called "Life on Steroids" because it probes the essence and meaning of life. The Son came to give us life to the full (Jn 10:10). But what does that really mean? We'll examine two intriguing texts that speak of the Son receiving his life from the Father (Jn 5:26; 6:57). What emerges from this chapter is a picture of eternal life as a superior kind of existence deeply rooted in an unbroken, intimate bond with God. The Father/Son relationship is the model in John of the relationship Jesus offers to all who believe in him and become God's children.

Chapter 8 is called "God's Big Secret." If Jesus is truly God, why did he never simply announce, "I am God, worship me!"? Why is the Father called God continuously, but Jesus is called God infrequently? In this chapter we'll discover the strategy behind God's slow reveal of Jesus' true identity and why the Father is called God more than the Son. Also, Jesus claims the Father has given his own name, Yahweh, to him (Jn 17:11–12). But where in John—or anywhere else—do we see Jesus addressed as Yahweh? This chapter enhances our understanding of the Bible by showing us how the OT and NT views of God fit together. We'll also find help for answering critics of Jesus' deity.

Chapter 9 is called "Earthquake of the Soul." Jesus' first disciples were all traditional Jews who grew up believing in one God and detesting the notion of worshiping any man. But by the end of John's Gospel, Jesus is hailed as Lord and God. What could have caused such a seismic shift within them? This chapter will explore divine oneness in John—a concept deeply rooted in the OT and also seen in other parts of the NT. We will study Jesus' famous words, "I and the Father are one" (10:30) and examine the astonishing confession of Thomas to the risen Jesus, "My Lord and my God" (20:28). We'll get further insight into how a Christ-follower is to pray and worship the one God who exists in three persons.

But what about the Holy Spirit? Why does Jesus seem to keep him in the shadows until the night before he dies? If God is really a Trinity, why is the Spirit not mentioned in John 1:1? In chapter 10 ("Enter the Holy Spirit"), we'll observe God's awesome strategy of revealing his identity throughout the history of biblical revelation. Is the Holy Spirit really a person? Is he God? What is the role of the Holy Spirit in the Trinity and in your life as a believer? This closing chapter will provide answers to these and other questions as we tie together our discussion on the Trinity and its relevance to your life.

John's Gospel lays the firm foundation for the later intricate explanation of the doctrine of the Trinity by theologians and church councils. Also, in his portrait of Jesus, John shows us what it means to live in dependence on God and to pursue intimacy with God within the Father/child relationship which Jesus made possible and models in John. The Gospel also illustrates for us that equality and submission can successfully coexist in human relationships such as marriage, the family, church, and the workplace. In the eternal communion among the members of the Trinity, genuine equality is shared while different roles are fulfilled within a relationship of infinite love and unity.

QUESTIONS FOR DISCUSSION

1. Which of the views of Jesus discussed above was new to you? Which makes the most sense to you?

2. Does it really matter to you if Jesus is God or less than God? Why or why not?

3. What do you hope to gain from reading this book? What questions do you hope to get answered?

A VERSE TO MEMORIZE

The Word became flesh and made his dwelling among us. We have seen his glory, the glory of the one and only Son, who came from the Father. (Jn 1:14)

APPLY WHAT YOU'VE LEARNED

Try reading through the Gospel of John in one sitting. Depending on how rapidly you can read, you may find this easier or harder than others. Do your best. For this exercise realize you are reading to get the big picture, not to make a careful study. Feel free to skim, if need be, to get the gist. Don't allow yourself to slow down or get stuck. Report to your group what you discovered as a result.

CHAPTER 2

The World Behind John's World

How many Gods are there? People answer this question in different ways. Three very influential world religions—Judaism, Christianity, and Islam—teach that there is only one true God. This belief is known as *monotheism*. It seems simple enough—one God and only one. But if you probe more deeply into the teachings of these three religions, you will find strikingly different conceptions of what God is like and even major disagreement as to what it means for God to be one. For example, Muslims and traditional Jews consider the Christian view of the Trinity (one God in three persons) to be a gross misunderstanding of God's oneness at best, and blasphemous idolatry at worst. Unlike Trinitarians, Jews and Muslims are *unitarian* in their view of God. As they see it, God exists as only one person. But even many who identify themselves as Christians take strong exception to the idea that God is somehow three in one. For example, JWs, Mormons, and Biblical Unitarians embrace the Bible as God's word and yet maintain it does *not* teach the Trinity. Could they be right?

Answering this question is huge for understanding Jesus as revealed in John's Gospel. To answer it, we need to explore how God is portrayed in the OT, particularly in regard to his oneness. The OT is the world behind John's world.

GOD MATTERS

Why does it matter if God is one in three or just one? It matters because God is the most important being in existence! If we want to know, love, and serve God, we must discover what he's like and how to approach and worship him.

This is not hair-splitting. For instance, if you believe Jesus is God, you will see the need to pray to him and worship him as God. On the other hand, if he's not God, but rather a created being, then to worship him as God is idolatry—a violation of the commandment to have no other gods before the LORD (Exod 20:3).

Even a casual acquaintance with the Bible is enough to understand that idolatry gets you into major trouble with God.[1] And yet if Jesus really is God but you reject him as God, then this too can be hazardous to your eternal health! Jesus claimed that embracing his true identity is crucial to salvation. He says, "[I]f you do not believe that I am he, you will indeed die in your sins" (Jn 8:24). So whichever viewpoint you take on God's oneness and Jesus' identity, the stakes are high. Embracing the fundamental truths about God's oneness is not just a luxury for scholars; it's a necessity for all Bible believers. It's crucial for knowing God as he truly is.

BACK TO BASICS

In this chapter we will explore what the OT writers mean when they assert that God is one. This is essential for understanding John's conception of God the Father and Jesus. John and all the NT writers were deeply submerged in the OT.[2] To grasp what they wrote about God, we must understand the foundations of their beliefs as rooted in the OT. To do so, we need to enter the worldview of the OT and probe passages that speak of other gods. Where do they fit in?

Many Christians believe there are only two categories—the one true God (Yahweh) and false gods (i.e., idols). But this idea is not accurate. The OT writers often speak of divine beings ("gods" and "sons of God") that are neither Yahweh nor false gods. We also need to look at some of the intriguing appearances of Yahweh in the OT that seem to hint that though he is one, there is somehow more to him than one person. The gist of this chapter is that while other gods indeed exist, there is only one being who ultimately deserves the title of God. And yet, even the one true God, Yahweh, is also, in some mysterious way, *more* than one. If this sounds strange and confusing, welcome to the weird yet wonderful world of the OT.

1. See, for example, Lev 26:30; Deut 32:16, 21; 1 Kgs 16:26; Ps 78:58; Isa 42:17; Jer 51:47; Ezek 6:4; Acts 7:43; 1 Jn 5:21.

2. Though the writers of the Gospels were impacted by various writings, the Hebrew Bible or *Tanakh* (what Christians call the OT) was by far the biggest literary influence. To explore the extent to which John and all the NT writers used and were influenced by the OT, see Beale and Carson, *Commentary on the New Testament Use of the Old Testament*.

THE ONE GOD OF THE BIBLE

God is the main character of the Bible. He shows up in the very first sentence as the Creator of the universe: "In the beginning God created the heavens and the earth" (Gen 1:1). But just who is the God of the Bible? If he introduced himself to you, what would he call himself?

God's Personal Name

Just as you have a personal name that sets you apart from others, so does God. In one of the iconic stories in the Bible, Moses asks God for his name. As we pick up the story, God has appeared to Moses in a burning bush on the slopes of Mount Horeb (also called Sinai) where he is commissioning Moses to lead the Israelites out of slavery in Egypt.

> Moses said to God, "Suppose I go to the Israelites and say to them, 'The God of your fathers has sent me to you,' and they ask me, 'What is his name?' Then what shall I tell them?" God said to Moses, "I AM WHO I AM. This is what you are to say to the Israelites: 'I AM has sent me to you.'" God also said to Moses, "Say to the Israelites, 'The LORD, the God of your fathers—the God of Abraham, the God of Isaac and the God of Jacob—has sent me to you.' "This is my name forever, the name you shall call me from generation to generation." (Exod 3:13-15)

We will visit this key text several times in this book. But for now, I'll make only two observations about it. First, notice the word "LORD." The OT was written mainly in Hebrew. Whenever you see "LORD" in all uppercase letters (as in most English translations), it indicates the Hebrew word underlying the English is *Yahweh*, God's personal name. The actual word as it appears in the Hebrew Bible is four consonants and no vowels: YHWH. Technically, scholars are still not positive how it was pronounced in OT days, but Yahweh is the best guess

All the other names of God in the OT are actually titles, such as "God," "Almighty," "Lord," "Most High," etc. But Yahweh is God's *personal* name, not simply his title. The difference is important. For instance, I have several titles that many other people also share (pastor, husband, dad, doctor, etc.). But my name, Randy Rheaume[3], uniquely singles me out. It appears on my driver's license, Social Security card, marriage license, etc. In the same way, the name Yahweh singles out the one true God as unique. It's his personal

---

3. My actual given first name is Randall, but I much prefer Randy.

name. Yahweh occurs over 6,800 times in the OT. It is *the* name of God. It belongs to him alone, and in this text he says it's his name forever.

Second, notice the words "I AM WHO I AM." In Hebrew the word translated "I AM" here is closely related to the word "Yahweh." The name Yahweh most likely means "he is," referring to God as the eternal one who is always present. "I AM" is simply Yahweh speaking his own name in the first person.[4] When "He Is" speaks in the first person, he says, "I AM." Of course, Yahweh doesn't normally use I AM to identify himself, but he does so here to help explain his name to Moses. It means "the one who is continually present." In other words, Yahweh is the God who *is*.

Yahweh Alone

From ancient times until today, religious Jews have recited an OT text twice a day known as the Shema.[5] The Shema opens with a striking declaration of Yahweh's oneness which the Jews have regarded as the cornerstone of their faith since ancient times. It begins, "Hear,[6] O Israel: The LORD our God, the LORD is one" (Deut 6:4). The Shema declares Yahweh to be Israel's one true God—the only legitimate object of worship for them. All the other nations worshiped many different gods, but Israel was to worship and serve only Yahweh.

This requirement is of such supreme importance that it's the first of Yahweh's Ten Commandments. The first commandment reads, "And God spoke all these words: 'I am the LORD [= Yahweh] your God, who brought you out of Egypt, out of the land of slavery. You shall have no other gods before me'" (Exod 20:1–3). Yahweh not only created the universe, but he also selected Israel from all the other nations as his chosen people. He considered Israel his prized and privileged firstborn son (Exod 4:22).

Yahweh was so passionately devoted to Israel that he entered into a sacred agreement with the nation called a *covenant* (see Exod 24:1–12). In this covenant, Yahweh and Yahweh alone was to be Israel's God. As such, he would lovingly protect and provide for Israel as his prized possession—a holy nation of priests for all the other nations (see Exod 19:3–8). For Israel's end of the bargain, the highest devotion was owed exclusively to Yahweh above all other persons, possessions, or foreign gods. As the Shema goes on

---

4. See Waltke and Yu, *Old Testament Theology*, 365–67; Durham, *Exodus*, 39.

5. As prescribed in the opening tractate of the *Mishnah* (*m. Ber.* 1–2)

6. The Hebrew word translated "hear" in this text is the word *shema*. "The Shema" became a shorthand way of referring collectively to this biblical text (Deut 6:4–9, as well as Deut 11:13–21 and Num 15:37–41).

to say, "Love the LORD your God with all your heart and with all your soul and with all your strength" (Deut 6:5). This exclusive devotion to Yahweh was to undergird every aspect of Israel's life, government, worship, family, and social interactions. When Israel persistently turned away from Yahweh and worshiped other gods, it constituted spiritual adultery, a serious breach of the sacred covenant. Consequently, with great regret and justified anger, Yahweh would severely discipline his treasured nation.

When we fast forward several centuries to Jesus' day, we discover the Jews were keenly aware of Yahweh's exclusive identity. Jesus himself emphasized the Shema as the most important commandment in Scripture. Note how he answers the question put to him:

> One of the teachers of the law came and . . . . he asked him, "Of all the commandments, which is the most important?" "The most important one," answered Jesus, "is this: 'Hear, O Israel: The Lord our God, the Lord is one. Love the Lord your God with all your heart and with all your soul and with all your mind and with all your strength.'" (Mk 12:28–30)

In this landmark dialogue, Jesus points to the opening words of the Shema as the top priority for all of his followers. And Jesus himself lived faithfully by this commandment in his own life. For instance, when Satan offered him the kingdoms of the world if he would bow down and worship him, Jesus responded, "Away from me, Satan! For it is written: 'Worship the Lord your God, and serve him only'"[7] (Matt 4:10; cf. also Lk 4:8). Pleasing his Father was his highest priority,[8] even to the point of laying down his life.[9] Jesus was a monotheist both in belief and practice.

The Jews in the first century were well known for their peculiar belief in only one God. As one scholar of the period put it, "The Greeks and Romans are universal in proclaiming Jewish worship of one God. . . . [T]he sources always emphasize how different the Jews are from other people, and they are especially astonished at the lack of imagery in Jewish worship."[10] A first-century Jewish writer named Philo put it this way:

> Let us, therefore, fix deeply in ourselves this first commandment as the most sacred of all commandments, to think that there is but one God, the most highest, and to honor him alone; and let not the polytheistical [sic] doctrine ever even touch the ears of

7. Here Jesus is loosely quoting Deuteronomy 6:13.

8. Jn 5:30; 8:29; 14:31.

9. Mk 14:36; Jn 10:18.

10. Grabbe, *Judaic Religion*, 218.

any man who is accustomed to seek for the truth, with purity and sincerity of heart.[11]

Coming from a Jewish background, the writers of the NT were likewise passionate about devotion to the one true God. While there was some variation among Jews in the first century as to how God's oneness was to be understood,[12] Jesus and his early followers were on the strict end of the spectrum.[13] The authors of the NT consider monotheism a given. For example, the NT writer James understands God's oneness to be such a bedrock truth that even the demons acknowledge it (Jas 1:19)! Likewise, born, raised, and educated a Jew, the apostle Paul believed "God is one" (Gal 3:20), "'there is no God but one'" (1 Cor 8:4), and "there is only one God" (Rom 3:30). In the context of each of these statements, Paul is echoing the Shema and using the fact of God's oneness as the foundation of his point.[14] Paul considers idolatry to be the deepest pit of mankind's fall from knowing the one true God (Rom 1:21–23).

John's Gospel is committed to monotheism, as well. "In terms of Jewish monotheism as it existed in the first century," writes biblical scholar James McGrath, "the evidence suggests that John was completely, undeniably, and without reservation a monotheist."[15] In John Jesus refers to his Father as "the only God" (5:44), and he says that eternal life consists of knowing "the only true God" (17:3). So strong are these monotheistic statements on Jesus' lips that some have argued they leave no room for anyone (including Jesus or the Holy Spirit) to share the Father's exclusive identity as the one true God.[16] As we will see later, this is overreaching, but we can all agree that John's Gospel is definitely monotheistic.

Identifying Your God

The message from the beginning to the end of the Bible is clear: God is one, and as such he is the only legitimate object of your worship, ultimate trust,

---

11. Philo, *Decal.* 65.

12. For a survey of Jewish and Christian monotheism in the first century, see Rheaume, *Exegetical and Theological Analysis*, 15–20, 44–62. Excellent book-length treatments include Hurtado, *One God, One Lord*; Bauckham, *Jesus and the God of Israel*; Fletcher-Louis, *Jesus Monotheism*.

13. McGrath, *Only True God*, 129n1; cf. also 53.

14. Rheaume, *Exegetical and Theological Analysis*, 51–52, 54–57.

15. McGrath, *Only True God*, 55.

16. E.g., Buzzard and Hunting, *Doctrine of the Trinity*, 38–41; McGrath, *Only True God*, 57.

and love. This bedrock truth of Scripture is crucial because it means that God is entitled to first place in our lives.

But how can we know if this is truly the case with us? From a biblical standpoint, you can discover what or who is truly your G/god by asking yourself, "What/who is most important to me? Is it my happiness, family, career, achievements, goals, etc.?" These can all be good things, but if any of them holds first place in your life, then *that* is your god and you are an idolater. What's most important to you?

To illustrate the relationship God seeks with us, take marriage as an analogy. When you vow your life to another person on your wedding day, it's a commitment to love and be faithful to that person uniquely and exclusively—"forsaking all others," as the traditional wedding vow says. A relationship with God is like a marriage commitment—only fuller, deeper, and more permanent. It's the ultimate commitment. As our Creator and Re-deemer, God has the exclusive right to ask this of his people. When Yahweh prohibited idols, he told Israel, "for I, the LORD your God, am a jealous God" (Exod 20:5). Yahweh won't tolerate an "open marriage"! His perfect love for his people is infinitely strong and passionate. When you enter into a relationship with him, you are accepting him as your God, your highest priority forever.

When we come to the NT, we see this command in a bright new light. Astonishingly, Jesus steps into the shoes of Yahweh and requires the same exclusive devotion to *him* from his followers. Jesus says,

> Whoever loves father or mother more than me is not worthy of me, and whoever loves son or daughter more than me is not wor-thy of me. And whoever does not take his cross and follow me is not worthy of me. Whoever finds his life will lose it, and whoever loses his life for my sake will find it. (Matt 10:37–39 ESV)

In this breathtaking text, Jesus is requiring "Shema-like" devotion to him from his followers. He must come before everyone and everything else. He must be the top priority. In other words, Jesus is asking us to treat him as Yahweh![17]

Question: If you had to give up everything in your life except one thing, what would it be? It's a scary question, isn't it? To answer it truthfully is to identify your G/god. In the Bible, monotheism is far more than a factual proposition to which a believer must assent. It's saying "I do" to God for an

---

17. The renowned Judaic scholar Jacob Neusner aptly recognizes this in Jesus' teachings. In his imaginary talk with Jesus' disciples, Neusner asks them, "'And is your master God?' For, now I realize, only God can demand of me what Jesus is asking" (Neusner, *A Rabbi Talks with Jesus*, 68).

everlasting marriage. Truly a match made in heaven! It's a life and eternity exclusively committed to the one true God as revealed in Jesus Christ.

MANY GODS IN THE BIBLE

Yet right now you might be wondering, "But doesn't the Bible mention other gods besides Yahweh—gods that actually exist?" It does indeed. In fact, look again at the First Commandment: "You shall have no other gods before me." Notice that even here Yahweh does not deny other gods exist; he simply prohibits worshiping them. In the ancient world of the OT, people thought in terms of many gods. Often a nation—say Moab or Ammon—would claim one god as its own national deity, but this did not mean the people of that nation thought only their god existed. On the contrary, all the nations acknowledged numerous gods.

According to this ancient mindset, there were two basic realms of reality: 1) the physical world, which we call the universe, and 2) the spirit world—the world of *elohim*,[18] the Hebrew word translated "God/gods." The singular form of this word is *el* (God or god); the plural form is *elohim* (God, god, or gods). It can be used in the singular or plural to refer to Yahweh or to other gods.

But here's where things get really weird for us who think of the term "God" as applying only to one being. In the world of the OT, the word *elohim* was used for *all* spirit beings. All nonphysical beings—angels, demons, Satan, and, of course, Yahweh God himself—were considered *elohim* or, in some instances, "*sons of elohim*."[19] Why? Because all of these beings, according to the ancient mindset, belong to the unseen spirit world. In this way of thinking, there are two realms of reality: 1) the physical universe, and 2) the *elohim* world. From the perspective of the people of the Ancient Near East—including Abraham and the Israelites— *elohim* was a general term for all spirit beings, not just for Yahweh.

Not Your Average God

Nevertheless, when Yahweh revealed himself to his people, he made it clear that he was unlike any of the *elohim* they had heard of or had worshiped

18. For deeper exploration into the topic discussed in this section, see Michael S. Heiser's insightful book, *Unseen Realm*, esp. 28–37.

19. E.g., Job 1:6; 2:1; 38:7; Ps 29:1–2. But note, English translations often render the Hebrew expression "sons of God" (*ben elohim*) as "angels," "heavenly beings," "divine beings," or something like this.

before. Yes, the term *elohim* certainly applied to him, for Yahweh was indeed a spirit being not of this world. But he was supreme and unique among the *elohim*. Note how Yahweh is compared as superior to the other *elohim*:

> Who among the gods [*elhim*]
>   is like you, LORD [Yahweh]?
> Who is like you—
>   majestic in holiness,
> awesome in glory,
>   working wonders? (Exod 15:11)

> Sovereign LORD [Yahweh], you have begun to show to your servant your greatness and your strong hand. For what god [*el*] is there in heaven or on earth who can do the deeds and mighty works you do? (Deut 3:24)

> LORD [Yahweh], the God of Israel, there is no God [*elohim*] like you in heaven above or on earth below. (1Kgs 8:23)

> For the LORD [Yahweh] is the great God [*el*],
>   the great King above all gods [*elohim*]. (Ps 95:3)

> God [*elohim*] has taken his place in the divine [*el*]
>   council;[20]
> in the midst of the gods [*elohim*] he holds judgment. . . . I said,
> "You are gods [*elohim*],
>   sons of the Most High, all of you." (Ps 82:1, 6 ESV)

Notice again that the existence of *elohim* other than Yahweh is assumed. And these are just a few examples; the OT contains many such texts. Nevertheless, in these passages and throughout the entire OT, Yahweh is always regarded as transcendent, unique, and highly superior to all the other *elohim*. Yahweh God is the Creator of *all* things—visible and invisible, including the other *elohim*—and thus he existed before them.[21] This is why, as we saw above, Yahweh commanded his people that of all the *elohim*, only Yahweh *Elohim* was to be served and worshiped.

---

20. The divine council mentioned in this text likely refers to an assembly of *elohim* (i.e., heavenly beings) over which Yahweh presides and with whom he chooses to confer. The ancient Ugaritic, Mesopotamian, and Egyptian cultures had their mythological concepts of this council, but in the Bible, Yahweh is its supreme head. Other clear scriptural references to the divine council include 1 Kings 22:19–23; Job 1:6; 2:1. A less-likely view takes the gods mentioned in Psalm 82 to be human judges or rulers (cf. Exod 21:6; 22:8; where *elohim* is rendered "judges" in the NIV). Other possible references to the divine council include Genesis 1:26; 3:22; 11:4; and Isaiah 6:8. Heiser's book, *Unseen Realm*, provides a thorough and very readable exploration of this subject.

21. See Ps 148:1–5; Neh 9:60; also Jn 1:1–3; Col 1:15–17.

In light of this, you might be wondering if Christians are right to claim that there is only one God, for clearly the Bible speaks of many other gods besides Yahweh. Some tell us that instead of calling themselves monotheists (those who believe in only one God), Christians would be more accurate to call themselves *henotheists*—those who believe many gods exist but worship and serve only one God.[22] In this view, only one God (i.e., Yahweh) is supreme and worthy of worship, but lesser deities indeed exist. Are they right? Is the biblical view actually henotheism rather than monotheism? I don't think so. While the term *henotheism* captures much of the truth of what we've explored so far, it's certainly not the best way to characterize the worldview of the biblical writers. Let's explore this question more deeply.

The One True God

As we read through the OT, it gradually becomes clear that while Yahweh and the writers of Holy Scripture often use the common *elohim* terminology in reference to all spirit beings, Yahweh resents sharing this term with others. As the story of the Bible unfolds over the centuries, Yahweh increasingly makes it plain that the word applies rightfully to him alone.

> You were shown these things so that you might know that the LORD is God [*elohim*]; besides him there is no other. . . . Acknowledge and take to heart this day that the LORD is God [*elohim*] in heaven above and on the earth below. There is no other. (Deut 4:35, 39)

> See now that I myself am he!
> There is no god [*elohim*]
>   besides me. (Deut 32:39)

> How great you are, Sovereign LORD! There is no one like you, and there is no God [*elohim*] but you, as we have heard with our own ears. (2 Sam 7:22)

> . . . so that all the peoples of the earth may know that the LORD is God [*elohim*] and that there is no other. (1 Kgs 8:60)

> There is no one like you, LORD, and there is no God [*elohim*] but you, as we have heard with our own ears. (1 Chr 17:20)

> "You are my witnesses,"
>   declares the LORD,

22. Biblical scholar Paula Fredriksen, for example, thinks the term "monotheism" in reference to the beliefs of ancient Jews and Christians, should be put into mandatory retirement and replaced by "henotheism." See "Mandatory Retirement," 35–38.

"and my servant whom I
have chosen,
so that you may know and
believe me
and understand that I am he.
Before me no god [*el*] was formed,
nor will there be one after me." (Isa 43:10)

This is what the LORD says—
Israel's King and Redeemer,
the LORD Almighty:
I am the first and I am the
last;
apart from me there is no
God [*elohim*]. (Isa 44:6)

I am the LORD, and there is no
other;
apart from me there is no
God [*elohim*]. (Isa 45:5)

Then you will know that I am
in Israel,
that I am the LORD your God [*elohim*],
and that there is no other. (Joel 2:27)

These texts, and others like them, insist emphatically that Yahweh alone is *elohim*. What are we to do with these texts? Do they contradict the passages we cited earlier that clearly show other *elohim* exist? No. The *elohim*-affirming texts occur together with the *elohim*-denying texts.[23]

There's a better explanation. Christian scholar Michael Heiser addresses this apparent discrepancy by noting that the "denial statements" don't rule out the existence of other *elohim*; they deny only that the other *elohim* can compare to Yahweh. Heiser observes that the same sort of denial language shows up when the arrogant cities Babylon and Nineveh boastfully claimed "there is none beside me" (Isa 47:8; Zeph 2:15).[24] Obviously, everyone knew other cities existed besides Babylon and Nineveh. The denial was a colorful way of bragging that no other city measured up or compared to these cities. Yahweh is doing the same with the other gods. Heiser's explanation is helpful.

---

23. For example, though Deuteronomy contains several *elohim* (other than Yahweh) denying texts (4:35, 39; 32:39), other texts in Deuteronomy presuppose the existence of other *elohim* (3:24; 5:7; 10:17).

24. Heiser, *Unseen Realm*, 35.

But we need to go a step further. The *elohim* denial statements nudge us to set a higher standard for how we speak about God. Through his prophets, Yahweh is, in effect, saying, "Instead of simply following the *elohim* jargon of the day, I want you to regard me and me alone as *elohim*—the only one who truly deserves the title." Yahweh is not denying that other spirit beings exist; he simply doesn't like sharing the same title with them. This point registered deeply with the Jews. When Jewish scholars of later generations translated the Hebrew Scriptures into Greek (a translation often called the Septuagint, or LXX for short), they sometimes rendered *elohim* as *angeloi* (i.e., angels) to avoid applying the word "god" (Greek *theos*) to beings other than Yahweh.[25]

The NT writers continue this trend. What were called *elohim* in many OT texts are in the NT exclusively referred to as angels, demons, Satan, or other creatures that make up God's heavenly council.[26] Unlike the OT, nowhere in the NT is the term "gods" used of spirit beings in a positive manner. The only exception is John 10:34–35, but here Psalm 82 is quoted, employing the older terminology. True, Paul once calls Satan "the god of this age" (2 Cor 4:4), but here he clearly means that Satan is a *false* god—a usurper that bears the title in a completely negative and illegitimate manner. Paul and the other NT writers are, of course, aware that the pagans regard spirit beings and their idols as gods, and so sometimes they refer to them using pagan terminology.[27] But it is also understood that only one being bears the title of "God" *legitimately*. The lords and gods that pagans worship are merely "so-called gods" (1 Cor 8:5). The angelic creatures that were once called *elohim* in the OT lingo, Paul now refers to as "things in heaven and on earth, visible and invisible, whether thrones or powers or rulers or authorities" (Col 1:16).[28]

Truly Divine

In two important passages, Paul shows us what separates the one true God from all the alleged gods. The first reads this way: "Formerly, when you did not know God, you were slaves to those who by nature are not gods" (Gal 4:8). Notice Paul's wording here. He says the gods the Galatians served before they became Christ-followers were not gods "*by nature*."[29] In other

25. E.g., LXX Job 1:6; 2:1; Pss 8:5; 97:7.

26. E.g., Rev 4:4–11.

27. E.g., Acts 14:11; 17:18; 28:6; 1 Cor 10:20; Gal 4:8; 2 Thess 2:4.

28. See also Eph 1:21; 3:10; 6:12.

29. The Greek term Paul uses in Galatians 4:8 translated "nature" is *physis*—a word

words, they were different in their very *being* (i.e., their most basic proper-
ties) from the one true God. They don't belong in the same category with
him. Just as a stone is fundamentally different in its nature (i.e., its essential
attributes) from a human being's *human* nature, these so-called gods don't
have the same nature as the true God.

In a similar text Paul pushes the contrast a bit further when he writes,
"They tell how you [the Christ-followers in Thessalonica] turned to God
from idols to serve the living and true God" (1 Thess 1:9). In stark contrast
to the real God, the pagan gods the Thessalonian Christians used to serve
were *non*living and *un*true. They lacked the essential attributes of life and
reality possessed by the true God. As Paul puts it elsewhere, they are only
"so-called gods" (1 Cor 8:5).

As far as Yahweh—the one eternal and uncreated God—is concerned,
the fact that both he and the other *elohim* are nonphysical spirit beings (as
conceived in the OT world) is not enough to justify lumping him into the
same category with created, temporal things, many of whom were utterly
wicked and sought to be worshiped in God's place. It's not that the old terminology was wrong; it was simply incomplete, imprecise, and subject to
dangerous misunderstanding. For Bible-believing Christ-followers, there is
only one *true* God.

How is this Relevant?

Why is it important to know this stuff? It shows us that God is passionate about keeping his identity distinct from everyone/thing else. He doesn't
want you to mistake something else for him. Also, God wants to keep clarifying and refining our perception of him, just as you keep fine-tuning your
focus when you watch a ballgame from the stands through a set of binocu-
lars. God wouldn't bother if he didn't intensely care about us.

This is not simply a matter of getting the facts right, as in learning the
correct way to spell a word or solve a math problem. The facts are vital, of
course, but God wants you to understand the truth about him so you can
know him personally and intimately as his precious child (Jn 1:12–13). "See
what great love the Father has lavished on us," John tells us, "that we should
be called children of God" (1 Jn 3:1). The scriptural facts about God are
aimed at developing our relationship with him as our Father. Just as lovers want to know everything about one another, lovers of God will want to
know about him. Finally, this discussion also provides essential background

---

that speaks of the ontological (i.e., the actual or existential) reality of a thing, not merely
its function. See Rheaume, *Exegetical and Theological Analysis*, 52–53.

information for comprehending the portrait of Jesus we encounter in John's Gospel.

THE INVISIBLE GOD

I've been asked many times by atheists, "If God exists, why doesn't he show himself?" But it's not just skeptics who wonder this. I too have often wished God would show up so that he and I could sit down and discuss my concerns face to face. Have you ever longed to see God? You may be surprised to discover that he wants you to see him. But there are some obstacles in the way.

God's Invisibility

The apostle John confirms what we've all experienced for ourselves when he writes, "No one has ever seen God" (Jn 1:18).[30] Paul ratchets it up a notch when he says God "lives in unapproachable light" and that "no one has seen or can see" him (1 Tim 6:16). Not only has it *never* happened, claims Paul, it *can't* happen!

The background for these statements is rooted in the OT. Yahweh makes it clear that seeing him would be lethal. Yahweh says to Moses, "Go down and warn the people so they do not force their way through to see the LORD and many of them perish" (Exod 19:21). The same rule applies to Moses himself. Yahweh tells him, "[Y]ou cannot see my face, for no one may see me and live" (Exod 33:20). God's glory is so infinitely awesome that getting even a glimpse of him can be deadly dangerous—as Moses (Exod 33:18–23), Job (42:5–6), Isaiah (6:5), Ezekiel (1:28), and others in the Bible testify.

Beyond the Universe

Because God is infinite, he transcends the universe. When Solomon completed Yahweh's temple in Jerusalem, he fully recognized that God cannot be contained in any building or even the universe: "But will God really dwell on earth? The heavens, even the highest heaven, cannot contain you. How much less this temple I have built!" (1 Kgs 8:27). As we saw back in chapter 1, God created the universe out of nothing by simply speaking it into existence. Thus Yahweh is neither part of the universe nor dependent on it. And

30. See also Jn 5:37; 6:46; and 1 Jn 4:12.

yet he is vitally present with all creation and is intimately aware of all that
goes on within it (Ps 139:1–17).

Technically, God is not *in* the universe (i.e., part of it); he transcends
it. When you look at a painting by a great artist, you don't see the artist but
his/her artwork. Still the artwork reveals the style, technique, and genius
of the artist. We don't see God because he created the universe; the beauty
and intricate design of the universe reveal his mind-bending artistry (Ps
19:1–6). He's not the artwork; he's the artist. God is both immanent and
transcendent. As Yahweh says in Jeremiah, "'Am I only a God nearby,' /de-
clares the LORD,/ 'and not a God far away'" (Jer 23:23)? He is not a physical
being; he's a spirit being (Jn 4:24) and thus invisible.[31]

THE VISIBLE GOD

But this raises a bit of a problem, at least for those of us who believe the
Bible contains no actual contradictions. Many other OT passages inform
us that Yahweh himself actually appeared to people who not only physically
saw him but also conversed with him, washed his feet, took walks with him,
ate dinner with him, and even wrestled with him! I'm not referring here
to visions or dreams of God, such as those seen by Ezekiel (10:20), Daniel
(7:9–14), and John (Rev 4:2–3). I'm talking about actual, live encounters
with Yahweh himself in physical, visible form—events in which the artist
somehow enters into his artwork. Let's consider a few notable examples.[32]

Yahweh's Appearance to Adam and Eve

The first recorded instance of such an experience happens with the original
human couple. After they disobeyed Yahweh by eating the forbidden fruit,
we're told, "Then the man and his wife heard the sound of the LORD God
as he was walking in the garden in the cool of the day, and they hid from the
LORD God among the trees of the garden in the cool of the day" (Gen 3:8).
Yahweh then calls to Adam (3:9), and a conversation follows (3:10–19). Notice that it's Yahweh himself ("the LORD") they hear walking. This is not just
a vision or dream about Yahweh. The text plainly says it's Yahweh himself
walking. They can hear him among the other tangible objects—"the trees of
the garden" experiencing "the cool of the day." Apparently they could hear

---

31. See Rom 1:20; Col 1:15; 1 Tim 1:17; Heb 11:27.

32. For more detailed discussion on appearances of Yahweh in the OT, see esp.
Brown, *Answering Jewish Objections* 2:25–37, and Heiser, *Unseen Realm*, 127–48.

his footsteps and perhaps the rustling of leaves as he brushed by the bushes. All of this assumes that Yahweh is physically present as he confronts the couple. Adam and Eve hide from Yahweh because of their guilt, but aside from this they don't seem particularly surprised to see and hear Yahweh physically.

This would seem to indicate that prior to this event it was customary for Yahweh to appear to the couple in a tangible form to fellowship with them.[33] Since Adam and Eve were the first humans, they serve as a prototype of God's intention for the human race as a whole. After they fall into sin, the rest of the Bible is about restoring the broken relationship. In the final chapter of the Bible (Rev 22), we see God's intention finally and fully realized. God and humans will once again enjoy fellowship together with Yahweh in tangible form, as did Adam and Eve..

Appearances to Abraham

Yahweh makes some of his most striking appearances to Abraham, the father of Israel and other nations. Genesis records Yahweh's original call to Abram (his name before God changed it to Abraham) in 12:1–3, where we're told Yahweh spoke to him. But in Stephen's speech to the Sanhedrin, he says, "The God of glory *appeared* to our father Abraham while he was still in Mesopotamia" (Acts 7:2; italics added). Genesis informs us that after Abram arrives in Canaan, Yahweh makes another appearance: "The LORD *appeared* to Abram and said, 'To your offspring I will give this land.' So he built an altar there to the LORD, who had *appeared* to him" (Gen 12:7; italics added). Yahweh is said to have appeared to Abraham on other occasions as well.[34]

The most detailed appearance is by far the most intriguing. In Genesis 18 we're told that Yahweh himself pays a visit to Abraham to converse with him and enjoy dinner together. The text plainly says that Yahweh "appeared to Abraham near the great trees of Mamre while he was sitting at the entrance to his tent in the heat of the day" (Gen 18:1). Three men visited Abraham at his tent on that warm day (18:2), and one of them was Yahweh in human form. Later in the story we discover the other two men were angels (19:1).

The text makes it clear Abraham was not merely experiencing a dream or a vision. This was a tangible experience in the physical world. Abraham hurried out of his tent to bow to these men (18:3); he offered to wash their

33. Wenham, *Genesis 1–15*, 76.
34. Gen 17:1; 18:1; cf. also 15:1, 17.

feet and feed them dinner, and they accepted (18:3–5). Imagine! Yahweh enjoyed a foot bath while he dined on freshly baked bread, roasted calf, and curds, and washed it down with milk (18:6–8). Wouldn't it be neat to be a fly on the tent wall that day! Throughout the conversation Yahweh, in human form, repeatedly speaks in the first person about his plan for miraculously enabling Abraham and his wife to conceive a child in their old age, as well as his planned response to the wickedness of Sodom and Gomorrah (18:13–33). After dinner Abraham takes a walk with the three men while continuing his conversation with the embodied Yahweh (18:16). At one point Abraham and Yahweh stop walking but keep talking, as the two other men (i.e., the angels) head towards Sodom (18:22). Here the conversation becomes quite intense, as Abraham pleads with Yahweh regarding Sodom's plight.

Does Abraham know he's actually speaking face to face with Yahweh in human form? While he never calls Yahweh by name (only by the reverential title "Lord"), Abraham clearly knows to whom he speaks. He addresses Yahweh as "the Judge of all the earth" who judges justly (18:25) and who will decide the fate of Sodom (18:22–32). Abraham knows he's speaking directly to God. We're not told how Abraham knew it was Yahweh, nor are we given any details about the appearance of the three visitors. Did they look unusual or just like ordinary men? Unfortunately, we're not told. What we do know is that Yahweh can and does enter his artwork to show up in human form, at least on some occasions.

Similar to the case of Adam and Eve, the appearances to Abraham reveal God's desire to fellowship closely with all his people—not just with super saints. In the NT, Abraham is called the father of all true believers in Jesus,[35] and thus God's relationship with Abraham reveals the relationship he desires for us, too.

Appearances to Isaac and Jacob

These appearances of Yahweh don't end with Abraham. He makes at least two more to Abraham's son Isaac, (Gen 26:2, 24), and a few to Isaac's son, Jacob.[36] One appearance to Jacob was in a dream (28:12–17). But in another very bizarre appearance, Yahweh apparently takes the form of a man to fight with Jacob in a wrestling match (32:22–32)! How's that for a tangible appearance? In this ultra-weird episode, Yahweh gives Jacob the name Israel and later Jacob exclaims, "I saw God face to face, and yet my life was spared"

35. E.g., Rom 4:11, 16; Gal 3:7.
36. Cf. Gen 35:1, 9; 48:3.

(32:30). Truly fascinating! But we cannot linger here. After Yahweh's appearances to the three great patriarchs—Abraham, Isaac, and Jacob—the recorded appearances cease for several centuries until the time of Moses.

Appearances to Moses

During the life of Moses, Yahweh initiates a whole new round of tangible appearances, but space limits us to discussing only two.

Dinner with Yahweh

The first appearance we'll discuss takes place as the Israelites are gathered below the slopes of Mount Sinai. One day Moses and the other Israelite leaders are summoned by Yahweh to meet with him to solemnize the covenant of the law:

> Then the LORD said to Moses, "Come up *to the LORD*, you and Aaron, Nadab and Abihu, and seventy of the elders of Israel. You are to worship at a distance but Moses alone is to *approach the LORD*; the others must not come near. And the people may not come up with him." . . . Moses and Aaron, Nadab and Abihu, and the seventy elders of Israel went up and *saw the God of Israel*. Under his *feet* was something like a pavement made of lapis lazuli, as bright blue as the sky. But God did not raise his *hand* against these leaders of the Israelites; *they saw God*, and they ate and drank. (Exod 24:1–2, 9–11; italics added)

This is one of the most dramatic appearances of Yahweh in the OT. Verse 1 makes it clear he is summoning Moses and the other leaders to meet directly with him: "Come up to the LORD," says Yahweh. Yet notice that Yahweh speaks of himself in the third person. Instead of saying "Come up to me," he says, "Come up to Yahweh," almost as though he's speaking of someone else. And yet it's clearly Yahweh at the meeting. We'll talk more about this below. Also intriguing is the fact that the seventy elders of Israel are invited to this meeting. They represent the nation of Israel, God's chosen people. Once again, Yahweh's desire to meet in person with his people is revealed. Next, notice caution is the order of the day. Only Moses can come close to Yahweh; the other leaders must keep their distance. If they're not meeting with Yahweh himself, why the need for such measures? The most startling statement is found in verse 10: they "saw the God of Israel," apparently in the form of a man, and yet only his feet (v. 10) and hand (v. 11) are mentioned. The blue pavement under his feet likely represents the sky, showing that Yahweh is sovereign over the whole earth.

Could this event be a dream or vision? No. The leaders had to travel to this meeting where Moses had performed a sacrifice on an altar and recorded the events in a book (see 24:3–8). Most amazingly, after the covenant ceremony, the elders enjoy a covenant meal in Yahweh's presence: "But God did not raise his hand against these leaders of the Israelites; *they saw God*, and they ate and drank" (24:11; italics added). Everything in this account points to an objective, real, live meeting with Yahweh in human form.

Yes, precautions had to be taken, but Yahweh clearly wants to fellowship in person with his people. Eating a meal together was a sign of friendship in the Ancient Near East—like going on a picnic together in our culture. In this setting, Moses and the elders not only see Yahweh, but they learn that Yahweh desires friendship and intimacy with his people[37]—a theme that reaches its zenith in Jesus.

Yahweh in the Bush

The second appearance to Moses we'll consider is his encounter with Yahweh at the burning bush on Mount Horeb. Look carefully at what Yahweh tells him: "Go, assemble the elders of Israel and say to them, 'The LORD, the God of your fathers—the God of Abraham, Isaac and Jacob—*appeared* to me. . .'" (Exod 3:16; italics added). In this case, Yahweh apparently does not take human form but appears as a fire within the bush (3:2).

Yet there can be little doubt this is Yahweh himself and that he is—in some sense—visible to Moses. As we saw earlier in this chapter, Yahweh uses this incident to unveil the meaning of his personal name with the words "I AM WHO I AM." Yahweh speaks in the first person throughout his conversation with Moses. The burning bush appearance is Yahweh's signature revelation of his name, not to mention his declaration to bring the Israelites out of slavery. If this isn't Yahweh himself, who is it?

But here's where the fascination level takes another quantum leap. At the beginning of the story, as Moses is about to approach the bush, we read, "There the angel of the LORD appeared to him in flames of fire from within a bush" (Exod 3:2). Note that it doesn't say "Yahweh appeared" but "the angel of the LORD [Yahweh] appeared." And yet right after this the narrative plainly portrays Yahweh himself as the one speaking to Moses from the burning bush. For example:

---

37. Likewise, Yahweh's stated purpose for the tabernacle was so that he could dwell among his people (Exod 25:8; 29:45–46).

> When the LORD saw that he had gone over to look, *God* called to him *from within the bush*, "Moses! Moses!" And Moses said, "Here I am." "Do not come any closer," God said. "Take off your sandals, for the place where you are standing is holy ground." Then he said, "I am the God of your father, the God of Abraham, the God of Isaac and the God of Jacob." At this, Moses hid his face, because he was afraid to *look at God.* (Exod 3:4–6; italics added)

What's going on here? In verse 1 it's the angel of Yahweh, but here it's Yahweh himself. Some answer by appealing to the cultural understanding of a messenger in the Ancient Near East. So closely was the messenger identified with the person who sent him that the messenger was treated as the sender. For example, if a king sent his messenger (what we would call an ambassador) to a neighboring nation to negotiate on the king's behalf, the messenger would represent and speak for the king. The one sent stands in the place of the sender. If he is mistreated, it is as though the king himself has been mistreated. The two persons (the king and his messenger) are regarded, for the purposes of the mission, as virtually one. This concept of a messenger (or "sent one") was well established in the world of the OT and among the Jews in the NT. It was a given that "a man's agent is like [the man] himself."[38] It's the same today when the president's press secretary speaks for the president.

Could the angel of Yahweh in the burning bush (and in similar encounters) simply be Yahweh's messenger and not Yahweh himself? Biblical scholars have researched the messenger concept endlessly.[39] Briefly, my answer is both yes and no.

On the one hand, the angel of Yahweh seems too closely identified with Yahweh himself to be a mere messenger. The OT prophets were Yahweh's messengers,[40] but they did not speak of themselves as though they were Yahweh. They didn't talk as Yahweh in the first person unless they made it clear in the context they were directly quoting Yahweh, such as with the expression, "This is what the LORD says. . ."[41] But at the burning bush, Moses is in Yahweh's actual presence. As Yahweh introduces himself to Mo-

---

38. *m. Ber.* 5:5. This quotation comes from the *Mishnah*—a collection of Jewish oral tradition that was put in writing around AD 200 but often reflects ideas from earlier periods, such as the time of Jesus.

39. E.g., Meier, *Messenger in the Ancient Semitic World*; Greene, *Role of the Messenger.*

40. E.g., 2 Chr 36:15–16; Isa 44:26; Hag 1:13.

41. This expression occurs about 170 times in the OT by many of the speaking and writing prophets. Never does a prophet apply God's name to himself, as the angel of Yahweh does in Exod 3:14–15.

ses, he warns him not to come any closer and to remove his sandals (Exod 3:5–6). We're told, "At this, Moses hid his face, because he was afraid to look at God" (3:6). When the angel of Yahweh shows up in other places in the OT, often in human form, he talks, acts, and is treated as Yahweh himself, just as in the burning bush incident.[42]

One strong indication that the angel of Yahweh is not merely a messenger but Yahweh himself is to compare Moses' status as Yahweh's spokesperson. Moses was God's top human representative in the OT, and yet he never speaks or acts as though he is Yahweh himself. When Moses first received his commission from Yahweh, he objected that he was not a good speaker. In response, Yahweh made Moses' brother Aaron his spokesman. Note these astonishing words: "He [Aaron] shall speak for you [Moses] to the people, and he shall be your mouth, and you shall be *as God* to him" (Exod 4:16; ESV; italic added). Moses was to represent God to Aaron, and Aaron was to represent Moses to the people. Even more surprising is when Yahweh grants Moses this same unique representative status before Pharaoh: "Then the LORD said to Moses, 'See, I have made you like God [*elohim*] to Pharaoh, and your brother Aaron will be your prophet'" (Exod 7:1). Actually the word "like" does not appear in the Hebrew. It literally reads "God" or perhaps "a god." In other words, Moses was to speak to Pharaoh as God himself—Yahweh's unique human messenger. This would elevate Moses to *elohim* status (a member of Yahweh's divine council!) when speaking to Pharaoh. Moses even gets his own prophet as part of the deal! Moses is functioning as Yahweh to both Aaron and Pharaoh. Nowhere else in the OT does Yahweh appoint a human to be "God" and give him a human prophet to speak for him.

Thus Moses is a good test case to compare with the angel of Yahweh. And yet, even in this special role, Moses never speaks to Aaron or Pharaoh as Yahweh in the first person, as though he is Yahweh himself. Instead, Moses introduces Yahweh's word to Pharaoh by saying, "This is what the LORD says. . ."[43] just as the other OT prophets do when speaking as Yahweh's messengers. Moses is never said to appear as Yahweh nor is there any chance of confusing him with Yahweh. Nor does Aaron ever speak to Moses or regard him as Yahweh. The distinction between Moses and Yahweh is always crystal clear. In other words, Moses never does what the angel of Yahweh continually does. If the angel of Yahweh were *merely* an angelic messenger, not Yahweh himself, we would expect him to speak and act as Moses does when

42. Some notable instances include Gen 16:7–13; 22:5–18; Judg 2:1–5; 6:11–24; 13:3–23; Zech 3:1–2.

43. Exod 4:22; 7:17; 8:1, 20.

addressing Pharaoh and Aaron. Instead, there's a stark contrast. It seems that the angel of Yahweh is much more than a mere messenger.

On the other hand, the angel of Yahweh does indeed seem to be distinct from Yahweh.[44] After all, he's called the *angel* of Yahweh—clearly implying he's speaking for Yahweh as a distinct person. If he *is* Yahweh, why send himself as a messenger? Thus many scholars see him not as truly Yahweh but only Yahweh's messenger.[45] And yet, if he's *only* a messenger, why does he speak and act like Yahweh? An answer may be found in Yahweh's appearance in Exodus 24:10. Recall that when Yahweh summoned Moses and the elders to meet with him, he spoke of himself in the third rather than the first person (Exod 24:1). In this case, it was plainly Yahweh himself, and yet there was also this third-person phraseology. Could the one Yahweh somehow be two?

Two Yahwehs?

In case you think this is nothing but Trinitarian slight-of-hand, attempting to smuggle Jesus into the OT, think again. The Jews before and after Jesus' time wrote and debated at length about the texts we've discussed above and many others like them. Some of the rabbis concluded that the one true God somehow exists in two forms.[46] They pointed to many OT passages that signified God's justice while other texts seemed to signify his mercy or conceive of Yahweh as an old man on some occasions and a young man on other occasions[47]—so much that some ancient Jewish scholars reasoned there are two (or more) distinct aspects or manifestations of the one true God! Others pointed to God in his transcendent form on the one hand, and his interactive form on the other, as we observed above. This viewpoint of two Yahwehs in one was arguably accepted as legitimate within Judaism until—with the widespread success of Christianity—it was eventually condemned by the rabbis. They derisively called it the "Two Powers" heresy.

But perhaps the advocates of this Two Powers idea were onto something. As we saw above, Scripture teaches, on the one hand, that Yahweh is unseeable and transcendent, but, on the other hand, Yahweh himself visited

---

44. E.g., Gen 21:17; 2 Chr 21:15–17; Zech 1:12.

45. E.g., Waltke and Yu, *Old Testament Theology*, 362–63

46. The classic study on this topic is by Alan Segal in *Two Powers in Heaven*. But many others have contributed to the discussion from various viewpoints—some more convincingly than others. See, for example, Barker, *Great Angel*; Boyarin, *Jewish Gospels*; Gieschen, *Angelomorphic Christology*; Heiser, *Unseen Realm*; Schäfer, *Jewish Jesus*.

47. One OT text the rabbis discussed at length was Dan 7:9–14, which describes both the old and young figures together in the same passage.

Abraham, Jacob, Moses, and Israel's elders in human form. And then there's the mysterious angel of Yahweh. Could there be more to the one Yahweh than just one person? The eye-opening answer awaits us in the next chapter as we venture into John's Gospel.

SO WHAT?

Before you move on to chapter 3, pause to consider the implications of what we've explored in this chapter. How does it strike you that the one, truly unique God of the universe is really interested in an exclusive relationship with you? Remember, God initiated his relationship with Adam and Eve, Abraham, and Moses. In the NT, Jesus assures us that God always initiates the relationship, never humans (Jn 6:44, 65). Though it may appear to us that we are seeking God, behind the scenes it is God who is seeking us (cf. Rom 3:10–12). And yet there are major obstacles to overcome. God is infinite; we are finite. He is holy; we are sinful. Nevertheless, God is determined to make it work. In the OT, he engineered creative means to meet and fellowship with humans. He revealed himself in numerous ways; he founded a nation of priests; he made covenants; he ordered the tabernacle and temple built; he established a sacrificial system for dealing with the sin barrier. This was a great start, but in the NT he takes it to a whole new level. That's where John's Gospel picks up.

QUESTIONS FOR DISCUSSION

1. What stood out to you most in this chapter and why?

2. Why do you think God originally allowed his people to apply the term *elohim* to beings other than him in OT times? Why did he eventually want them to change this practice?

3. Some people are taken aback by Yahweh calling himself a "jealous God" (Exod 20:5). Why do you think he uses the word "jealous?"

VERSES TO MEMORIZE

Hear, O Israel: The LORD our God, the LORD is one. Love the LORD your God with all your heart and with all your soul and with all your strength. (Deut 6:4–5)

APPLY WHAT YOU'VE LEARNED

Try identifying your G/god, your number one priority in life. Let's say you could keep the clothes on your body, but you were forced to give up everything else—God, family, home, career, health, investments, etc.—except for only one of those things. Honestly, what would you keep? Try imagining your life with only that one thing. Does this exercise reveal changes you need to make in your lifestyle?

CHAPTER 3

God's Feature Film

When Debbie and I go to the movies, we usually try to skip most of the trailers before the feature film. We're pretty selective about the movies we watch, but even when the feature is wholesome, often the trailers are not. And so I like using the trailer time to visit the restroom and purchase our popcorn. But I must admit, some trailers are fun to watch and get me pumped to see an upcoming release, like, say the next *Star Wars* episode. When a trailer is well done, it provides a small taste of the forthcoming film to make you hungry for more, yet without any spoilers. A good trailer leaves you wanting and wondering about the coming feature.

The feature film of God's appearances on earth is the life of Jesus as recorded in the four NT Gospels. The OT appearances were a bit like trailers for the feature. They revealed Yahweh and his desire and intention to interact personally with his people. But like a good trailer, they leave us wanting more and wondering about what's ahead.

In this chapter we dive headfirst into God's revelation of himself as recounted in John's Gospel, particularly 1:18. The aim of this chapter is to show that in Jesus Christ, God himself is truly revealed as never before—not simply through secondary messengers, but by Yahweh himself. Jesus is Yahweh revealed in human flesh. He's the blockbuster feature film.

MYSTERY SOLVED

The appearances of Yahweh in the OT leave us scratching our heads just as they did for the ancient rabbis. But John's Gospel clears up the mystery for us. The Word—God's voice as we called him in chapter 1—is both the official spokesperson for God (his press secretary, we might say) and is God himself. This matches up very neatly with the appearances of Yahweh in the OT.

But John connects the dots for us like no other Scripture author when he writes,

> No one has ever seen God. The one and only Son, who is himself God and is at the Father's side—he has revealed him. (Jn 1:18 CSB)

This verse is of monumental importance for understanding John's Gospel and the history of God's revelation to humans. In this chapter we will examine it closely. Some of the discussion in this chapter gets a bit technical, but I've kicked most of the details down into the footnotes where you can find tools to dig more deeply if you wish.

Seeing the Unseeable

As we observed back in chapter 2, John 1:18 declares God has never been seen by humans—"ever"! At first this appears in hopeless contradiction to the passages we studied which emphatically insist people such as Adam and Eve, Abraham, Moses, and the elders of Israel did indeed see Yahweh, the one true God, not merely in dreams or visions, but in actual, tangible, live encounters. But then the next part of John 1:18 both clears up the contradiction and solves the mystery of the so-called two Yahwehs. God's one and only Son, whom we know as Jesus Christ, is the visible spokesperson for the invisible God. John says God has never been seen, but the Son, who is God, has revealed the Father.

Notice that two persons in John 1:18 are called "God" (Greek *theos*). The first turns out to be the Father. "No one has ever seen God" says John, but the Son has revealed the Father. This squares with the usage of the word "God" in John 1:1 which we looked at briefly in chapter 1. When the word "God" is used with no qualification as to which divine person is meant, the

Father is understood to be the referent by default. The Father is God, no question, but as in John 1:1, another person is also called "God" in John 1:18—"the one and only Son." John has parsed for us the difference between the unseeable Yahweh and the seeable Yahweh. Within the one God are two persons. The Father is the unseeable person and the Son is the seeable—the one who has revealed the Father. This helps answer the mystery of the unseeable and the seeable God we've been discussing. But it also raises some new questions.

Trouble with Translations

You may have noticed English translations differ somewhat in rendering John 1:18. Two differences especially stand out. First, some read "Son" in reference to Jesus whereas others also call him "God." Notice how the *GOD'S WORD* version renders John 1:18 compared to the CSB above: "No one has ever seen God. *God's only Son*, the one who is closest to the Father's heart, has made him known" (italics added). Here the Son is not called "God"[1] but simply "God's only Son." Which translation is correct?

A full answer gets pretty technical,[2] but most scholars (and English translations) conclude that when John originally wrote these words, he called the Son "God" at this point.[3] If so, then it is perfectly legitimate to speak of Jesus as "God the Son," which John in effect does in 1:18. But why do some translations differ on this crucial wording? The problem exists because some of our ancient Greek manuscripts of John 1:18 read "God" but others read "Son." The main reason the "God" reading is generally preferred is that the earliest and best Greek manuscripts of John read this way. It's also easier to explain how "God" could get altered to "Son" than vice versa.

Another reason is that the "God" reading makes better sense of the structure of John's prologue to his Gospel (1:1–18), as well as the structure of the entire book. John 1:1 clearly calls the Word "God." At the end of the book

1. English translations that do not read "God" in reference to the Son in Jn 1:18 include KJV, NKJV, and *GOD'S WORD*.

2. For a detailed explanation, see Murray Harris, *Jesus as God*, 74–83. In a nutshell, the Greek words for "God," *theos*, and "Son," *huios*, are easily confused as they appear in early NT manuscripts—which had to be hand copied by scribes. Many Greek manuscripts read "*huios*" (i.e., "Son") in Jn 1:18, but the earliest and best read *theos* (i.e., "God"). Since the expression in question in 1:18 is so similar to 3:16 and 18 (where it reads "Son"), it's more likely a scribe would change "God" to "Son" than "Son" to "God"—whether it happened accidentally or intentionally.

3. English translations that read "God" in reference to the Son in Jn 1:18 include NIV, CEB, CSB, ESV, NAB, NASB, NET©, NLT, NRSV, and NIrV.

Jesus is directly called "God" by Thomas (20:28).[4] These two occurrences of Jesus as God serve to bracket John's Gospel, showing the importance of Jesus' identity—just as two opposite bookends on a bookshelf or two opposite pieces of bread in a sandwich put the contents together into a unit. This sandwiching technique (called *inclusio*) was widely used by ancient writers to emphasize important themes. And in the case of John 1:18, if the "God" reading is accepted, the same sandwich exists at opposite sides of the prologue (1:1–18) as exists at the far sides of the Gospel as a whole. The prologue is bracketed by two declarations that Jesus is God, both of which emphasize that God's spokesperson—who is God, too—has uniquely revealed God to us. The prologue is beautifully structured and balanced. Like a good speech writer or essayist, John returns to his opening idea at the end by reiterating and enhancing the central theme. John 1:18 is a unit stressing the Son's deity and his role as the revealer of God the Father.

"One and Only" or "Only Begotten?"

Another noteworthy difference among English Bible translations of John 1:18 concerns these two expressions. What do these words really mean? The Greek word underlying these expressions is *monogenēs*.[5] Does it mean "one and only Son,"[6] as in many English translations, or "only begotten," as in others? (If you were raised using the familiar King James Version of the Bible, the expression "only begotten" in John 3:16—as well as 1:18—may be firmly glued in your memory.) When scholars debate the precise meaning of *monogenēs*, it gets pretty technical. The difference itself between the two senses is real yet not terribly significant. But explaining it a bit really helps to highlight an important aspect of John 1:18. It's worth learning about.

---

4. After Thomas's confession in 20:28, the Gospel wraps up (see 20:30–31). John 21 is an epilogue that he may have added later—though it is certainly part of the Gospel.

5. The Greek word *monogenēs* also occurs in John's writings in 1:14; 3:16, 18; 1 Jn 4:9 and in the rest of the NT in Lk 7:12; 8:42; 9:38; Heb 11:17.

6. As the NIV, CSB, and NIrV read. Similarly, *GOD'S WORD* reads "God's only Son;" NRSV, NAB, and CEB read "the only Son." I am in agreement with those scholars and English Bible translations that conclude sonship is implied in *monogenēs* —hence "one and only Son" (or the like), rather than simply "only," or "one and only," or "unique." See Rheaume, *Exegetical and Theological Analysis*, 114–16.

Both meanings ("one and only Son" and "only begotten") emphasize that Jesus is uniquely God's true Son, that he and he alone is God's *actual* Son. He's not simply *called* God's Son, figuratively. He's not merely *adopted* as God's Son, as in the case of his followers.[7] He actually *is* God's Son. John knows, of course, that many other beings were called "sons of God" in his day and in the Hebrew Scriptures. In chapter 2 we saw that angelic beings were sometimes referred to as "sons of God" in the OT. Since mankind is made in the image and likeness of God, Adam can be called "the son of God" (Lk 3:38).[8] To be God's son signifies a special relationship with him and the calling to represent him. Yahweh referred to the nation of Israel as his "firstborn son."[9] The Davidic kings were also considered Yahweh's sons[10] because they were commissioned to rule the nation as his representatives. Finally, in the well-known Jewish literature of Jesus' day, godly people could be called "sons of God."[11] Jesus himself referred to his disciples this way.[12] But when John applies the title "Son" to Jesus, he has something different and richer in mind. What John is saying is that Jesus is the real-deal Son. He's not just the Son of God metaphorically, like all the others.

For now, let's get back to "one and only Son" versus "only begotten Son." Which is right and what's the difference? The two possible senses of *monogenēs* are quite close in meaning, and so we have to split hairs a bit to distinguish them. But observing this intricate distinction is worth the effort. Without going too deep into the weeds, here's how they differ: The "one and only" meaning stresses that Jesus belongs to a class of his own; he's absolutely one-of-a-kind, period. No other is like him. The emphasis is on uniqueness. In fact, some who adopt this meaning translate *monogenēs* as "unique" in John 1:18.[13] On the other hand, the "only begotten" meaning stresses the natural Father-Son relationship. The Son is *from* the Father like no other. Just as a human son is *from* his father by natural descent, Jesus the Son is God's "natural" offspring—a mind-boggling thought, to be sure!

Until quite recently I was pretty sure the "one and only son" rendering of *monogenēs* was best—as most modern English translations have it. I considered the matter fairly settled. But a newer study has reopened the issue

7. True believers in Christ are called "sons" (or "children" in some translations) by adoption (Rom 8:15, 23; Gal 4:5; Eph 1:5).

8. Compare Gen 1:26–27 with 5:1–3. See Goldsworthy, *Son of God*, 59–82.

9. Exod 4:22–23. See also Deut 14:1; 32:6; Isa 1:2; 30:1, 9; 45:11; Wis 12:21; 16:10, 26.

10. 1 Sam 7:14; 2 Chr 28:6; Ps 2:7, 12.

11 Wis 2:18; 5:5; Sir 4:10; *Pss. Sol.* 13:9, 18:4.

12. Matt 5:9, 45; Lk 6:35.

13. NLT translates *monogenēs* "the unique One."

by making a good case for "only begotten."[14] At present I'm not strongly persuaded either way, and I'm open to go where the evidence leads. Fortunately, you can breathe a sigh of relief, because the difference doesn't matter to the big picture of Jesus' sonship as portrayed by John. What counts is what *both* renderings tell us: Jesus is God's Son in a way that no one else is. He is God's actual Son. Later in this book we'll see how important this fact is.

But you may be wondering, "How can Jesus be God's *actual* Son? What exactly does that mean? How can God have a Son and how did it happen?" That's a ginormous question which many stellar minds have probed and pondered deeply. Later, we'll explore it more in depth, but here it's vital to note both the Father and the Son are called "God" in the very same verse (Jn 1:18), just as in John 1:1. Thus we have God the Father and God the Son. In the Son's case, his sonship is absolutely unique. He's not "son of God" the way angels or a Davidic king or a pious Jew might bear that title. He's God's *actual* Son.

But you ask, "Weren't sons in Jesus' day regarded as subordinate to their fathers?" They were indeed. This understanding is taken for granted in John's narrative world,[15] and Jesus insists it's true for him as well. "[T]he Father is greater than I" (Jn 14:28), he assures his disciples. But if so, how can the Son be truly God and yet subordinate to God the Father? We'll return to this vital question later. But for now, let's get back to John 1:18.

"AT THE FATHER'S SIDE"

This little phrase in John 1:18 (as rendered in the CSB) is easy to skim over and miss, but it deserves attention. The Greek word used here is *kolpos*. It refers to the part of your body between your arms—in other words, your chest. As the NKJV translates it here, "The only begotten Son, who is in the bosom of the Father. . ." John is depicting the Son snuggled up next to the Father's chest sitting on his lap. It's a picture of love, tenderness, and closeness—a relationship of serene intimacy. If you've ever had the wondrous experience of snuggling your tiny child to your chest, this is the picture John paints for us here. For me, some of the dearest memories I have with my three children, when they were little, was the joy of holding them like this. And now that they're grown up, I still hug them close, and it never fails to warm my heart. If you're not a parent, perhaps you can remember far

14. See Irons, "Lexical Defense," 98–116. The view that *monogenēs* means "only" (or the like) is defended in Moody "God's Only Son," 213–19, whose lead many scholars have followed and defended further.

15. Jn 4:12; 8:53.

enough back to when your mom or dad cuddled you closely as a child and you felt loved and secure. That's the sense of tenderness and affection we see in John 1:18 between the Son and the Father.

Teacher's Pet

What's so amazing for us personally is that this is the sort of closeness God desires to have with us who believe in and follow Jesus! Incredible as it may sound, it's true. Allow me to explain briefly. Later in John's Gospel, a mysterious character shows up called "the disciple whom Jesus loved."[16] Obviously Jesus loved all his disciples,[17] but John portrays this particular disciple as especially close to Jesus. He experienced Jesus' love on a deeper and more personal level than the others. He's often referred to as "the beloved disciple," but we'll call him the BD for short.

The most striking example of the BD's extra-close relationship with Jesus is seen at the dinner table the night before Jesus died. At one point Jesus announces that one of those gathered is about to betray him. The baffled disciples stare at each other, clueless as to what he means and of whom he speaks. They have no idea that Judas, one of the twelve apostles sitting right there, will leave the room to perform his foul deed. At this point in the story we witness a fascinating exchange found only in John:

> One of his disciples, the one Jesus loved, was reclining close beside Jesus. Simon Peter motioned to him to find out who it was He was talking about. So he leaned back against Jesus and asked him, "Lord, who is it?" Jesus replied, "He's the one I give the piece of bread to after I have dipped it." When he had dipped the bread, he gave it to Judas, Simon Iscariot's son. (Jn 13:23–26 CSB)

Notice that the BD is at the table "reclining close beside Jesus" (13:23). Amazingly, this is the same expression—using the Greek word *kolpos* (literally "in the bosom of Jesus," AT)—that we find in John 1:18 where the Son is "in the bosom of the Father" (NKJV). John is sending his readers a mental text message recalling the intimate relationship between the Father and the Son described in John 1:18. What does such a relationship entail for the BD? Notice Peter motions to the BD to ask Jesus whom he's talking about. If you're familiar with the Gospels, you'll remember Peter is the leader

16. He is referred to this way in Jn 13:23; 19:26; 20:2; 21:7, 17, 20,. But he may also be the unnamed disciple mentioned in 1:37; 18:15–16.

17. See Jn 13:1, 34; 15:9, 12.

among the twelve apostles and one of Jesus' inner-circle of three disciples, consisting of him, James, and John. This threesome was closer to Jesus and witnessed events the others didn't see.[18] Yet at the dinner table on this momentous evening it's the BD, not Peter, who is sitting right next to Jesus in a place of extra-special friendship. Apparently Peter thinks this disciple has a better chance of getting insider information from Jesus than he has. "If I really want Jesus to tell us, I'll ask the teacher's pet!" Peter's hunch is right. As the BD speaks the question to Jesus—likely in a whisper—Jesus quietly provides the answer—which, by the way, the BD does not reveal to the others. The BD is really tight with Jesus! With him Jesus shares his secrets.

Unmasking the BD

Who is this BD? Actually, he claims to be the disciple who witnessed the events of the Gospel and later wrote them down. At the end of the Gospel's epilogue, he says, "This is the disciple who testifies to these things and who wrote them down" (Jn 21:24; cf. v. 20). The BD has traditionally been identified as the apostle John and for good reason. But since the BD functions as an ideal Jesus follower in John, some scholars have concluded that he's not a real person but simply a literary character created to illustrate discipleship at its very best. "After all," they say, "if he were really the apostle John, why wouldn't he clearly identify himself? And why would he portray himself as the model disciple? It sounds braggadocious!"

But this entirely misses the point John is making. What if it happens to be true that John was Jesus' closest friend and disciple? What if John did indeed enjoy a closeness with Jesus that illustrates the best of what discipleship is all about? If so, wouldn't John want to convey this in his Gospel so that his readers could seek the same sort of relationship with Jesus? Wouldn't this deeply enrich his account of Jesus' life by showing for us the kind of relationship Jesus desires to have with us? This seems perfectly reasonable to me. And yet on the other hand, how could John communicate this without sounding prideful, puffed up, and full of himself? Certainly a godly man who enjoys a richly deep relationship with the Lord is not going to brag about it. He will be humble and unassuming. It seems to me that the perfect way for John to "have his cake and eat it too" would be to tell the story the way it happened—so the lesson can be learned and appreciated—and yet keep himself anonymous when he tells it. If someone really wants to know the BD's identity, John has left enough clues to piece the puzzle together. But the point is not his identity; the point is that the rich relationship he enjoyed

18. E.g., Mk 5:37; 9:2; 14:33.

with Jesus is the model for us. It's like Jesus' relationship with his Father, and John is very interested in driving this point home to us in his Gospel. We will revisit this vital theme later. But for now, we need to get back to John 1:18.

"HE HAS REVEALED HIM"

These final words in John 1:18 tie together the whole verse. Unlike anyone else, the Son is in a unique position to reveal the Father. As Jesus will later say about himself, "No one has seen the Father except the one who is from God; only he has seen the Father" (Jn 6:46). Likewise, on another occasion Jesus said, "I am telling you what I have seen in the Father's presence" (Jn 8:38). These statements allude back to what John told us in 1:18. From his superb vantage point of closeness and intimacy with the Father, the Son comes to reveal God as never witnessed before.

But is it really like never before? Haven't we seen numerous examples of God showing up in human form? Isn't the life of Jesus just another appearance, the same as those we studied in the OT, except that it lasted longer? The answer to this question is important, but it involves the nuance of both a positive and negative response. First, let's probe the positive part of the answer: The Son did indeed show up in the OT.

Jesus in the OT

Actually this heading is subject to misunderstanding, but I use it to make a point. Strictly speaking, Jesus *never* shows up in the OT or any time before his birth. How so? Because "Jesus" is the *human* name given to the Son of God born to Mary. Before he was conceived in Mary's womb, he was not the man Jesus but the unembodied Word (Jn 1:1) or, as we'll show later, the eternal Son of God. To speak of "Jesus" in the OT is like talking about Columbus discovering America. It wasn't called "America" when Columbus arrived. This is what's known as an anachronism, like depicting Abraham Lincoln using a smart phone! Some speak of the appearances of Yahweh in the OT as the "preincarnate Christ." But technically this is anachronistic as well. "Christ" (or "Messiah") is a title that presupposes his humanity. I typically prefer to speak of him in the OT appearances as either the Word, the Son, the angel of the LORD, or Yahweh in human form, but "Jesus" is shorter. And so, whenever I speak of "Jesus" or "Christ" in the OT, please understand I mean the prehuman Son of God.

"But wait!" I can hear someone saying. "Aren't you getting ahead of yourself? Regardless of what you call him, how do you know it was really the Son in the OT Yahweh appearances? Couldn't it have been the Father or the Holy Spirit?" The quick answer is found in John 1:18. It couldn't have been the Father, because no one has seen him at any time. John is emphatic on this point.[19] As for the Holy Spirit, he's never associated in John or elsewhere with making appearances in human form.[20] But when it comes to the Son, John emphasizes that Jesus is the visible revelation of the Father.[21] Also, the Word, as we discovered back in chapter 1, is God's official voice, his spokesperson, whose declarations brought the universe into existence as recorded in Genesis 1. It makes sense that he would be the one to show up in OT days, just as John 1:18 says he reveals the Father in Jesus' human life. These factors make it likely that it was the Son who made the OT Yahweh appearances. But there's more to it than this.

Abraham Meets Jesus

Later in the Gospel of John, both Jesus and John confirm that it was the Son who appeared in the OT as Yahweh. Our first instance occurs as Jesus is in the middle of a heated debate with his opponents:

> "Your father Abraham was overjoyed to see my day, and he saw it and was glad." Then the Judeans replied, "You are not yet fifty years old! Have you seen Abraham?" Jesus said to them, "I tell you the solemn truth, before Abraham came into existence, I am!" Then they picked up stones to throw at him, but Jesus hid himself and went out from the temple area. (Jn 8:56–59 NET©)

So much is going on in this fascinating passage, but here we can only unpack a few pertinent points. To understand the background, it's important to remember that Abraham lived about two thousand years before Jesus, and yet Jesus claims that somehow Abraham saw Jesus' day. Hearing this, his enemies are convinced he's delusional.

But knowing who Jesus is, we naturally ask, "When did Abraham see Jesus?" The wording in this text is puzzling. How did Abraham see Jesus' "day?" Did Abraham see a vision of Jesus' future ministry? If he did, nothing in Genesis or the rest of Scripture even hints at it. Jesus seems to be referencing an event the Jews in his time could recognize from Scripture—otherwise

---

19. See also Jn 6:46; 1 Jn 4:12.

20. cf. Jn 14:17. The Spirit does, however, appear as a dove (Jn 1:35).

21. E.g., Jn 1:14; 6:36; 14:7–9; 20:29; cf. also 1 Jn 1:1–3; 4:14.

the premise of his claim would seem totally baseless to them. The only clue Jesus provides is his reference to Abraham rejoicing to see Jesus' day.

The sole instance in the Genesis account of Abraham that comes anywhere close to rejoicing and gladness takes place, ironically, during one of Yahweh's appearances to Abraham. We're told, "When Abram was ninety-nine years old, the LORD appeared to him and said, 'I am God Almighty; walk before me faithfully and be blameless'" (Gen 17:1).[22] During this appearance, Yahweh reveals the startling news that Abraham's wife, Sarah, is going to conceive a child in her old age. At this, Abraham suddenly bursts out in a fit of laughter: "Abraham fell facedown; he laughed and said to himself, 'Will a son be born to a man a hundred years old? Will Sarah bear a child at the age of ninety?'" (Gen 17:17).

Could this be what Jesus meant by rejoicing to see his day? At first it seems unlikely. After all, Abraham's laughter is apparently spawned more out of incredulity at the idea of a pregnant old woman than out of rejoicing for the good news of a soon-to-be baby boy. But let's not jump to conclusions. Abraham's first reaction to the surprising news may indeed have sparked a doubtful laugh. A ninety-year-old pregnant woman would get a laugh out of me! How about you? You have to admit, it's funny. On the other hand, Abraham and Sarah had patiently waited and trusted God for nearly twenty-five agonizing years, struggling and even quarrelling with each other over God's promise to provide them with an heir. Such momentous news must have produced a flood of powerful and even conflicting emotions within Abraham. To assume he was howling with laughter out of pure mockery and doubt is inconsistent with everything else we know about him. Here's the apostle Paul's inspired take on the incident:

> Without weakening in his faith, [Abraham] faced the fact that his body was as good as dead—since he was about a hundred years old—and that Sarah's womb was also dead. Yet he did not waver through unbelief regarding the promise of God, but was strengthened in his faith and gave glory to God, being fully persuaded that God had power to do what he had promised. (Rom 4:19–21)

Paul is convinced Abraham's reaction was more about faith than a funny farce.

But there's still more to this laughing matter. In Genesis 18, Yahweh appears again to Abraham—a passage we discussed in chapter 2. On this occasion, Sarah overhears Yahweh reiterate his prediction of her impending

22. Like the Genesis 18 appearance studied in chapter 2, the characteristics of this Yahweh appearance indicate it was likely not a dream or a vision (17:3, 17, 22).

pregnancy. Like her husband in the previous encounter, Sarah immediately laughs to herself when she hears of it (18:12–15). If you put yourself in Sarah's sandals, the promise must have sounded too good (and hilarious!) to be true. A year or so later, when Sarah's baby boy is born, Abraham names him "Isaac," which means in Hebrew "he laughs." After the initial shock and surprise of the pregnancy announcement wore off, Abraham and Sarah must have been delirious with joy over their miracle son. By naming him "He Laughs," they were fondly remembering their stunned-turned-ecstatic response when the impossible became a reality. And yet "He Laughs" was born out of (pun intended!) two appearances of Yahweh. For Abraham and Sarah, these days were likely the most memorable and happy of their lives. With this background in mind, Jesus' statement in John 8:56 fits these events in Abraham's life better than anything else. The "day" Jesus refers to is likely his remarkable birth-announcement visits to the elderly couple.

But there's one more bit of evidence to which we can point. When Jesus' opponents scoff at the notion that the young man standing before them somehow met Abraham two thousand years earlier, he makes this stunning declaration: "I tell you the solemn truth, before Abraham came into existence, I am!" (8:58 NET©). Does the expression "I am" sound familiar? It's a clear reference to the explanation of Yahweh's name (cf. Exod 3:14–15) we discussed in chapter 2. We'll explore this text in greater length in an upcoming chapter. But here notice that Jesus applies the divine title "I am" to himself, claiming to be Yahweh. Jesus is saying, "Seeing Abraham two thousand years ago? That's nothing! Long before Abraham existed, I am!" Notice he doesn't say "I was" but "I am." Jesus is not simply claiming to have existed before Abraham, which would be true if he were merely an angel. No, Jesus' words lay claim to the eternal present tense of Yahweh's true identity. Jesus' enemies clearly get his point; they react by attempting to stone him because they believe he has profaned the sacred name of Yahweh by applying it to himself (Jn 8:59). But if we see Jesus' declaration within the context of the debate about Abraham, we can better understand what he meant. Abraham could see Jesus' "day" because as the eternal Word he is present every day throughout time—including in his appearances to the great patriarch and his wife.

Isaiah Meets Jesus

Another reference to Jesus making a Yahweh appearance in the OT comes from John as he provides inspired commentary on Jesus' ministry. John is lamenting the rejection Jesus received from so many of his fellow Jews, despite all the miracles he performed:

> Even after Jesus had performed so many signs in their presence, they still would not believe in him. This was to fulfill the word of Isaiah the prophet: "Lord, who has believed our message and to whom has the arm of the Lord been revealed?" For this reason they could not believe, because, as Isaiah says elsewhere: "He has blinded their eyes and hardened their hearts, so they can neither see with their eyes, nor understand with their hearts, nor turn—and I would heal them." Isaiah said this because he saw Jesus' glory and spoke about him. (Jn 12:37–41)

This text requires a close look and a bit of unpacking. John informs us the Jewish rejection of Jesus was sad but not surprising. He proves this by quoting two texts from the OT prophet Isaiah, who lived and wrote many centuries before Jesus' birth. John's first quotation comes from Isaiah 53 where the Servant of Yahweh (whom the NT identifies as Jesus) faces stubborn rejection from Israel. This stunning prophecy is the clearest and most detailed prediction of Jesus' rejection and death found anywhere in the OT.

But then John quotes another text from the Book of Isaiah, this time from chapter 6. Like the first quotation, Isaiah speaks of Israel's stubborn unbelief using the vivid language of blinded eyes and hardened hearts. What's so amazing is what many readers of John miss when they come to these momentous words: "Isaiah said this because he saw Jesus'[23] glory and spoke about him" (Jn 12:37). When did Isaiah see Jesus' glory? Back in Isaiah 6, from which John is quoting, we discover another appearance of Yahweh, and in this case his glory is prominently featured:

> In the year that King Uzziah died, I saw the Lord, high and exalted, seated on a throne; and the train of his robe filled the temple. Above him were seraphim, each with six wings: With two wings they covered their faces, with two they covered their feet, and with two they were flying. And they were calling to one another: "Holy, holy, holy is the LORD Almighty; the whole earth is full of his glory." At the sound of their voices the doorposts and thresholds shook and the temple was filled with smoke. "Woe to me!" I cried. "I am ruined! For I am a man of unclean lips, and I live among a people of unclean lips, and my eyes have seen the King, the LORD Almighty." (Isa 6:1–5)

---

23. In the Greek text, the word "Jesus'" does not appear here, as it does in the NIV. It simply reads "his." The NIV translators supply the name to make plain what the context clearly reveals.

This is one of the OT's most awesome Yahweh appearances. Unlike some cases, in which Yahweh shows up in the somewhat plain look of a man, here Yahweh is seated on a glorious throne, high and lifted up, surrounded by angelic creatures (i.e., the seraphim) that are sounding his praises and afraid even to look at him. Verse 5 confirms that Isaiah is seeing Yahweh himself. So fearful and flabbergasted is Isaiah at this glorious sight that he shrieks at his impending doom! He remembers that no one can see Yahweh's face and live (Exod 33:20). Thankfully, Isaiah lives to tell of this spectacular encounter, but before the appearance is over, Yahweh imparts to Isaiah the prophecy that John quotes. Clearly the glory Isaiah saw and to which John refers is Yahweh's glory revealed in Isaiah 6. And in case there's any doubt about this, recall the words of the angelic creatures near Yahweh, "Holy, holy, holy is the LORD Almighty; the whole earth is full of *his glory*" (Isa 6:3; italics added). Yet John says that what Isaiah saw was Jesus himself and *his* glory! Like Jesus' allusion to the Abraham episode, John's quote from Isaiah 6 identifies an OT appearance of Yahweh as the preincarnate Son.

And so, when John declares in 1:18 that God the Son has revealed God the Father, he's not referring exclusively to Jesus' life as recorded in John. From John's perspective, the Son has always exercised his role as the Word, God's spokesperson who is also God himself. When God shows up visibly, he comes in the person of his Son.[24]

Why Trailers Can't Compare

Yet with all our excitement over the OT appearances of Yahweh, John would be quick to remind us that the trailers can't compare to the feature film. For John, the definitive revelation of God is found not in OT appearances, but in Jesus Christ, the Word who "became flesh and made his dwelling among us" (Jn 1:14). When John says in 1:18 that the Son revealed the Father, he's speaking *primarily* of this unique event, which Christians call the *incarnation*.

Nothing in the OT compares with it.[25] To see Jesus is not just to see an appearance of Yahweh, the Son, but also the perfect representation of God

24. A word of clarification is appropriate here: Because the Son is the member of the Trinity that makes the visible appearances, we should not conclude that he is not as glorious as God the Father or the Holy Spirit, or that he does not also exist as a nonphysical, invisible spirit. In his divine nature, the Son shares the same eternal glory as the Father possesses (Jn 17:5) and is omnipresent (Jn 14:23; Matt 18:20; 28:20; Eph 4:10).

25. Some scholars advise that postulating OT appearances of the Son in the OT diminishes the uniqueness of the incarnation (e.g., Sanders, *Triune God*, 224–26). But

the Father. As Jesus said, "The one who looks at me is seeing the one who sent me" (Jn 12:45). Two for the price of one! In Jesus, God didn't visit the planet for a fleeting appearance in a temporary human form[26] as in the OT visits. In Jesus, God entered the human race by joining himself permanently with humanity.[27] Nothing of this wondrous magnitude had ever occurred before. Unlike the OT appearances, Jesus is God's light not only for a select few OT believers, but for all mankind so that all may believe and be saved.[28] And the grand finale of this supreme revelation is Jesus' death on the cross for our sins, followed by his resurrection and ascension. Jesus refers to this as his being "lifted up"[29]—an event of cosmic significance in John's Gospel. Unlike the OT appearances, Jesus came into the world as God's ultimate gift, so that "whoever believes in him shall not perish but have eternal life" (Jn 3:16).

True, Jesus' human life did not come with the stunning special effects of glory,[30] as many of the OT appearances did. But the quality of the revelation was of much greater significance. And when Jesus returns in power and great glory to raise the dead and fully establish his kingdom, he will consummate the glorious revelation he began when he became flesh.[31] This is the ultimate hope of every Christ-follower. The final chapter of the Bible sums up this unfathomable climax by saying, "They will see his face" (Rev 22:4).

---

while due caution is in order, it seems the OT preincarnate appearances are warranted by the biblical evidence, especially in John.

26. The tangible human forms in which Yahweh appeared in the OT were temporary—as in the case of angels that appeared as humans. Unlike Jesus, they were not conceived and physically born, nor did they experience a human life and death.

27. Contrary to common misconception, Jesus did not dispense with his humanity or his body when he ascended to heaven. He will return just as he left (Acts 1:11). He is still a man (1 Tim 2:5)—though now with a glorified human body (Phil 3:21)—and remains a descendent of Judah and David (Rev 5:5; 22:16).

28. Jn 1:4, 7; 3:19–21; 8:12; 9:5.

29. Jn 3:14; 8:28; 12:32, 34. This expression "lifted up" is an allusion to Isaiah's prophecy of Yahweh's Servant who is lifted up in glory after suffering horribly (Isa 52:13–15). John uses it as a double entendre to refer both to Jesus' being lifted up on the cross and in glory.

30. According to John, Jesus' presence (1:14) and miracles (2:11) showed his glory to his disciples, but he otherwise appeared as simply human to onlookers. The other NT Gospels record Jesus' transfiguration as an exception to the rule (Matt 17:1–8; Mk 9:2–8; Lk 9:28–36).

31. Jn 5:27–29; 1 Jn 3:2; Rev 1:7; 11:15–19; 19:11–21; 21–22.

HOW DOES THIS APPLY TODAY?

As we've seen in this chapter, the history of God's dealings with humankind shows God's desire to fellowship closely in human form with us—so we can see, touch, and enjoy him—just as the BD did. But our sin and human frailties are formidable obstacles that only God himself can overcome. His solution, in one word, is Jesus.

God wanted to show himself to us and be with us so badly he crossed an immeasurable divide to become one of us! On the cross he paid the penalty for our sins so that the deadly obstacles could be permanently removed. If you want to know how much God desires your company, look at the life of Jesus. If you want to see the depth of his love, look at the cross of Jesus. If you want to see the future he's prepared for you, look at the resurrection and promised return of Jesus.

Think of what this means! When you go to the Lord in prayer, you can do so with the confidence that he really desires your companionship. Think of your prayer time not simply as communicating information to God, but as a private meeting with a dearly cherished yet highly revered friend. When you feel lonely or left out, remember that the Lord is always present to comfort, strengthen, and refresh you. When you're loaded down with guilt and feelings of failure, remember what he's done to rescue and restore you—his death and resurrection. Confess your sins to him in simple faith and humble repentance, and he will soothe your soul and repair your spirit. When you're suffering and discouraged with your circumstances, remember his promise to return and remake you in a recreated universe where, in everlasting glory, you will see his face.

QUESTIONS FOR DISCUSSION

1. What stands out to you in this chapter?

2. In some of the OT appearances of Yahweh, those who see him are fearful (e.g., Moses at the burning bush and Isaiah) while others are not (e.g., Abraham and Sarah). Why do you think this is?

3. What are some practical ramifications of this chapter for your life beyond those noted at the end?

A VERSE TO MEMORIZE

No one has ever seen God. The one and only Son, who is himself God and is at the Father's side—he has revealed him. (Jn 1:18 CSB)

APPLY WHAT YOU'VE LEARNED

Try to find other appearances of Yahweh (or the angel of Yahweh) in the OT that were not discussed in this chapter. You may want to use a Bible concordance to help you. What can you learn from these appearances?

CHAPTER 4

God's Equal

In a conversation I heard many years ago, a woman was asked, "If you saw your dog was drowning, and at the same time a human you didn't know was drowning, and you only had time to rescue one of them, which would you save?" The woman didn't hesitate. "I would save my dog, of course!" I suppose many people in our culture would respond the same way. But still her answer shocked and sickened me. Don't get me wrong. I know what it's like to cherish a dog dearly. Debbie and I own a dog that's getting up in years now, and we dread the day she leaves us. But a human being is incomparably more valuable than any animal[1]—no matter how much we may be attached to the pet and no matter how little we may know or like the human.

A fundamental teaching of Scripture and Christian theology is that because humans are created in God's image,[2] they are therefore of greater inherent worth than any object or animal on the planet. This is true no matter how young or old, good or bad a human may be. Just as a crumpled, worn-out twenty-dollar bill is worth the same as a new, fresh one, so the value of a human life is not determined by its condition or age. All humans are of equal value—even though one may be much smarter, kinder, healthier, better educated, better looking, and better known to you than another. You may like one much more than another, but they both have the same

1. See Jesus' remarks in Matt 10:31; 12:12; Lk 12:7.

2. See Gen 1:26–27; 9:6; Jas 3:9. Being made in God's image does not mean humans physically look like God; he is a nonphysical being (Jn 4:24). It basically means that humans are God's physical representatives on earth to rule over it responsibly for him (Gen 1:28). A human being is not a facsimile of God but a representation of him—as the American flag represents our country and stands for its founding values but doesn't actually look like America. For more on "the image and likeness of God," see Waltke and Yu, *Old Testament Theology*, 215–22.

inherent value before God because they both share the same nature—the nature of humanness. Humans differ greatly in size, shape, color, race, etc., but we are all of the same species; we all have human DNA. We all have a human soul/spirit. We're all made in God's image and are loved by him, and therefore we are all of equal and inherent value and dignity by nature.

So far in this book we've seen that the Father and the Son are both called and treated as "Yahweh" and "God" in the Bible. But are they equal? Some believe—such as the JWs—the Son is not equal to God the Father. Though they believe the Son is a god, they consider him to be a lower-grade deity compared to Almighty God, the Father. Could they be right? Alternatively, Biblical Unitarians[3] (BUs for short) believe the Bible presents us with a Jesus who did not exist before his earthly life. He is God or Yahweh only in the sense that he perfectly represents God the Father and is empowered by the Spirit to act in his place. Could they be right? On the other hand, classical Christianity affirms the Father and the Son are coequal. Both are truly God by nature, just as two humans are human by nature and therefore equal.

In this chapter we probe the equality question by looking carefully at the very first verse of John's Gospel. We will discover that when John 1:1 is understood in its literary, cultural, and biblical context, this verse affirms the Word (or Son) is God by *nature* and therefore coequal with God the Father. We'll also discover why this teaching is of such ginormous importance to your life. A savior who is less than truly God is a poor substitute for the Savior we find in the Jesus of the Bible.

A PERSONAL WORD

We now return to our discussion of the opening of John's Gospel that we started in chapter 1. Once again, John begins as follows: "In the beginning was the Word, and the Word was with God, and the Word was God" (Jn 1:1). If you keep reading, you discover the pronouns "he" and "him" are applied to the Word in verses 2–4 by nearly all English translations, indicating the Word is a person: "*He* was with God in the beginning. Through *him* all things were made; without *him* nothing was made that has been made. In

---

3. An alternate term often used to describe this belief system is Socinianism, named after Fausto Sozzini (or Socinus)—a sixteenth-century theologian who rejected the Trinity and espoused a form of unitarianism that he and his followers believed was thoroughly biblical. Biblical Unitarianism should not be confused with Unitarian Universalism—a liberal, pluralistic religious movement (often called simply Unitarianism) with no specific doctrinal creed or view of God.

him was life, and that life was the light of all mankind" (1:2–4; italics added). The Word is clearly a person, not simply a thing.

The BUs' Impersonal Word

But some argue this is a biased translation of the Greek. The pronouns can and should be taken as neuter and thus translated "it" instead of "he/him."[4] Also, though the Greek term translated "Word," *logos*, is grammatically masculine, a "word" is not normally thought of as a person but rather an impersonal object. This view, then, understands the Word of John 1:1 not to be a distinct person with God the Father at the beginning of creation but the expression of God's activity. BUs and some well-known NT scholars[5] understand John 1:1–4 this way. In chapter 1, we called the Word "the voice." But a BU might ask, "Why should we assume God's voice is a distinct person? After all, every human person has a voice, but it's not a separate person. Why should we assume God's voice is a person?" It's a fair question that deserves a good answer.

BUs take the Word to be God's "self-expressed activity"[6] through which the universe was created. "It" was not a person but God's "creative activity" at work. If we read John 1 with this understanding, they say, we get a much simpler and more sensible view of God and Jesus than the complicated Trinitarian scenario. In the beginning, God spoke the universe into existence using his Word (i.e., his powerful voice)—just as Genesis 1 and John 1:1–3 tell us. The declaration in 1:14—where we're told "[t]he Word became flesh and made his dwelling among us"—simply means God's expression of himself (i.e., the Word) came upon the man Jesus to make him the embodiment of God's activity on earth.[7] When did this happen? BUs (and some NT scholars) often point to Jesus' baptism when the Spirit descended upon him and empowered him for his ministry (Jn 1:32–34).

Thus, BUs claim, the man Jesus is not *God* the Son, but the Son of God—an otherwise ordinary man upon whom the Word/Spirit descended

4. Buzzard and Hunting, *Doctrine of the Trinity*, 192–93, 283–84.

5. See, for example, Robinson, *Priority of John*, 379–94; Sidebottom, *Christ of the Fourth Gospel*, 161–63, 194–97; Dunn, *Did the First Christians?* 117–23 (though Dunn's view is nuanced in other publications). See my detailed interaction with these and other scholars on this topic in Rheaume, *Exegetical and Theological Analysis*, 211–36.

6. Buzzard and Hunting use a variety of terms to describe their understanding of the Word, including God's "self-expressed activity," "eternal plan," "creative activity," and "design" or "intention," as in the mind of an architect (*Doctrine of the Trinity*, 190, 286).

7. Ibid., 196, 259–60, 287.

and who became the embodiment of Yahweh on earth. He's called "Son of God," they say, because his virgin mother, Mary, was impregnated supernaturally by God (Lk 1:35).[8] The Son of God began to exist when he was conceived; he did not preexist with the Father before the creation of the universe. What preexisted was the impersonal Word. Why did Jesus speak and act like God? BUs answer that just as a messenger (in the ancient world) represents, speaks for, and should be treated like his sender—Jesus represents, speaks for, and should be treated like the Father who sent him.[9] But he was certainly not a preexistent, distinct person, equal to God. He is God's perfect representative, not God himself. Could the BUs be right?

Taking this Personally

For several good reasons, this understanding of the *logos* (i.e., Word) in John 1 should be rejected as badly mistaken. The first hint the Word is a person—not merely an impersonal object, power, or expression—comes in John 1:1 where we read, "the Word was *with* God" (italics added). The Greek preposition translated "with" (*pros*) in this construction implies a close personal relationship between the Word and God: "the Word was face to face with God,"[10] or perhaps better, "the Word was in close company with God."[11] This would indicate the *logos* is not an impersonal object but a cognizant person. Of course, if this were the only indication of personhood, we might conclude John was figuratively personifying the *logos* in this instance.

But the case for the Word's personhood only gets stronger as John continues. In chapter 3 we learned that John 1:18 depicts the Son as "in the bosom of" the Father—signifying close, personal relations. But when does this relationship take place? Is John talking about before, during, or after the Son's life on earth? John provides some clues. An awkwardly literal translation of the Greek reads, "the one being in the bosom of the Father" (AT). John's usage of the Greek present participle (i.e., *ho ōn*, "the one being") here most likely signifies a timeless sense.[12] In other words, John is locating the Son's place in and outside of time right at the Father's heart in the closest, personal communion. Remember the bookends (or sandwich) effect in John 1:1 and 1:18 we discussed in chapter 3? John calls the Word/Son "God" at the beginning and ending of his prologue, creating a bookend effect that

8. Ibid., 70–72.

9. Ibid., 43–44, 261, 291.

10. Robertson, *Grammar of the Greek New Testament*, 623.

11. Wallace, *Greek Grammar Beyond the Basics*, 358–59; BDF, §2391

12. Rheaume, *Exegetical and Theological Analysis*, 120–23.

highlights Jesus' deity. Most likely these bookends also emphasize the close, personal relationship between God the Father and the Word/Son. Notice on one side we read, "the Word was in close company with God" (1:1), and similarly on the other side, "the one being in the bosom of the Father." Since John 1:1 is clearly before the Son's earthly life, this indicates he preexisted as the personal *logos*—not simply the impersonal expression of God's activity.

But what seals the deal are the numerous references throughout John where Jesus refers back to his relationship with his Father *before* he came into the world. Consider a few examples:

> "For I have come down from heaven not to do my will but to do the will of him who sent me." (Jn 6:38)

> "No one has seen the Father except the one who is from God; only he has seen the Father." (Jn 6:46)

> "I am telling you what I have seen in the Father's presence, and you are doing what you have heard from your father." (Jn 8:38)

> "I came from the Father and entered the world; now I am leaving the world and going back to the Father." (Jn 16:28)

> "And now, Father, glorify me in your presence with the glory I had with you before the world began." (Jn 17:5)

Clearly Jesus is recollecting his preexistent state (before the incarnation) with the Father. He remembers being there with him! This cannot be explained by appealing to the Father's foreknowledge of the Son in the distant past (as if he had an *ideal* but not *real* existence) because the Son speaks of himself in the first person in the Father's presence before creation.[13] This confirms that the preexistent, personal relationship indicated in John 1:1 and 1:18 is to be taken at face value. But there's still more to the story.

The Logos in John's World

Here we need to step back for a moment to ask why John refers to the Son as the *logos* in his preexistent state with the Father. Biblical scholars have probed this question deeply since ancient times.[14]

One possibility is that John is tapping into the Jewish concept of Yahweh's wisdom personified, which—like the *logos* in John 1—existed with

---

13. To this we can add John 8:58, in which Jesus claims—using the emphatic first person pronoun *egō* ("I")—to have existed before Abraham: "Before Abraham was born, I am."

14. For a survey of recent scholarly views, see Rheaume, *Exegetical and Theological Analysis*, 91–97.

God at creation.[15] In some texts, wisdom almost seems to be a person distinct from Yahweh.

Other scholars have pointed to the way in which *logos* was discussed in John's day among the Greek philosophers—the divine principle that brought structure to the universe and was the essence of human rationality. A Jewish philosopher in Jesus' day named Philo was influenced by this thinking and spoke of the *logos* as God's purposeful interaction with creation.[16] Perhaps John was using the word *logos* to build a bridge to his non-Jewish audience.

Other scholars have connected John's *logos* with the Jewish use of the Aramaic term *memra* (i.e., "utterance" or "word of God").[17] Some ancient Jewish teachers used "the Memra" in place of God's sacred name, Yahweh, or perhaps as a personified attribute of Yahweh or even a virtual person that interacted with creation on his behalf. If John's meaning of *logos* emerged out of this background, it would fit well with how he associates Jesus with the divine name, as we saw in chapter 3.

Alternatively, perhaps John was familiar with all of these concepts associated with the term *logos* and wanted to use it in his Gospel in his own unique way (similar yet different to these concepts) in order to connect with a wide variety of people. This is possible.

The Pre-Jesus Word

So then, why did John use *logos* for the preincarnate Son? The most likely answer, as I see it, is because of the way Yahweh's word is portrayed in the OT, as we discussed in chapter 1. As we discovered, God used his word to bring the universe into existence:

> By the word of the LORD
>   the heavens were made,
>   their starry host by the
>   breath of his mouth. . .
> For he spoke, and it came to be;
>   he commanded, and it stood firm. (Ps 33:6, 9)

---

15. E.g., Prov 3:19; 8:22–31; Sir 1:1–30; 24:6, 8; Wis 7:22, 25; 9:2, 9. A scholar who pursues this approach is Ben Witherington in *John's Wisdom.*

16. A scholar who pursues this approach is C. H. Dodd in *Interpretation of the Fourth Gospel*, 276–85.

17. A scholar who pursues this approach is John Ronning in *Jewish Targums*, esp. 1–45.

Like Genesis 1, this psalm says Yahweh's "word" brought creation into being. True, this Scripture does not indicate the word is a person, but there's more to the story.

Fascinatingly, a few of Yahweh's OT visual appearances speak of him as "the word of Yahweh."[18] Notice: "After this, *the word* of the LORD came to Abram in a vision: 'Do not be afraid, Abram. I am your shield, your very great reward'" (Gen 15:1; italics added). We're told here that Abram was seeing a vision, in other words, something he could see (during his dream or trance-like state). He's not just hearing a voice; he's seeing someone. But how does one *see* a word? Evidently this "word of Yahweh" was not an impersonal object but a person who could talk and be seen. At first we might suppose this is a messenger (or angel) sent from Yahweh. But this won't do. Notice this "word" speaks in the first person as Yahweh himself: "*I* am your shield. . ." (italics added). Later in the same passage we read, "Then *the word* of the LORD came to him: 'This man will not be your heir . . .'" (Gen 15:4; italics added). Twice this person is identified as "the word of Yahweh," and yet throughout the passage he continues to speak as Yahweh himself. In verse 5, the word takes Abram outside. Whether Abram is still in a visionary state or now acting in the tangible world, somehow *the word* of Yahweh visibly leads him. In verse 7, Yahweh says, "I am the LORD . . ." In verse 8, Abram says to the word of Yahweh, "Sovereign LORD, how can I know . . . ?" In verse 9, we read, "So the LORD said to him . . ." The point here is that Yahweh and the word of Yahweh are one and the same!

But this remarkable manifestation of "the word of Yahweh" is not an isolated incident. In 1 Samuel 3:1 and 7, "the word" of Yahweh makes another visual appearance. At first Samuel only hears Yahweh's voice. But then Yahweh appears to the young boy Samuel. The text says, "The LORD came and stood there . . ." (3:10); apparently this involved an appearance of Yahweh in human form. As with Abram, Yahweh speaks to Samuel in the first person (3:11–14). In 3:21, the author doubles down on this by stressing that Yahweh "continued to *appear*" to Samuel "and *revealed himself*...through his *word*" (italics added). Again, just as with Abram, the word of Yahweh shows up, speaks, and acts as Yahweh himself.

The prophet Jeremiah has the same sort of experience. He writes, "*The word* of the LORD came to me, saying, 'Before I formed you in the womb I knew you. . .'" (Jer 1:4–5; italics added). Again note that it's the word of Yahweh who speaks as Yahweh himself ("I"). But remarkably, a few verses later Jeremiah says, "Then the LORD reached out his hand and touched my

18. For my discussion of these appearances, I am indebted to Heiser, *Unseen Realm*, 128–32.

mouth and said to me, 'I have put my words in your mouth. . .'" (Jer 1:9)
Fascinating! Yahweh has a hand that touches Jeremiah's mouth! The *word*
of Yahweh—who identifies himself *as* Yahweh—has appeared to Jeremiah
apparently in human form, just as he did to Abram and Samuel.

We have already seen in chapter 2 that John portrays the preincarnate
Jesus as making OT Yahweh appearances, but now we discover some OT
Yahweh appearances in which he is identified as "the word of the LORD."
John may have had a number of reasons for referring to the preexistent Son
as the Word, but the most likely and prominent background is the specialized OT usage of "the word of Yahweh" who creates the universe and, as a
distinct person, speaks and acts as Yahweh himself. This is precisely what we
find in the Jesus of John's Gospel.

GOD'S DNA

Yet at this point a thoughtful person might ask, "Okay, but might the Logos/
Word simply be Yahweh's representative, such as a lower-grade god or chief
angel? After all, John 1:1 clearly speaks of two persons. If there is only one
true God, then only one person can *truly* be Almighty God, Yahweh himself, correct?" These are hugely important questions.

Recall our discussion at the beginning of this chapter. All human beings are of the same species and possess human nature (i.e., the essential
attributes of humanness). Humans are all created in God's image and therefore equal by nature. Likewise, if there is only one true God *by nature*[19]
(i.e., one being who alone possesses God's nature—the essential attributes
of Yahweh)—then the Word can only be the true God if he has the nature
of Yahweh—the "divine DNA."[20] If he does not possess the nature of the one
true God, you can *call* him anything you like, but there's no way he's truly
Yahweh himself. At best he may be *functioning* as Yahweh—as his representative or an angel or a secondary god—but he cannot actually *be* God
himself. Remember, there are many "so-called gods," but there is only one
God by nature.

Is Jesus God by nature? That's the million-dollar question! The term
scholars often use to speak of "the nature of something" is *ontological*—referring not just to the *function* of a thing but to its *being*. To be God ontologically is to be really and truly God in actual fact. And so the real question

---

19. See the discussion in chapter 2 under "Truly Divine."

20. As a nonphysical being, of course, God has no DNA. No irreverence is intended
here. I'm using the genetic analogy only to illustrate natural relation.

becomes: Is the Son ontologically God or only functionally God? John 1:1 provides the answer.[21]

Does it Really Matter?

If your head is beginning to spin or your eyes are crossing, don't panic. Unless you've studied this topic in some depth, this discussion may seem complicated and unnecessary. Is it worth it to read on? Should you skip this section? A Christian woman once asked me, "Why does it matter if Jesus was really God? What difference does it make?" It's a fair question.

Allow me to ask a question in return: Does it matter to you if God himself actually came to save you or if he sent a stand-in to do it for him? Think of a leader or artist or entertainer you've always respected, admired, and dreamed of meeting. Which would mean more to you—for this person to visit you personally or for a representative to come in his/her place? You have to admit, for God to come personally shows a much deeper commitment and love on his part, does it not? It literally means God has skin in the game. He didn't just mail in his concern; he came himself. He doesn't just know about human pain, shame, and temptation; he experienced it himself. He didn't just care about humans; he became one. He doesn't just sympathize with you; he empathizes. He too felt hunger, thirst, cold, sweat, tiredness, muscle cramps, the need to relieve himself, wrenching heartache, mental anguish, and the copious loss of his own blood. He died a more horrible, painful, and shameful death than has the vast majority of people who've inhabited the planet. If God actually visited this planet as a genuine human being, it's a game changer for the way we understand his love for us.

But there's an even more basic question involved here: How can the death of only one man atone for the sins of all people? If Jesus is only a man, then his life would be no more valuable than any other human life. How could he alone substitute for the lives of all humanity? Many Christian thinkers throughout church history have recognized that only God himself could pay the sin debt we owe. On the other hand, only humanity deserves to pay this debt, since it is humanity that has violated God's commands and accrued the debt. It's a catch twenty-two: Only man *should* pay, but only God *could* pay. The psalm writer put it this way:

---

21. Many NT scholars shy away from talk of ontology in the NT and prefer to speak in terms of the divine function or identity of Christ. I see this as generally correct, but in John 1:1 (and some other NT texts regarding Jesus' deity), the ontological nature of the Word is the issue. See Harris, *Jesus as God*, esp. 288–91; Rheaume, *Exegetical and Theological Analysis*, 101–7.

> No one can redeem the life of another
>   or give to God a ransom for them—
> the ransom for a life is costly,
>   no payment is ever enough—
> so that they should live on forever
>   and not see decay. (Ps 49:7–9)

According to this text, God will not accept anything in exchange to redeem a human being from death. The cost of a human life is too much. And yet Jesus once said about himself, "For even the Son of Man did not come to be served, but to serve, and to give his life as a ransom for many" (Mk 10:45). According to the NT, Jesus' atoning death paid this ransom from sin and death for us.[22] But surely this is impossible according to Psalm 49, is it not? No human can do this! Thankfully, the psalm writer goes on to provide the answer: "But God will redeem me from the realm of the dead; he will surely take me to himself" (49:15).

What no one else can do, God himself can and does do in Jesus Christ. He himself provides redemption. In becoming a true man, he was able to die in our place. But because he was also truly God, his life was of infinite value and could pay the ransom for all humanity. Does it really matter if Jesus is truly God? Nothing could matter more.

Was the Word "a god?"

John 1:1 speaks of the Word as God, but in what sense? The BU idea of an impersonal Word does not fit the evidence. But what about the JW concept of a lesser god? Could the Word/Son be god in a lesser sense, as in some of the OT instances of *elohim* we discussed in chapter 2? Such a god could theoretically be the perfect representative of the Father to speak and act on his behalf. One might call him "god" in the same sense Yahweh referred to the gods in Psalm 82:1 and 82:6. Of course, such a god would not be Yahweh himself, who is uncreated and has no beginning. He would be God functionally, but not ontologically. Though he may represent God and—on occasion—speak, act, and be treated like God, he would in fact not be Yahweh by nature.

To use a crude illustration, if the Word as a god had DNA, it would not be Yahweh DNA; it would be, in this view, angel or *elohim* (in the older sense discussed in chapter 2) DNA. Or let's put it another way: everything that exists falls into one of two categories—Yahweh and his creation. If the

22. E.g., Mk 14:24; Jn 6:32–33; 10:10–18; Rom 5:6–19; Gal 3:13–14; Heb 2:14–15; 1 Pet 1:2–5, 18–19; Rev 1:5–6.

Word is a god but not truly Yahweh, then he's on the creation side of the line. Could this be what's going on in John 1:1? To answer we must look closely at John's wording to unpack his precise meaning. Some of the discussion here may get a bit technical, but I'll do my best to keep it clear, simple, and accurate. Please stay with me; it's worth it!

The best way to distinguish what John *is* saying from what he's *not* saying is to look at the Greek of John 1:1 using my awkwardly literal English translation underneath it:

En   archē   ēn   ho logos,   kai ho logos
In   (the) beginning was   the Logos,   and the Logos

ēn   pros ton theon, kai   theos ēn   ho logos.
was   with the God,   and   God   was   the Logos.

Notice the first occurrence of "God" is preceded by the English definite article "the" (*ton*). The article does not appear in English translations because our language doesn't typically use the definite article before God in a sentence like this. But why then is it present in the Greek here? The article emphasizes that "the God" is not simply any old god (i.e., "a god") but *the* God whom Jesus so often calls the Father. Without question, "the God" is the OT Yahweh, Israel's one and only true God. The Greek article also distinguishes "the God" from the Word when John writes "the *logos* was God." If John had written, "the *logos* was the God," he would be saying the God and the Logos are the same person, which wouldn't make any sense in the sentence. The Word is *with* the God and also *is* the God? Hopeless! But what John actually wrote differentiates them as two distinct persons—the Logos and the God.

But here's where some people get really confused. In the last five words of John 1:1 (which we will call 1:1c), the Greek article is conspicuously *absent* before "God" (*theos*). Unlike English, NT Greek does not have an indefinite article ("a" or "an"). When Greek writers wanted to speak of "*a* something," they would write the noun *without* the article. For example, to say in NT Greek "the man," you might write *ho anēr* (with the article), but if you wanted to say "a man," you would simply write *anēr* (without the article). On this basis, some people—such as the JWs—maintain that John 1:1c should be translated, "the Word was a god."[23] It is indeed true that *theos* without the article can sometimes properly be

23. The JWs' New World Translation (2013 ed.) may be viewed online at Watch Tower Bible and Tract Society of Pennsylvania. https://www.jw.org/en/publications/bible/nwt/, accessed May 9, 2018. For the JWs' defense of this rendering, see Watch Tower Bible and Tract Society of Pennsylvania. "Is Jesus God?" https://www.jw.org/en/publications/magazines/wp20090401/is-jesus-god/, accessed March 21, 2018. For a more detailed defense, see Stafford, *Jehovah's Witnesses Defended*, 308–32.

translated "a god." One such instance is when the pagan natives of Malta observed that Paul had no ill effects from a deadly snake bite. We read, "[T]hey changed their minds and said he was a god" (Acts 28:6). Here the word "god" has no article in Greek.

But it's erroneous to conclude that a Greek word without the article must *always* be indefinite and translated into English with an "a." What counts in translation is the author's usage patterns, the grammatical construction, and the context in which the term is used. Interestingly, in John 1:2-18, for example, the Greek word *theos* ("God") is used six times—five of which do not have the article. In the following verses *theos* clearly refers to God the Father, but it does *not* have the article:

> There was a man sent from God whose name was John. (1:6)
> ... he gave the right to become children of God (1:12)
> ... children born not of natural descent, nor of human decision or a husband's will, but born of God. (1:13)
> No one has ever seen God, but the one and only Son... (1:18)

No competent translator would render these occurrences of *theos* as "a god," even though they do not have the article. Indeed, the JWs in their New World Translation, correctly render each of these instances "God" (or "God's" in verse 12), conceding, in effect, that *theos* without the article does not necessitate an "a god" translation in every instance. So where does this leave us?

... and the Word was Rearranged

How can we determine if John 1:1c should be rendered "the Word was God" or "a god?" Is it simply a matter of Trinitarian or non-Trinitarian bias that determines the translation? Is there any objective reason to take it one way or the other? Fortunately, the subject has been studied in depth by many outstanding NT Greek scholars, some of whom embrace the Trinity as taught in the NT and others of whom do not. The overwhelming consensus of scholars in this field is that John 1:1 means that "the Word was God"—not the same person as "the God," (i.e., the Father) but sharing the nature of God (his "DNA").

A key factor in unlocking John's meaning in 1:1c is the word order. Word order in Greek is not as important as it is in English, but often it helps us distinguish between shades of meaning and emphasis. In this section we'll look at the Greek word order John actually used (let's call it Option A) compared to the other options John could have used. Bear with me as

I attempt to explain very technical information in an uncomplicated way. My hope is to make it simple without oversimplifying. If you hang in there, you'll see how important this is.

Back in chapter 1, we discussed various ways Jesus is understood in relation to God. One such viewpoint is what I dubbed "God's Three Faces," which says the Son is the same person as the Father, rather than a distinct person. It is only in respect to his mission to save humanity as a man that he is the Son of God. This viewpoint rejects the Trinitarian understanding of God in favor of what is often called the "Oneness" or "Jesus Only" perspective. God is not three persons in one God, says this view, but one person who manifests himself three different ways—sometimes as the Father, sometimes as the Son, and sometimes as the Holy Spirit. If John held to this perspective and wanted to convey it clearly, how might he have written John 1:1? (Let's call this Option B.) Would he use the word order as we find it or would he use a different word order? On the other hand, the JWs believe the Son is not Yahweh God, but a separate, lower god created by Yahweh (or "Jehovah," as JWs call him). As we saw, they translate John 1:1c, "the Word was a god." (Let's call this Option C.) If John wanted to say this, how would he most clearly convey it? Would he write John 1:1c the way we find it in the Greek NT or would he likely put it differently? Or let's say John believed, as Trinitarians do, that the Father and the Word are two distinct persons and yet both share the nature of God and are therefore both equally God. To bring out this emphasis, would John write John 1:1 the way he did or would he arrange the wording differently to express this viewpoint? Examining the word order John chose versus the other options he had available to him is quite revealing.

In a highly regarded study on John's word order in John 1:1c, NT scholar Philip Harner lays out the clearest way to convey each of the options outlined above if John had meant to do so.[24] Harner's results are significant.

24. Harner, "Qualitative Anarthrous Predicate Nouns," 82–87. For the purpose of this discussion, I have transliterated the Greek characters into English and adjusted the order in which Harner presents the options. Though Harner was by no means the first to argue that the predicate noun *theos* in Jn 1:1c bears a qualitative force, stressing the nature of the Logos, his important study helped confirm the work of previous NT Greek scholars.

Option A: *theos ēn   ho logos*. (as in the Greek NT)
God was the Logos.

Option B: *ho theos ēn   ho logos*.
the God   was the Logos.

Option C: *ho logos ēn   theos*.
the Logos was a god.

Based on a careful study of how John uses the article in his Gospel, Harner concluded that John's chosen order (Option A) reveals he did not mean the Word was the same person as God (Option B) or that the Word was a secondary god that was inferior to "the God" (Option C). Instead John chose to place *theos* without the article before the verb (*ēn*), emphasizing that the Word is not the same person as "the God" but possesses the same nature as God. This view is represented in the well-known translation, "the Word was God."[25] To bring out the meaning of the clause, Harner suggests the translation, "the Word had the same nature as God," because this shows that the Logos' nature was identical to "the God" mentioned earlier in the sentence.[26] Harner is addressing the issue from the standpoint of Greek grammar and word usage,[27] and yet his conclusion is precisely what Trinitarians have classically claimed about the deity of the Word/Son. The Father and the Son are two distinct persons who each share the nature of genuine deity and are therefore equal by nature.

What's just as revealing is that John actually had an alternative for expressing Option A as it reads above. If John wanted to convey the idea that "the Word—not anyone else—was God by nature," he could have placed *ho logos* at the beginning of the clause instead of the end. This would have meant basically the same thing but with only a slightly different emphasis—that *the Word* (not someone else) was God (i.e., had the nature of God). But instead John chose to place *theos* at the beginning of the clause to emphasize that the Word was *God by nature* (not something else). John chose the order that would most highlight that the Logos is God by nature—not a lesser or inferior god of some kind.[28] He's of the same *kind* as God. He has Yahweh

25. You may wonder why the English word order does not follow the Greek word order. It's because in Greek the Logos is the subject of this clause, but if we render the clause, "God was the Word" (following the Greek word order), this makes God the subject of the English clause and changes the intended meaning.

26. Ibid., 87.

27. Subsequent studies by outstanding NT Greek authorities have confirmed and built upon Harner's conclusions. E.g., see Harris, *Jesus as God*, 51–71; Wallace, *Greek Grammar Beyond the Basics*, 266–70.

28. Unfortunately, some of those arguing for the BU position (Buzzard and Hunting, *Doctrine of the Trinity*, 285–87) and for the JW translation (Stafford, *Jehovah's*

DNA, not angel or any other DNA. This is precisely what Trinitarians have always said about the Son, that he and the Father are both God by nature. Just as two humans share human nature and are equally human, the Father and the Son share "God nature" and are thus equally God. John 1:1 presents the Word as a distinct person from God the Father but equal in the "godness" (divine nature) they share.

Admittedly, this is not an easy concept to grasp, but the critical point is that this is what John meant. We dare not choose a simpler meaning just because it's easier to understand. The true Bible believer wants to understand what the original writer of Scripture meant, whether it's easy, hard, fun, or dangerous to believe. When it comes to understanding Scripture, we need to check our biases at the door as best we can and allow the text to speak for itself.

Various English Translations of John 1:1c

Fortunately for us, many excellent English translations of the Bible have been produced by top-notch scholars from a wide variety of backgrounds. When it comes to John 1:1, some of these translations really help bring out John's meaning as I have explained it above. A huge majority of English translations render John 1:1c "the Word was God."[29] This is a very good rendering of the Greek, but the potential exists for taking the two occurrences of "God" to mean the exact same thing—which, as we have seen, is not what John intended.

Because John is conveying a difficult concept, some English translations have attempted to paraphrase the rendering slightly in order to bring out the subtleties in meaning. I'll share a few here in the hope of making John's meaning clearer. The NET© renders John 1:1c "the Word was fully God." The term "fully" brings out the fact that the deity (or godness) the Word possesses is equal to that of "the God" mentioned earlier in the sentence. Another excellent rendering of this verse is the CEV which reads, "The Word was with God and was truly God." The addition of the word "truly" emphasizes that the Word's deity is as genuine as it gets. Finally, the

---

Witnesses Defended, 316–33) of John 1:1 have failed to understand the meaning and full import of the qualitative sense of *theos* in this text, even when they interact with the works of credible scholars on the subject.

29. Some of these include KJV, NKJV, NASB, ESV, NIV, CEB, CSB, NLT, NRSV, *GOD'S WORD*, NAB, LEB, and GNT. Many others could be added to this list, as a visit to https://www.biblegateway.com/ will confirm. Collectively, these English translations represent the work of thousands of specialists in the original languages of the Bible from countries all over the world and diverse religious backgrounds.

NEB and REB translate it, "what God was, the Word was." While this is a paraphrase, it nicely conveys that God and the Word share the same godness, which is another fine way of restating what John meant.

Creator, Not Creature

But perhaps you're a JW reading this or simply a person unsure about how to understand Jesus in relation to God. At this point you may be thinking, "Without knowing NT Greek for myself, how can I know whether this Randy guy is telling the truth or is just trying to pull the wool over my eyes? After all the technical explanations, we're still left with two persons in John 1:1. How can I know in nontechnical terms that these two persons are both equally God?" Fair questions![30]

John himself must have anticipated questions like these. What he goes on to write in 1:2–3 confirms the Word is truly God, rather than a created being. Speaking of the Word, John says, "He was with God in the beginning. Through him all things were made; without him nothing was made that has been made." The Word is before all creation! In others words, of the two categories we noted above (Yahweh and his creation), the Word is on the Yahweh side of the line. John says all things, without exception, were created "through" the Word. The preposition translated "through" here indicates agency.[31] The Word was the agent who caused all things to exist, and God the Father was the initiator of the project. To use an analogy, the Father was the architect and the Son was the builder.

"But," you may say, "perhaps John is speaking here only of the creation of the material universe. Perhaps God created the Word *before* he made the universe. Maybe John 1:3 really means, 'Through him all [*other*] things were made'—i.e., things beside himself." But this won't work! First, John does not say "all *other* things." His language is plain enough. Second, the next part of the sentence rules out this "other" suggestion where John says, "without him nothing was made that has been made." It's as if John is saying, "In case you're thinking—'He doesn't really mean *all* created things; he's leaving out the Word himself, of course'—forget it!" Absolutely nothing was created unless the Word created it! Zilch! Zero! John couldn't have made it clearer. The Word is no creature!

---

30. In addition to what I write here, I would encourage questioning readers to do your own investigation. I only ask you give each side a fair hearing. Check out the sources I cite. Don't go easy on any view (including your own). Examine each view using the strongest case that can be made for it.

31. Harris, *Exegetical Guide*, 22.

Also, if you'll allow me to delve back into the Greek for a moment, the case gets even stronger! When we compare the verb used for God and the Word to the verb used for created things in 1:1–3, we see John is hammering the point home. The verb *eimi* (rendered "was" in vv. 1–3) is consistently applied to "the God" and "the Word" in the imperfect tense (*ēn*). By itself this is not significant, but in this context John seems to be contrasting *eimi* with the verb *ginomai*, which he applies to creation.[32] *Ginomai* means "become or come to exist." Placed next to each other like this, the contrast is vivid. Creation *came to be*, but the Word, like God the Father, already *was*! What's also fascinating is that John switches the verbs when he first speaks of the Word's human nature: "The Word *became* [*ginomai*] flesh" (1:14; italics added). The Word's God nature has continual, eternal existence, but his human nature "*came to be*" in space and time. At the incarnation the eternal God took on a finite human nature. The Logos—the Word—is not a created thing; he's the eternal Yahweh God, and he has visited us as one of us!

"ARE WE THERE YET?"

If you've ever driven small children a distance of more than a city block, you've heard this question recited endlessly! Here I need to say to my readers what I used to tell my three kids when they were little munchkins: "We still have a ways to go yet, so enjoy the ride."

So far in this book I've argued that both the OT and John affirm that there is only one true God, one being alone who truly deserves the title "God"—the almighty Yahweh ("the LORD" in most English translations). I've also showed that the Bible presents Yahweh as both unseeable and seeable without explaining the apparent contradiction. We discussed several OT appearances of Yahweh in human form and have seen that John understands these to be preincarnate appearances of the Son of God. John clears up the seeming discrepancy of unseeable versus seeable by presenting God the Father as unseeable and God the Son as the person who makes the visible appearances. In this chapter, we learned that John 1:1 presents us with two distinct persons—the Word and (the) God (i.e., the Father)—and that both share the same nature.

But we still have a ways to go. If the Son is truly Yahweh along with God the Father, how can we say with a straight face that there's only one God? If there are two persons, doesn't that unavoidably make two Gods (or three, if you count the Holy Spirit)? Also, on a more practical note, if the Father and the Son are both God, whom do I address when I pray? Whom

---

32. Carson, *Gospel According to John*, 114.

do I worship? We're in deep water here, and so we need to pace ourselves, taking one issue at a time, if we hope to swim safely to the shore.

First, we need to tackle the matter of the Son's subordination to the Father spelled out so plainly in John. That question looms every time the issue of equality comes up. How can the Son be equal to God the Father if he's under his authority? It is to this matter we must turn in the next chapter.

BUT WAIT!

Before you move on to chapter 5, take some time to ponder what we've learned in this chapter and the implications for your life. Recently I was thinking about what it will be like to stand in God's presence. What will go through my mind the instant I see Jesus in heaven? On this occasion, I suddenly was struck with an overwhelming realization. I was literally on the floor in our front room, when I realized, "I can't wait to fall on my face before the Lord Jesus in worship and thank him profusely for saving me." Suddenly—like never before, I confess—this simple yet weighty realization struck me with a new and profound force. God himself came to save *me*— yes, sinful and unworthy *me*! If he'll permit me and if I can do it before crumbling into a pile, I want to look him straight in the face and thank him from the bottom of my heart. While on my knees before him, I want to examine the wounds in his hands that were pierced when he died in my place. I want to thank him for those wounds. "If you hadn't come for me," I hope to say, "I'd be forever lost!"

I don't know when that time will come, but because God came for me, I know it will come. I want to live my whole life—every moment of it—in light of that realization. How about you?

QUESTIONS FOR DISCUSSION

1. What's the most important thing you learned in this chapter? Why is it important? What questions remain for you?

2. If you are a Christ-follower, what difference would it make in your spiritual life if you discovered that Jesus is not truly God but that the BU or JW concept of Jesus is true?

3. How would you explain to a small child that both the Father and the Son are God? If you've had some experience with this, what was the conversation like?

A VERSE TO MEMORIZE

In the beginning was the Word, and the Word was with God, and the Word was God. (Jn 1:1)

APPLY WHAT YOU'VE LEARNED

For a thought experiment, imagine that you view Jesus the way either a sincere JW or BU views him. Yahweh God did *not* become a man to save you; he sent someone else. This exercise is not about bashing people who believe differently! It's about comparing some of the practical ramifications of our views about God. How would it change your prayer life and worship habits? Imagine yourself thanking God for Christ's sacrificial death. How would this be different than doing so as a Trinitarian? Imagine how you would see Jesus' birth. How might you view a personal relationship with Jesus differently? How would it change the way you communicate your faith to a nonbeliever? Do you know a JW or a BU you might ask? Discuss all this with your group.

CHAPTER 5

God's Junior Partner

In the front room of our home hangs an artwork print portraying Jesus as a small boy playing in the workshop of Joseph, his adoptive father. While Joseph works at his carpentry bench, boy Jesus plays nearby on the floor with some large spikes. The light shining in from an open window transforms Jesus' shadow into an image of a cross on the floor next to him. That artwork hangs near the chair where I read my Bible each morning. It's a stirring reminder to me that Jesus' entire life pointed him forward to the cross. It also graphically reminds me of Jesus' very human and ordinary upbringing in a small Galilean village.

Years before Jesus began his public ministry he likely worked side by side with his adoptive dad on building projects. In the Jewish culture of that day, sons nearly always followed their fathers into the same occupation. While growing up, a son would typically serve as an apprentice or junior partner under his dad in the family trade or business. That idea may seem a bit foreign to our typical mental image of Jesus, but it's the picture Jesus himself paints for us to illustrate some of the deepest and most profound truths in John's Gospel about his relationship with his heavenly Father.

SETTING THE SCENE

In John 5, Jesus speaks of watching his Father work and then performing the same task, just as a Jewish boy would learn his dad's trade by watching and assisting him. We pick up the story as Jesus has just healed a man who had been disabled for thirty-eight years. Because he performed this miracle on the Sabbath, the Jewish leaders are outraged:

> In his defense Jesus said to them, "My Father is always at his work to this very day, and I too am working." For this reason they [the Jewish leaders] tried all the more to kill him; not only was he breaking the Sabbath, but he was even calling God his own Father, making himself equal with God. Jesus gave them this answer: "Very truly I tell you, the Son can do nothing by himself; he can do only what he sees his Father doing, because whatever the Father does the Son also does. For the Father loves the Son and shows him all he does. Yes, and he will show him even greater works than these, so that you will be amazed." (Jn 5:17–20)

In this chapter we will examine Jesus' monologue in John 5 to see how it contributes to the developing portrait of the Son's relationship to the Father as painted by John. So far we've seen that though John certainly embraces the monotheism of his Jewish background, he includes the Father and Son as equal members within the nature of the one God. We've also learned that because John presents him as the actual, unique (or only begotten) Son of God, this would communicate to John's first-century readers the Son's full equality to the Father (sharing the same being/nature) as well as his subordinate role as a Son. In this chapter, we will learn more about how this relationship works by looking carefully at Jesus' explanation in John 5.

John 5 is a fascinating chapter for numerous reasons. Jesus defends his miraculous healing on the Sabbath by claiming, "My Father is always at his work to this very day, and I too am working" (v. 17). This claim sets off an explosion of outrage among the Jewish leaders. Why so? To our ears their reaction may seem way overblown. They claim Jesus violated the Sabbath and, even worse, called God "his own Father, making himself equal with God" (v. 18). This is an extremely serious charge, meriting, in that culture, the death penalty. How do the authorities jump all the way to this startling conclusion from Jesus' simple statement about working alongside his Father (v. 17)? The charge leveled against Jesus in John 5:18 prompts one of the most enlightening talks he ever gave on his relationship to the Father. I call it the "Father/Son Talk" (or FST for short).

THE CHARGE AGAINST JESUS

What are we to make of the accusation that Jesus was equating himself with God? It's important to point out that in v. 18 John is reporting the charge of the Jewish leaders. Does John agree with them? Does John think Jesus made himself equal to God? Does he want his readers to agree? Does Jesus agree?

Was Jesus actually claiming equality with God? After what we've learned so far, the answer may seem to be a no-brainer. In chapter 4, we saw that the Father and Son are indeed equal; both are God by nature. And yet when it comes to the charge against Jesus in John 5:18, biblical scholars differ.

"Not Guilty!"

Some biblical scholars argue that the FST shows Jesus does *not* agree with the equality charge.[1] According to this interpretation, Jesus disavows the notion of equality with God but claims only to be God's obedient Son. Jesus says he can do nothing unless he first gets the nod from his Father (v. 19). Far from declaring equality with the Father, Jesus maintains he's in complete subjection to him. We must admit Jesus cites some telling examples of his complete dependence on the Father in the FST. And then he forcefully declares, "By myself I can do nothing; I judge only as I hear, and my judgment is just, for I seek not to please myself but him who sent me" (Jn 5:30). If Jesus is truly equal to his Father, why would he say this?

Scholars who take this approach typically acknowledge Jesus' full deity from other texts in John. In other words, they are not denying John's Jesus is fully God. But they argue that in Jesus' day and culture the expression "making himself equal to God" would be heard to mean he was declaring his independence from God as a rebellious son blows off his parents. It would be understood to mean that Jesus considered himself a rival god, a blasphemous claim to be sure (cf. Deut 13:6–18). To refute this misinformed charge, Jesus explains that he's the obedient Son of the Father, not a rebellious child. In this interpretation of the FST, Jesus is not addressing the issue of his equality of nature to the Father (which is declared elsewhere in John), but refuting the twisted notion that he's hijacking his Father's authority. In other words, Jesus is only claiming the submissive role of an obedient Son who works alongside his Father.

"Guilty with an Explanation"

But with all due respect to the fine scholars who take this approach, a better case can be made that in John 5 Jesus boldly affirms both his equality and submission to the Father.[2] If we look closely at the FST, Jesus says nothing

1. E.g., Keener, *Gospel of John* 1:646–48. Cf. Rheaume, *Exegetical and Theological Analysis*, 186–87.

2. See Barrett, "Father is Greater Than I," 23–24.

to deny that he's equal in his nature to God. Quite to the contrary! He continues to assert his equality. But, on the other hand, he does clarify that as God's Son he is totally committed to following his Father's lead. This is why John 5 is so vital to our study.

Here an analogy might help. My son Jonathan is fully equal to me as a human being, but growing up in our home, he has always looked up to his parents for leadership. When Jesus was growing up, he submitted himself obediently to his parents, Joseph and Mary (Lk 2:51). Did this role difference mean they were superior beings to Jesus? Certainly not! Children in first-century Jewish culture considered their parents to outrank them in authority, even though they were all equal humans made in the image of God. As we'll see, equality of being can coexist with a hierarchy of roles.

In John 5, Jesus reiterates his equality with the Father, but he also provides two important caveats: 1) Jesus did not "*make* himself equal to God," as though he's only a self-proclaimed upstart who's assumed the title "Son" without the Father's approval, and 2) Jesus' equality with the Father is not absolute equality. He's fully equal in one sense (his deity) but fully subordinate in another (his role as Son).

Jesus' Rap Sheet

Since the accusation in John 5:18 reflects the charges of the Jewish leaders, how might we know whether Jesus would plead guilty or not guilty to these charges? First, it's enlightening to compare this accusation with others the Jewish leaders made against Jesus. When we do, a clear pattern emerges. Note the striking similarities in the wording of the following charges leveled against Jesus in John:[3]

> For this reason they tried all the more to kill him; not only was he breaking the Sabbath, but he was even calling God his own Father, *making himself* equal with God. (Jn 5:18; italics added)

> Are you greater than our father Abraham, who died? And the prophets died! Who do you *make yourself* out to be?" (Jn 8:53 ESV; italics added)

> The Jews answered him, "It is not for a good work that we are going to stone you but for blasphemy, because you, being a man, *make yourself* God." (Jn 10:33 ESV; italics added)

3. Neyrey, *Gospel of John*, 106–7.

The Jews answered him, "We have a law, and according to that law he ought to die because he has *made himself* the Son of God." (Jn 19:7 ESV; italics added)

From then on Pilate sought to release him, but the Jews cried out, "If you release this man, you are not Caesar's friend. Everyone who makes himself a king opposes Caesar." (Jn 19:12 ESV; italics added)

Notice that in each accusation the Jewish leaders are disputing the lofty claims they believe Jesus has blasphemously made for himself. In the original Greek the words translated "make(s) himself/yourself" are the same, aside from minor variations in form. Significantly, each accusation applies a position or title to Jesus that John's readers know from the rest of the book is certainly true of Jesus, but without the antagonistic connotation.

Leaving aside 5:18 for the moment, let's consider the other accusations one by one. First, in 8:53, John's readers already know that Jesus is indeed greater than Abraham, and, as we shall see in chapter 8, he is claiming God's sacred name. Secondly, in 10:33, the readers know from John 1:1, and 1:18 that John has already declared Jesus to be "God" in the full sense, and Thomas will do so climactically in 20:28. The point that John would dispute, of course, is that Jesus is blasphemously *making* himself God. Thirdly, likewise, in 19:7 and 19:12, John certainly agrees that Jesus is the Son of God and a king, but again, he would not agree that Jesus was only a wannabe claimant to these titles and would also differ with the accusers on the precise meaning of the titles. John accepts the basic point but without the sinister twist.

If this pattern is in force back at 5:18, then it follows that John affirms the basic claim of Jesus' equality with the Father, but with important clarifications. John wants his readers to say to themselves, based on what they've read so far in his Gospel, "Jesus is not *making* himself equal with God; he *is* equal with God." This is precisely what we find in Jesus' FST, which begins in 5:19. But before we jump into Jesus' speech, we need to further our discussion of how sonship was understood in Jesus' Jewish context.

THE BONE OF CONTENTION

What the Jewish leaders find particularly offensive is that Jesus referred to God as "his *own* Father" (5:18; italics added). He spoke of God as "*my* Father" and claimed that by healing the disabled man he was working in tandem with his Father on the Sabbath (5:17). From the creation account in Genesis 1–2, the Jews believed that God rested from creating the world on the seventh day of the week (i.e., the Sabbath). But if so, how did he keep the world running on the Sabbath, as he obviously did? In pondering this question, many Jews reasoned that God did indeed maintain his creation even on the seventh day, and in this sense, God worked on the Sabbath.[4] God's people were required to rest, but God worked in this way on the Sabbath.

This background helps us to understand Jesus' words, "My Father is working right now, and so am I" (Jn 5:17 GOD'S WORD). Remember, Jesus is saying this to justify healing a man on the Sabbath. It doesn't take rocket science to understand Jesus is claiming to work alongside his Father, doing the work on the Sabbath that only God is allowed to do. To the Jews these are fighting words, because Jesus is claiming a prerogative exclusive to God. Only God can do this on the Sabbath. By claiming to be working on this healing "project" with his Father, Jesus is implying that he is on God's side of the line that separates him from all creation! On this basis, Jesus claims his miraculous cure is justified on the Sabbath.

From this the Jewish leaders rightly conclude Jesus' basic meaning: he is claiming to be God's Son not simply in a metaphorical sense as Adam, angels, a Davidic king, and pious believers were understood to be "son(s) of God" in that day (see below). No, Jesus is going much further than a mere analogy or figure of speech. He's somehow claiming to be God's *real* Son, *actually related* to God in *what* he is, as though he belongs in the same class, kind, or family with God. Spot on! This is indeed what John has been showing us, his readers, since the very first verse of his Gospel. But to the Jewish leaders standing around him, it is an outrageous affront to God and must be roundly rejected and punished as blasphemy. In this light, the accusation in 5:18 makes perfect sense: Jesus is indeed claiming equality with God.

Son of an X!

To grasp the full weight of this claim, we need to consider how sonship was understood in Jewish parlance back in Jesus' day. As noted above, most sons in the ancient world followed the vocation of their fathers. Because of this, a son typically took on the work and lifestyle characteristics of his dad, not simply his biological features. Thus to be a "son of X" could convey a meaning beyond a mere biological relationship.

Since OT times, the expression "son of X" was a common idiom that illustrated a direct association with whomever or whatever the person was said to be the "son of."[5] In other words, besides the literal biological

4. See Philo *Cherubim* 2 §86–90; Carson, *Gospel According to John*, 247.

5. See esp. Carson's book *Jesus the Son of God*, 19–27. Some of Carson's ideas and examples are used here.

sense of "son of X," this expression was also used to convey an association or relationship between the son and the X that was real but nonbiological. English translations of the OT often hide this Hebrew idiom by conveying the intended *meaning* of the figure of speech rather than rendering its literalistic sense. For example, a man condemned to death might be called a "son of death" (1 Sam 20:31), as though death were his father. But since "son of death" doesn't make much sense in English, an English translation will typically paraphrase the metaphor by saying, "he must die" (NIV) or "he's a dead man!" (CEB) Likewise, a one-year-old male is literally a "son of one year" (Ex 12:5). In Ezra 4:1, the expression "sons of captivity" actually *means* "exiles," and Lamentations 3:13 refers to arrows as "sons of the quiver." In Psalm 89:22, a wicked person is literally "a son of malice," as though he was sired by malice. In each case, the son shares the characteristics of the father, not in a biological but in a metaphorical yet very real sense.

Jesus and the NT writers also make use of this way of speaking. Jesus gives the sons of Zebedee the nickname "sons of thunder" (Mk 3:17) because he apparently saw them as boisterous and perhaps contentious men, as though thunder were their father! A Christ-follower named Joseph is given the nickname Barnabas—an Aramaic word that Luke explains as "son of encouragement" (Acts 4:36). Apparently Barnabas was so encouraging, you'd think he was raised by encouragement itself! Likewise, both Paul and Luke's Gospel speak of God's people as "sons [and daughters] of light."[6]

We see this phenomenon in John's Gospel as well. John's Jesus uses this idiom to speak of Judas as "the son of damnation" (17:12) and believers as "sons [and daughters] of light" (12:36 AT). According to John's Jesus, "like begets like." In other words, what is born is the same as the father (or begetter) who sired him/her (3:6). This clarifies Jesus' meaning when he calls his opponents the devil's offspring rather than Abraham's (8:39–45). Jesus is saying that their behavioral characteristics serve as a spiritual paternity test, showing that their nonbiological father is Satan. We see remnants of the "son of X" idiom today in English when people speak of a "son of a gun" or more disgustingly a "son of a b____." Thus, a son of X, in a nonbiological sense, is one who shares the characteristics of X.

Sons of God

It's this sort of thinking that lies behind the Jewish notion of divine sonship, i.e., talk of son(s) of God. It's not a physical sonship, as in Greek mythology in which Zeus, for example, has sexual relations with a mortal woman and

6. 1 Thess 5:5; Lk 16:8.

produces a "son of a god." Rather, the Jewish concept of divine sonship we see in Scripture is a nonbiological kinship of characteristics or behavior. This is the sense in which angels, Davidic kings, and pious people can be sometimes called sons (or daughters) of God, because they are seen as having a special relationship with God, representing him and carrying out his purposes. It is in this sense that Jesus says, for example:

> Blessed are the peacemakers, for they shall be called *sons of God*" (Matt 5:9 ESV; italics added).

> But I say to you, Love your enemies and pray for those who persecute you, so that you may be *sons of your Father* who is in heaven. For he makes his sun rise on the evil and on the good, and sends rain on the just and on the unjust. (Matt 5:44–45 ESV; italics added)

In these two cases, Jesus' disciples are called "sons [and daughters] of God" because in the first instance, they—like God—are peacemakers, and in the second instance, because they—like the Father—show love to their enemies. They are his sons because they share his characteristics. To be a son of God in a metaphorical sense meant to be *like* God in some significant way—just as Adam, the angels, the Davidic kings, and godly persons were sometimes described..

In Jesus' day this kind of talk was completely acceptable among the Jews, including the Jewish teachers and leaders. But if this is so, why then did the Jewish authorities find Jesus' claim to be the Son of God so outrageously offensive and blasphemous? In other words, why did they have a cow over Jesus calling himself God's Son if it was not blasphemous in Jewish culture to do so? This crucial question brings us back to look again at the incident in John 5 that generated so much controversy.

The Son Par Excellence

The most likely answer to this question is that Jesus' enemies rightly perceive his claim to signify a much different sort of divine sonship—one that goes beyond mere analogous characteristics to an actual sameness of being or kind. As Jesus responds to their charge of breaking the Sabbath, his enemies quickly gather that he's speaking about God as his Father in an exclusive manner, as though God is his *own* Father, in a much deeper and greater way than he is the Father of anyone else (5:18). "This guy is claiming," they deduce, "not simply to be *a* son of God (i.e., a pious Israelite), but *the* Son of God, in a class by himself. It's unheard of! He thinks he's *the* Son of God

par excellence!" It was perfectly acceptable to refer to God as one's Father
in a figurative, metaphorical way. Yahweh himself spoke of his relationship
to Israel in these terms (Exod 4:22–23). But Jesus is talking about an *actual*
Father-Son relationship, not simply a *figurative* one. He's calling God his
actual, natural Father. The concept was unprecedented in Jesus' day. It went
beyond the acceptable Jewish categories of divine sonship.

In effect, Jesus was hinting that he was actually sired (or begotten)
by God the Father. This could *not* mean a biological siring because Jesus
himself, like the rest of Scripture, taught that "God is Spirit," (4:24) i.e., he's
a nonphysical being. As we know from chapter 4, the sonship Jesus speaks
of means that he and the Father are *of the same kind.* "Like begets like" is a
truism Jesus himself embraces (Jn 3:6). A dog sires a dog, and thus son dog
is just as much dog as daddy dog. They share all the attributes of dogness
equally. A cat sires a cat, and thus the son of a cat is just as much cat as daddy
cat. They share catness equally. A human son is just as human as his dad
because they share humanness equally. In the same way, the one and only
Son of God shares all the same attributes of godness as his Father. From
Jesus' words in 5:17 (and possibly 2:16), the Jewish authorities have gotten a
whiff of Jesus' true meaning of his sonship, and it has enraged them. But for
John's readers, this understanding has been developing since John 1 where
Jesus is called "the one and only" (or "only begotten") Son of God.

JESUS' DEFENSE

With this understanding of the charge leveled against Jesus, the Jewish concept of sonship, and Jesus' unique view of his divine sonship—we're in a
good position to understand Jesus' FST in John 5. If Jesus is indeed equal
to his Father in the godness they share, what are we to make of all Jesus'
striking statements in the FST about his total dependence on his Father and
full submission to him?

Claiming His Rights

As we've seen, Jesus is charged with making himself equal to God (5:18). In
Jesus' FST he will argue that though he has full rights as a Son to act as his
Father acts, he does so as an obedient Son who's been given permission by
the Father to do so. It's important to understand that in this talk (5:19–30),
Jesus lays claim to prerogatives (or rights) the ancient Jews believed were
reserved for God alone—namely creating and ruling over all things. By
carefully examining the OT and the ancient Jewish literature that followed it

until Jesus' time, scholars have discovered that, from the Jewish perspective, God reserved these two actions for himself alone.[7] Though God delegated many secondary tasks to his agents (angelic and human), only he: 1) created the cosmos,[8] and only he could 2) rule and judge universally.[9] When it came to these actions, God insisted on being hands on, but in the FST, it is precisely these two prerogatives that Jesus claims the Father has granted to him.

For starters Jesus maintains that he works side by side with his Father on everything. He says, "Whatever the Father does the Son also does" (Jn 5:19). We readers of John's Gospel will recall that in John 1 the Son (there called "the Word") was the co-Creator of all things with the Father in the beginning (1:1–3). Jesus' words in 5:19 would seem to include this. But Jesus gets even more explicit when he claims to have the right from his Father to give life and to be the universal judge of all mankind:

> For just as the Father raises the dead and gives them life, even so the Son gives life to whom he is pleased to give it. Moreover, the Father judges no one, but has entrusted all judgment to the Son, that all may honor the Son just as they honor the Father. Whoever does not honor the Son does not honor the Father, who sent him. "Very truly I tell you, whoever hears my word and believes him who sent me has eternal life and will not be judged but has crossed over from death to life. Very truly I tell you, a time is coming and has now come when the dead will hear the voice of the Son of God and those who hear will live. For as the Father has life in himself, so he has granted the Son also to have life in himself. And he has given him authority to judge because he is the Son of Man. (Jn 5:21–26)

It's vital to grasp two crucial facts from these startling words. First, Jesus is claiming the prerogatives that his listeners knew belonged only to God. Only one on par with God could do everything the Father does (5:19)! Both in the OT and in Jewish writings in Jesus' day, giving life was understood as God's sole prerogative.[10] Life was his greatest creation. True,

7. E.g., Neyrey, *Gospel of John*, 108–109.

8. See, for example, Gen 1:1; Isa 40:26, 28; 44:24; 45:12; 48:13; Neh 9:6; Bel 5; 2 Macc 1:24; Sir 43:33; *Sib. Or.* 3:19–35; *2 En.* 47:3–5; 66:4; *Apoc. Ab.* 7:10.

9. See, for example, Gen 18:25; Pss 82:1, 8; 83:18; 96:13; 98:9; Dan 4:34–35; Bel 5; 3 Macc 2:2–3; 6:2; Sir 18:1–3; *Sib. Or.* 3:10, 19; *1 En.* 9:5; 84:2–3; Josephus, *Ant.* 1:155–56; Acts 17:31; Rom 3:6. While 1 Corinthians 6:2 indeed says believers will one day judge the world, this authority will not be universal but divided up, under God, among these future judges (cf. Matt 19:28; Lk 22:30; Rev 1:6). The same is true now with fallible rulers (cf. Gen 1:28; Pss 8:5–8; 82:1; Rom 13:1–4).

10. Gen 2:7; Num 16:22; Deut 32:39; 2 Kgs 5:7; Neh 9:6; Ps 71:20; Philo, *Creation*

some of the prophets and apostles raised the dead,[11] but the accounts of these astounding events made it clear that the power of life did not reside in them, but in God alone to whom these godly people prayed. But in the FST, Jesus goes way beyond this. "The Son," he maintains, "gives life to whom he is pleased to give it" (v. 21). The power of life is in his hands. What's more, Jesus claims the power of life resides within himself (5:26)! He's not merely an empty pipe through which God's life flows to others or a vessel into which God pours his life, like the prophets were. No, he himself is the reservoir of divine life. Clearly Jesus is laying claim to a prerogative that belonged to God alone.

Notice too that Jesus also claims the right to judge all humanity. He says "all judgment" has been entrusted to the Son (v. 22). In other words, the Father has appointed his Son to be *the* Supreme Court over all creation. To what purpose? Incredibly, it's so that "all may honor the Son just as they honor the Father" (v. 23). To a first-century Jew, this statement was staggering! No angel, human, or other created thing could ever legitimately be honored in the same way Yahweh God was. Such an idea was unthinkable![12] The fact that Jesus so clearly lays claim to the sole prerogatives of God shows that he is surely not denying the equality charge in 5:18. He is indeed equal to his Father, but not in every respect.

Equal Yet Subordinate

The second vital fact we need to note in the FST is that Jesus is just as determined to qualify his equality with the Father as he is to affirm it. Jesus is a true Son of the Father, performing the same tasks that only God can do. On the other hand, he's not a rebellious Son acting independently of the Father. In everything, he follows his Father's lead (5:19) and exercises his rights only as the Father grants him permission to do so.

In the culture of Jesus' day, it was universally understood that a son was in a subordinate role to his father. They were equally human, but the father was considered the leader. Just as a loving, earthly father labors with his

---

135; *Jos. Asen.* 12:1–2.

11. 1 Kgs 17:19–23; 2 Kgs 4:32–37; Acts 9:40–43; 20:8–10.

12. See, for example, Exod 20:1–3; Deut 6:13. Scholars debate the extent to which exalted or idealized figures in Jewish writings (such as Adam, Enoch, Moses, the Son of Man, or certain angels) may have been worshiped or shared God's attributes or identity. See Hurtado, *One God, One Lord,* 17–39, 93–124. But in Jesus' case, here was a real, flesh-and-blood man (a lowly Galilean carpenter, no less!) standing in front of his opponents making these claims—not a legendary hero from the distant past in a work of fiction.

son in the workshop, God the Father takes the initiative to show his Son the work to be done so the Son can follow (5:20). When the Son raises the dead, it's because he has followed the lead of his Father (v. 21). When it comes to judging, the Father has delegated that job completely over to the Son (v. 22). Thus Jesus is claiming that all of the many OT texts declaring that God will one day judge the world will actually be handled solely by the Son.

We can only imagine the jaws of the bystanders dropping open at Jesus' astonishing claim. Jesus declares that this authority from the Father is given to him "because he is the Son of Man" (5:27). Claiming this title would have done little to cool the tempers of his outraged opponents. Jesus' reference to "Son of Man" points back to a mysterious figure seen in a prophetic vision who will be given universal authority by God himself and worshiped by everyone (Dan 7:13–14). Without apology, Jesus is declaring his divine rights before the astonished crowd. And yet, he insists that he will exercise these rights as a fully subordinate Son following the lead and will of his Father.

Summing Up the FST

What emerges so far from our study of the FST may be summed up as follows: If "like begets like" (which all affirm), and if Jesus is calling God "his own Father" (5:18), then he is claiming to be God's Son in a unique manner unheard of in the Hebrew Scriptures. In effect, by saying he is a true Son (in the same class, kind, or family as the Father), he is indeed claiming equality with God. In the talk that follows, Jesus reaffirms this equality by claiming God's honor and exclusive prerogatives. On the other hand, Jesus carefully qualifies his equality by stressing that he exercises all his divine rights as an obedient Son in full submission to the Father.

In chapter 7, we will return to the FST to examine Jesus' intriguing declaration that he receives his life from the Father (5:26). What exactly does this mean? But for now, we must show how this understanding of Jesus' sonship makes sense in some other key passages in John.

WHAT A SON!

This understanding of Jesus' unique kind of sonship enlightens our understanding of what at first may seem to be puzzling words found elsewhere in John. Look closely at another famous exchange Jesus has with the Jewish authorities:

"I and the Father are one." Again his Jewish opponents picked
up stones to stone him, but Jesus said to them, "I have shown
you many good works from the Father. For which of these do
you stone me?" "We are not stoning you for any good work,"
they replied, "but for blasphemy, because *you, a mere man, claim
to be God*." Jesus answered them, "Is it not written in your Law,
'I have said you are *"gods"?*'" If he called them 'gods,' to whom the
word of God came—and Scripture cannot be set aside—what
about the one whom the Father set apart as his very own and
sent into the world? Why then do you accuse me of blasphemy
because I said, *'I am God's Son?'* . . . . Again they tried to seize
him, but he escaped their grasp. (Jn 10:30–36, 39; italics added)

In this incredible passage Jesus claims to be one with the Father, an
astonishing assertion which alludes to the Shema, as we'll see in a later chapter. But here we need to deal with an objection that is often brought up by
those who deny or play down Jesus' deity. Note carefully Jesus' enemies want
to stone him for blasphemy for claiming he's God (10:33). Is that what Jesus
has been doing? According to some, Jesus goes out of his way here to refute
he's claiming to be God. "On the contrary," they object, "he's not God but the
Son of God." This view says the Jews wanting to stone Jesus have badly misunderstood him, and so Jesus quotes and comments on Psalm 82:6, where
God refers to the rulers of the nations as "gods" (v. 34). Jesus, they claim,
is saying, "If God can call these fallen rulers 'gods,' then surely it's okay for
me to refer to myself as 'God's Son.'" In other words, Jesus did not claim to
be God but *only* God's Son—a "god" like the rulers mentioned in Psalm 82.
And so, Jesus wants the charge reduced way down from claiming to be God
to saying he's just the Son of God.

But when we understand the unique sonship Jesus has been claiming
for himself in John's Gospel, this view doesn't add up. Jesus' sonship is not
the same as the angels, kings, or pious Jews, who were all created beings
inferior to God. When Jesus says in v. 34 that he's the Son of God, he's talking in the same terms of divine sonship as he did back in John 5. He is *the*
true and unique Son of the Father—of the same kind, class, or family—just
as John has argued since John 1. His quotation of Psalm 82 only serves to
underscore his point: If fallen beings can be called "gods," then surely the
title is infinitely more appropriate for God's true and only Son!

This discussion in John 10 takes place in Jerusalem, as did Jesus'
monologue in John 5. Jesus' enemies certainly remember what Jesus means
by calling God "his Father" and himself "the Son." They understood the
implications in John 5 just as surely as they do in John 10. If Jesus meant
to disavow a claim to deity in vv. 34–36 by only claiming to be God's Son

like, say, the angels in the OT, why did his opponents still seek to kill him after hearing his clarification (v. 39)? Why didn't they simply say, "Oh, we misunderstood you! So sorry! We thought you were claiming to be God, but now it's obvious you only meant to say you're God's son"? Answer: Because they understood correctly that Jesus was speaking of a unique kind of divine sonship that implied equality with God—just as we've seen in John 1 and 5.

If there's any doubt about this, note the words these same religious authorities spoke to Pilate during Jesus' trial: "The Jews answered him, 'We have a law, and according to that law he ought to die because he has made himself the Son of God'" (Jn 19:7 ESV). The Jews claim Jesus has violated Jewish law by claiming to be God's Son. Question: Was calling yourself a son of God a crime worthy of death in the Jewish understanding? Did the Hebrew Scriptures condemn a person to death who claimed to be a son of God? No way. Not, as we saw above, if you meant it the way the title was typically used and understood by Jews in Jesus' day. It might get you some strange looks or a stern rebuke or two for sounding presumptuous or braggadocious, but not the death penalty. If Jesus had simply claimed to be a son of God in the sense that the Messiah—the Davidic King—was called this in the OT, surely this was not against OT law. The Jews were hoping and looking for such a person in fulfillment of the OT (see Jn 7:42). In Jesus' case, however, the Jewish authorities speaking to Pilate have understood—since the events of John 5—that Jesus speaks of a unique kind of sonship that implies equality with his Father. Since they take him to be an imposter, this claim is unquestionably blasphemous and worthy of death.[13]

WRAPPING UP

Remember the picture I described at the beginning of this chapter? The universe is, we might say, the Father's workshop. Jesus is his Father's true Son, working alongside of him and following his Father's lead. As we've seen throughout our study, Jesus is both equal and subordinate to his Father. But when Jesus speaks of this relationship with his Father, is he only referring to his life on earth as a man or does this apply to his eternal relationship with the Father outside of time and space? That's the question we'll begin to address in chapter 6.

13. No evidence exists that claiming to be the messianic "son of God" in the metaphorical sense discussed above was a capital offense under Jewish law in Jesus' day (Brown, *Death of the Messiah*, 1:534–35). But a claim to divine sonship as viewed in the unique way John has been developing it since 1:1 would indeed be regarded as blasphemous and worthy of death. See Bock, "Jesus as Blasphemer," 76–81, 90–91; cf. Exod 22:28; Lev 24:11–16; Deut 13:6–18; *m. Sanh.* 7:5.

But before we move on to the next chapter, let's pause for a moment to consider some of the practical lessons we can learn from God's Junior Partner in this chapter. Imagine living your own life following the lead of Jesus—a life of intimate closeness and complete dependence on God. Jesus did nothing unless he saw his Father doing it first (Jn 5:19). Imagine a life so close to God that you could actually live depending on the Father like that.

Perhaps you're thinking, "But that was Jesus, God in the flesh! He doesn't expect us to have that sort of intimate interaction with the Father, does he?" I might agree with you if we only had John 5, where Jesus says this only about himself. There's nothing in the FST to suggest that Jesus is our model or pattern for this tight relationship with God. But when we pull the camera back to get a wide-angle look at John's Gospel, we see that the broader picture sets up Jesus' relationship with his Father as the model for us. The Son came to give believers the right to become God's children (1:12–13). The person who trusts in Jesus is born from God's Spirit.[14] As the Son is tucked snugly at the Father's side (1:18), so is the BD at Jesus' side (13:23). As the Son receives life from the Father (5:26), so do believers receive life from Jesus (6:57). Jesus' close relationship with his Father is indeed the model for us, the goal to pursue as we seek to know and obey him each day.

QUESTIONS FOR DISCUSSION

1. What stands out more to you in the FST: Jesus' equality or submission to his Father?

2. Does the idea of equality and subordination coexisting within a relationship sound less than ideal to you? If this kind of relationship exists between two perfect persons, what are the implications for human relationships?

3. Jesus looked to his Father for every word he spoke and every action he performed. How can a Christ-follower do the same?

A VERSE TO MEMORIZE

Jesus gave them this answer: "Very truly I tell you, the Son can do nothing by himself; he can do only what he sees his Father doing, because whatever the Father does the Son also does." (Jn 5:19)

14. Jn 3:3, 5, 16.

APPLY WHAT YOU'VE LEARNED

Make a list people that are in a higher position than you, people to whom you must submit, whether in your workplace, family, or the government. Then list some people in a lower position than you. Are not the people on both lists created in God's image? Discuss in your group how equality and subordination work in your life, good or bad.

CHAPTER 6

The Son Before the Sun

When I was growing up, my dad and I were not particularly close. He had dozens of noble qualities. He was a man of principle, a faithful husband, a good provider, well educated, well liked, generous, hospitable, and good to his kids. And yet, as a young boy, I frequently—for no good reason—found myself resenting him. Though he was not heavy-handed, I disliked his authority over me. I often felt judged and inferior in his presence. Neither of us was a Christ-follower at the time. He had been raised Catholic, but I knew him as an agnostic. On the rare occasion he attended church (perhaps on an Easter Sunday), he would bring along a book to read to pass the time—and it wasn't the Bible!

But when I became a Christ-follower as a teenager, I made it a goal to see my dad come to know the Jesus I knew and loved. My mother and brothers, who had also become Christ-followers, were part of the effort. We prayed for him constantly and regularly shared our faith with him, sometimes in long conversations late into the night. He was never antagonistic. In fact, he liked the positive transformation he observed in our lives since we had become Christ-followers. And yet his unbelief remained unbudging.

But that all changed in the wake of a heart attack which landed him in the hospital and prompted a reevaluation of his life and the claims of Jesus. In that hospital bed he received Christ as Lord and Savior. His newfound faith began to transform his life radically and with that our relationship. We gradually got closer. In the early years of my ministry, as I planted and pastored two churches, my dad was by my side every step of the way. I couldn't have asked for a more loyal encourager and faithful supporter, always beaming with joy and optimism. As the Lord brought us together, the old resentment melted away. I was now his pastor, and he reveled in his role as a church member. He was so openly proud of me that at times it was embarrassing! Nonetheless, he was still my father, and though we were good friends, I still looked up to him as my dad. I can't imagine ever doing otherwise. When my dad died, I counted it one of the highest privileges of my life to officiate at his funeral, difficult as it was. With each passing year, I miss him more and am eager to see him again in heaven. But when I do, will we still be father and son? Will I still look up to him and respect him as my dad? Will he still affectionately call me son, or will role distinctions like these forever be behind us?

The question before us in this chapter is much larger and more profound, though it also has implications for how we answer questions about authority and role relationships in our lives. Since we are made in God's image, are human role relationships involving authority a necessary evil (a consequence of sin), or might they simply reflect the way God created us to be forever? The members of the Trinity are the perfect model. But was Jesus' relationship to his Father a temporary or eternal arrangement? Was he always the Son of God or is that only a role he assumed when he took on his earthly mission of coming into the world to save us? Will the Son always defer to the Father's authority or are there no first-among-equals in eternity?

Back in chapter 1, I introduced a view I respectfully dubbed "God at the Round Table"—a perspective of the Trinity held by some Christian scholars. This viewpoint sees the Father, Son, and Holy Spirit as totally equal in authority, seated as it were at a round table, rather than a rectangular table headed by a chairperson. The only exception to this arrangement, says this view, is during the Son's earthly mission and role in bringing salvation to the world as the Messiah, Jesus Christ. In this capacity, the Son voluntarily defers to the Father. In becoming a man, he freely chose to humble and greatly limit himself in an awesome demonstration of divine love, even to the point of dying a tortuous death (Phil 2:5–8). But then God the Father fully vindicated his Son by raising him from the dead and exalting him to the highest place of honor as Lord (i.e., Yahweh) over all creation (Phil 2:9–11).

I agree totally with this scenario the Son's earthly mission! No argument. But here's the million-dollar question: Does the Son *eternally* submit to the Father, or was that just a temporary arrangement during his earthly mission? Answering this question from John's perspective is the goal of this chapter.

FATHERS IN JESUS' WORLD

In Jesus' day it was taken for granted throughout the known world that the father was the head of the family.[1] The assumption in society—both Jewish and non-Jewish—was that wives and children were legal dependents of the husband and father of the household. If you lived in Jesus' day and culture, your dad was your origin and future, your provider and protector, and your leader and trainer in life. What's important for our study is that each of the primary assumptions about fathers in Israelite culture was also understood to be true, in the best sense, of God as Father.[2] Here we will focus on a few of these fatherly traits.

Dad Determines Identity

Today we tell one Joe or Jane apart from another by their last names. But if you were living in Jesus' culture, you were distinguished by your father's name, such as "Jesus. . . son of Joseph" (Jn 1:42), "James son of Zebedee" (Matt 4:12), "Anna. . . daughter of Penuel" (Lk 2:36), "Simon son of Jonah" (Matt 16:17), "Sarah. . . daughter of Raguel" (Tob 3:7 NRSV), "John son of Zechariah" (Lk 3:2), or "Judas. . . son of Simon Iscariot" (Jn 6:71). This was nothing new. It was standard practice throughout the history of the OT. And it wasn't merely at home. Israel's national identity as a whole was rooted in its forefathers—the patriarchs Abraham, Isaac, and Jacob—who founded the nation and had entered into the sacred covenant with Yahweh which set Israel apart from other nations.[3] In Jewish life, the father not only provided the identity of the family/clan, but also the inheritance when he passed away. Dad was the key to your past as well as the provider for your future.

What's noteworthy here is that the OT speaks of God's fatherhood in the same terms. As a human father is the founder of the family/clan who provides an inheritance, likewise God is the Father of Israel in that he brought the nation into being,[4] "fathered" it via redemption,[5] and bequeaths it with an inheritance.[6]

---

1. See Matthews, "Marriage and Family," 1–3; Reeder, "Family," 263. The subject of fatherhood in the NT world and John is treated in more detail in Rheaume, *Exegetical and Theological Analysis*, 147–85.

2. Thompson, *Promise of the Father*, 39–48;

3. E.g., Exod 3:6; Num 32:11; Deut 1:8; 1 Kgs 18:36.

4. Deut 32:4–6; Isa 64:8–9; Jer 31:9.

5. Deut 32:18; Isa 63:15–16.

6. Isa 61:7–10; Jer 3:19; 31:9; Zech 9:12.

Dad's in Charge

The OT and NT were pretty clear-cut about dad's place in the family. He was the head of the home,[7] the family priest,[8] as well as the educator and disciplinarian of the children.[9] He had veto power over oaths taken by the women of his household (Num 30:3–16). As one expert on this subject put it, "Father connotes a social relationship in which 'father' and 'children' are not equals; this is not a democratic relationship of peers. Fathers require obedience and honor."[10] This was all the more the case regarding God as Father. Yahweh's son Israel was obligated to obey him for the loving Father he was.[11]

Among fathers and sons in Jesus' Jewish culture, there were certain features of the relationship that were well established. According to NT scholar Anthony Harvey, there were three defining aspects of the father-son relationship in first-century Israel: 1) a son's obedience to his father, 2) a son serving as an apprentice under his father, and 3) a son as an agent of his father.[12] Of these three the first was the most basic.[13] As Harvey observes, "[W]hen men were called sons of God in the Bible or in later Jewish literature, it was this quality of obedience which was primarily suggested by the metaphor."[14] For Harvey obedience is an *essential* characteristic of Jesus' sonship. "To say, therefore, that Jesus was 'son of God' was to say, first and foremost, that he showed perfect obedience to the divine will."[15]

Dad Stays Dad

The parent/child relationship was considered permanent. In the Jewish sources of the period, adults forever remain children to their parents. Grown-up children were considered duty bound to provide for their elderly parents. The obligation to serve them never ceased. Adult children were even

---

7. Josh 24:15; Eph 5:22–24; Col 3:18; 1 Pet 3:1–6. Likewise, in the *Mishnah*, "The father comes before over the mother under all circumstances, because both he and his mother are liable to pay honor to his father" (*m. Ker.* 6:9).

8. Exod 12:3; Job 1:5.

9. Deut 6:7; 32:7, 46; Prov 4:1–4; Eph 6:4.

10. Thompson, *God of the Gospel of John*, 62.

11. Jer 31:9, 18, 20; Hos 11:1, 3, 4; Mal 1:6.

12. Harvey, *Jesus and the Constraints of History*, 159–63.

13. The latter two traits proposed by Harvey are dealt with elsewhere in this book.

14. Ibid., 159.

15. Ibid., 159.

obligated to honor a father who had lost his senses.[16] Dad was to be treated with the same respect even after he had ceased to function in his fatherly duties. Forefathers long dead were still revered and considered "greater" than their offspring.[17] Even in the afterlife, the notorious rich man in Jesus' story respectfully calls his ancestor, "Father Abraham,"[18] and Abraham calls him, "son."[19] Once a dad, always a dad; once a son, always a son. As Jesus says, "[A] son is part of the family forever" (Jn 8:35 NLT). Likewise, Yahweh remains Israel's Father and the nation his son throughout the generations.[20]

THE FATHER AND SON IN JOHN

John's striking portrait of the Father and the Son must be seen against the backdrop of the Jewish view of fathers as well as the OT portrayal of Yahweh as Israel's Father. As we saw in chapter 3, John calls Jesus "the one and only" (or "only begotten") Son of God the Father (1:18). His divine sonship is unique because he shares the Father's same being (or nature). We found in chapter 5 that Jesus speaks of God as "his own Father" (5:18), and that while he is equal to God in one sense, he is without exception a submissive Son to his Father.

Two Undeniable Facts

John declares Jesus' deity in his Gospel as boldly and clearly as any other NT writer—arguably more so. Yet this equality and submission is a double-edged sword. On one side of the sword, the Logos is audaciously called God in John's opening sentence (1:1), the one through whom all creation came to be (1:3). The Gospel climaxes with Thomas's dramatic confession of faith in which Jesus is hailed as his Lord and God (20:28). But the other side of the sword is equally sharp. The Son can do nothing by himself (5:30) apart from what he sees the Father doing (5:19). He can't perform the simplest deed or even utter a syllable without a nod from his Father.[21] Strikingly, the Father is

16. Sir 3:12–13; Balla, *Child-Parent Relationship*, 104.

17. Jn 4:12; 8:53.

18. Lk 16:24, 27, 30.

19. Lk 16:25. The Greek (*teknon*) may also be translated "child."

20. God is referred to as "Father" fifteen times in the OT (Deut 32:6; 2 Sam 7:14; 1 Chr 17:13; 22:10; 28:6; Pss 68:5; 89:26; Isa 63:16²; 64:8; Jer 3:4,19; 31:9; Mal 1:6; 2:10), not counting the instances in which he is compared to a human father (e.g., Deut 1:31; 8:5; Ps 103:13) or Israel is called his son (e.g., Exod 4:22; Hos 11:1).

21. Jn 8:28; 12:49–50. This is not to say Jesus waited minute-by-minute on orders

not only greater than the Son (14:28), but he is the Son's God (20:17) as well! John highlights Jesus' subordination to the Father as much as, if not more than, any other NT writer. Both sides of the sword are razor sharp.

It is sometimes argued that this portrayal is balanced in John by instances of the Father deferring and submitting to the Son. But there is no such instance.[22] The idea of mutual submission between the Father and the Son has no basis in John. It's a one-way street. Where in John is the Father ever said to "do the will of"[23] or keep the "command"[24] of the Son? Harder yet to imagine, where in John is the Son ever said to be greater than the Father (cf. 14:28) or the God of the Father (cf. 20:17)? Nothing remotely approaching this is seen anywhere in John, only the opposite. The Son always defers to the Father, never the reverse.

A Match Made in Heaven

On the other hand, though the Son invariably submits to the Father, there isn't the slightest hint in John that anything but the deepest love, affection, and devotion exist between the two persons. The Father is no autocrat, nor is the Son his slave. On the contrary, the Father and Son share perfect, unbroken love together. Note in the following texts the devotion they have toward each other:

> The Father loves the Son and has placed everything in his hands. (Jn 3:35)

> For the Father loves the Son and shows him all he does. (Jn 5:20)

> He [the devil] has no hold over me [Jesus], but he comes so that the world may learn that I love the Father and do exactly what my Father has commanded me. (Jn 14:30–31)

> As the Father has loved me, so have I loved you. Now remain in my love. If you keep my commands, you will remain in my love,

---

from God, as though he were a mindless robot. Jesus lived in such close communion with his Father that he instinctively knew everything he said and did had God's approval (cf. 8:29). Some other noteworthy examples of Jesus' unilateral submission to the Father in John include 5:19, 30; 6:38; 7:16, 28; 10:32; 14:28, 31; 17:4; 20:17.

22. Royce Gruenler argues for mutual submission between the Father and the Son and cites John 3:35 as an example of the Father's deference to the Son (*Trinity in the Gospel of John*, 23, 33, 45, 51–53, 59, 64). But this verse plainly makes no such claim. See Rheaume, *Exegetical and Theological Analysis*, 174–75; 216n16.

23. Cf. Jn 4:34; 6:38.

24. Cf. Jn 10:18; 12:49–50.

just as I have kept my Father's commands and remain in his love. (Jn 15:9–10)

And now, Father, glorify me in your presence with the glory I had with you before the world began. (Jn 17:5)

Then the world will know that you sent me and have loved them [Jesus' disciples] even as you have loved me. Father, I want those you have given me to be with me where I am, and to see my glory, the glory you have given me because you loved me before the creation of the world. (Jn 17:23–24)

This is the perfect model of a loving father/son relationship. They do everything together. As far as the Father is concerned, what belongs to him belongs to his Son. The Son's service to the Father is not out of servility but adoring deference. So united are they in heart and purpose that Jesus can say they are "one"[25] and that the Father is somehow "in" him and he is somehow "in" the Father.[26] These enigmatic "mutual indwelling sayings," as scholars call them, express an intimacy between the Father and the Son that is so profound that their full meaning remains somewhat of a mystery. And yet it is this perfect unity and love between the Father and the Son that Jesus holds up as the model for relationships between believers. Note Jesus' words: "May they all be one, as you, Father, are in me and I am in you. May they also be one in us, so the world may believe you sent me" (Jn 17:21 CSB).

Inheriting the Name

We learned above that in Jewish culture the father determines the identity and inheritance of his children. Similarly, in our culture children typically inherit the surname of their fathers. I am Randy Rheaume because my dad was John Rheaume. I inherited his surname, not my mom's maiden name. In John, Jesus tells us that the Father has given his name to his Son:

And I am no longer in the world, but they are in the world, and I am coming to you. Holy Father, keep them in *your name, which you have given me*, that they may be one, even as we are one. While I was with them, I kept them in *your name, which you have given me*. (Jn 17:11–12 ESV; italics added)

---

25. Jn 10:30; 17:11, 21–22. In chapter 9 we will explore what Jesus means when he says he is one with the Father.

26. Jn 10:38; 14:10–11; cf. 14:20; 17:21.

Note that Jesus twice specifically says he has been given the Father's own name: "your name, which you have given me." What is the Father's name? It can't be "Father"; strictly speaking, that's a title, not a name. Recall our discussion back in chapter 2. God's personal name is the sacred name, Yahweh.

Are there any instances in John where Jesus is called by the name Yahweh? Yes and no. No, because Yahweh is a Hebrew word, and yet John (and the entire NT) is written in Greek. Strictly speaking, the Hebrew name Yahweh appears nowhere in the NT.

On the other hand, there are strong indications that Jesus is identified by the name of Yahweh in John, as well as in other places in the NT. One indication is featured especially in John. As we saw in chapter 2, Yahweh revealed the meaning of his name to Moses by calling himself "I AM" (Exod 3:14–15). We learned that "I AM" is simply Yahweh speaking his own name ("He Is") in the first person. We also saw that Jesus applied this title to himself when he declared, "Before Abraham was born, I am" (Jn 8:58). By doing this, Jesus was applying the name Yahweh in the first person to himself. Though Jesus does not use the proper noun "Yahweh," he applies a verbal form of it to himself. We will delve more deeply into this topic in chapter 8, but for now note that Jesus is claiming the name Yahweh for himself. By calling himself "I am," Jesus was accepting and using the name which the Father had given to him (Jn 17:11–12). But if the Father gave his name to the Son, this is further indication of the Father's leadership position over the Son. The Son is identified by the Father's name. The Father grants it to the Son so that we may know the Son by the same name we know the Father.

And so we have seen that like the father/son relationship portrayed in Jesus' culture and in the OT, Jesus submits fully to the authority of his Father and is known by his name. And yet the relationship is one of supreme love and unity. The Son submits not out of servility, but devoted service. The Father leads, but never lords it over the Son.

TEMPORARY ROLES?

But wait! Perhaps the submission on the Son's part is only in his capacity as Jesus the Messiah. Could this perfect model of leadership and submission between the Father and the Son be only a temporary voluntary arrangement? Some evangelical scholars believe this is the case.[27] Might they be right?

27. NT scholar Michael Bird claims the egalitarian view of the Trinity is the "evangelical consensus." See "Preface: Theologians of a Lesser Son," p. 11.

Not Really Equal

Can there be genuine equality between equals when there's a permanent hierarchy of authority? Some say absolutely not! If the Son is eternally subordinate to the Father in his authority, he is *de facto* unequal and therefore inferior to the Father. Some claim the notion of an eternally submissive Son is a dangerous teaching bordering on (or even tantamount to) the ancient heresy of Arianism—the fourth-century doctrine that the Son is inferior *by nature* to the Father. This view is often called Subordinationism (with a capital S), and it is incompatible with Trinitarianism. What are we to make of this extremely serious charge? Those who make it claim that if the Son is by necessity eternally subordinate in authority to the Father, then they are not truly equal by nature, no matter how much we may claim that they are. For the sake of our discussion, I will refer to those who believe there is no eternal hierarchy between the Father and Son as Egalitarian Trinitarians (or ETs for short).

Some ETs suggest that the hierarchy we witness in John and the rest of the NT between the members of the Trinity is the result of a mutual and voluntary agreement the Father, Son, and Holy Spirit made before they enacted the plan of salvation.[28] Outside of this temporary agreement, they are the "God at the Round Table," as I call it, with no one in authority over another. No leader is needed because they are perfectly united; no leader is possible because they are totally equal. The only way they differ is that the Son is *from* (or eternally *begotten of*) the Father, and the Holy Spirit eternally *proceeds* from God.[29] But in every way—including their authority within the Trinity—they are absolutely equal. Could the ETs be right? Does John give us any clues?

Seeking Answers

When I was a new believer, I read a book by a scholar who argued that the second Person of the Trinity was only the Son of God when he became a human being Before that he was the Word (Logos) of John 1:1–3 and was therefore not in the submissive sonship role in which we see him later. God and the Logos were totally equal apart from the mission of salvation. In

---

28. See Erickson, *Who's Tampering with the Trinity?* 57, 122, 187, following Warfield, "Biblical Doctrine of the Trinity," 54–55; Boettner, *Studies in Theology*, 116–21.

29. See Giles, *Eternal Generation*. ET scholar Millard Erickson, however, regards the doctrine of the eternal generation of the Son to be problematic (*Who's Tampering with the Trinity?*, 251).

other words, his sonship was strictly limited to his role as the human Messiah. In that sense only was he the Son of God. This view made a lot of sense to me. It helped me reconcile the declarations of Christ's deity in Scripture with those of his subordination to the Father.

But as I studied the NT more closely over the years, I found that this view created more problems than it solved. Why, for example, does the apostle Paul speak about the Father and Son as he does in the text below, after the mission of salvation is completed?

> Then *the end will come*, when he [Christ] hands over the kingdom to God the Father *after* he has destroyed all dominion, authority and power. For he must reign until he has put all his enemies under his feet. The last enemy to be destroyed is death. For he "has put everything under his feet." Now when it says that "everything" has been put under him, it is clear that this does not include God himself, who put everything under Christ. When he has done this, then *the Son himself will be made subject to him* who put everything under him, so that God may be all in all. (1 Cor 15:24–28; italics added)

As I stared hard and long at this passage, I realized it contradicted my view that the Son's submission to the Father is only temporary.[30] In this text, the Son not only remains the Son in eternity but is "made subject" to the Father forever! Could this passage still be speaking of Jesus' role as a glorified man in relation to humans and not in his relationship to the Father? It doesn't seem so. But I finally realized that the most likely place to find a definitive answer is in John's Gospel, where the Father/Son relationship is highlighted more than in any other biblical book.

Was He Always the Son?

Might the Son submit to the Father in time but be equal in authority in eternity? If so, it would be a Father/Son relationship like none other in the Bible—including the relationship they share during the Son's mission of salvation. As we've seen, the father/son relationship in the ancient world always assumed the father to be the leader of the son. We've also seen that Jesus claimed complete submission to the Father numerous times in John. But could these roles be only temporary? Some ETs think the Father and

---

30. This text is a major problem passage for ET s. E.g., Erickson, *Who's Tampering with the Trinity?*, 136–38.

Son roles may not apply in their eternal relationships.[31] In other words, outside of time and space they are not Father and Son but more like twin siblings. Other ETs believe the Father/Son relationship is eternal but with no hierarchy of authority. Perhaps in eternity, to be Father and Son is more like modern egalitarian relationships than the ancient hierarchical arrangement.

Yet if this is the case, we might wonder why God would use the Father/Son terminology in a setting where it would be so easily misunderstood. But let's say he did so anyway. Could we reasonably expect God to make it clear that this particular Father/Son relationship is one in which there is no leader? I say *reasonably* because apart from an explanation, we would naturally assume that since the ancient father/son relationship—even the one between Jesus (on earth) and the Father—universally presupposes the father as the leader, the same would naturally be the case between the Father and the Son in eternity. Apart from an explanation, wouldn't this be a reasonable assumption? On the other hand, if they are only Father and Son in time but not in eternity, are there clues of this in John?

FATHER AND SON FOREVER

Do we find an explanation in John clarifying that this unique Father/Son relationship functions one way (i.e., with a hierarchy) during the Son's earthly mission and a much different way (i.e., with no hierarchy) during his preexistent and future states? Or even apart from an explanation, are there any discernable hints of this? Or do we find that the Father and Son consistently share the same sort of relationship, with the hierarchy fully intact, as far as the eye can see in the past and into the future? In what follows, we will see that the Father/Son relationship remains the same whether Jesus speaks of his preexistent life with the Father, his mission on earth, or his position when he returns to glory with his Father. No explanation is given in John that the Father/Son relationship is different outside of Jesus' mission. By all indications it's the same.

The Logos/Son Before Creation

John opens his Gospel by saying, "In the beginning was the Word. . ." Note that John does not say "*From* the beginning"—in other words, starting at the beginning of creation—but "*In* the beginning." The preposition John

---

31. One evangelical scholar who defends this approach is Linda Belleville in "'Son' Christology," 73–75.

chose indicates he means *before* creation.[32] Scholars have also observed that John's use of the verb "was" here implies the Word "already existed" before the beginning.[33] This would have to be the case anyway, since we are told in 1:3 that absolutely *nothing* came into being apart from the Word's act of creating. We learned in chapter 4 that when John says "the Logos was God," it means that he is God by nature and thus ontologically equal to the Father. But significantly, also notice that before and during creation the Logos is in a mediating position between God the Father and all created things. John says, "All things were made *through* him" (1:3 ESV; italics added). In other words, as God's agent, the Logos is acting on his behalf to create all things. And so, before and during creation, the Logos is in a secondary role following the lead of God the Father, just as we see during Jesus' earthly mission.

We find a couple other references in John to their relationship before creation—this time from the lips of Jesus himself. The night before his crucifixion, Jesus speaks of his relationship with the Father before they made the universe:

> And now, Father, glorify me in your presence with the glory I had with you before the world began . . . . Father, I want those you have given me to be with me where I am, and to see my glory, the glory you have given me because you loved me before the creation of the world. (Jn 17:5, 24)

Amazing! Jesus recalls back before the beginning of time when he was in the Father's presence. Notice he contrasts his earthly experience with his glorious experience in the Father's presence. During his earthly life his divine glory was largely concealed. To people who saw him he appeared as a normal man who would not necessarily stand out in a crowd. This squares with what we learned about Jesus in Philippians 2:5–11 back in chapter 1. When the Son was on earth, he limited his divine abilities to live as a true man. But notice in the passage quoted above that the Father/Son relationship is mentioned, but no indication is given of any difference other than glory. The Son asks for his glory back but not his equal position of authority. The Father is still the Father, and the Son is still the Son. Minus any explanation, it's natural to assume the Father/Son relationship is the same as it has been throughout the Gospel.

---

32. Harris, *Exegetical Guide*, 18.

33. Some English translations of John 1:1 have brought this sense out by rendering it, "the Word already existed" (NLT, *GOD'S WORD*) or "the Word was already there" (NIrV). Though paraphrastic, these renderings bring out John's meaning. See Ibid., 18; Hamerton-Kelly, *Preexistence, Wisdom, and the Son*, 24.

But perhaps you're thinking, "Randy, this is an argument from silence. The relationship *could* have been different in the ageless past—with no one person in authority—but Jesus simply doesn't mention it here." Possibly. But minus an explanation, the burden of proof is on the ET to show the relationship was different.

The Son on a Mission

Another indication that the Father/Son hierarchy is eternal is the constant reference to the Son as *given* and *sent by* the Father. The Father is always the initiator. Note this in the following examples:

> For God so loved the world that he *gave* his one and only Son, that whoever believes in him shall not perish but have eternal life. For God did not *send* his Son into the world to condemn the world, but to save the world through him. (Jn 3:16–17; italics added)

> Jesus answered, "My teaching is not my own. It comes from the one who sent me." (Jn 7:16)

> Jesus said, "I am with you for only a short time, and then I am going to the one who sent me." (Jn 7:33)

> The one who sent me is with me; he has not left me alone, for I always do what pleases him." (Jn 8:29)

> Then Jesus cried out, "Whoever believes in me does not believe in me only, but in the one who sent me." (Jn 12:44)

> "The one who looks at me is seeing the one who sent me." (Jn 12:45)

In each case it is the Father who does the giving or sending and the Son who is sent. Nowhere does Jesus indicate that they mutually decided on this course of action before he came. The initiation is always on the Father's part.

Yet perhaps you're thinking, "But Randy, couldn't these texts refer to Jesus once he was already on earth as a man? It doesn't say this giving and sending took place *before* the Word became flesh (1:14). After all, John the Baptist says he was sent by God (Jn 1:33), but no one says he came from a preexistent state."[34] Good observation! But John makes it clear the Son was sent *before* he came into the world. Speaking about himself, Jesus says,

---

34. To my knowledge the strongest case against Jesus' personal preexistence in John has been made by John Robinson in *Priority of John*, 379–94. See my rebuttal in Rheaume, *Exegetical and Theological Analysis*, 219–36.

"[D]o you say of him whom the Father consecrated and sent into the world, 'You are blaspheming,' because I said, 'I am the Son of God?'" (Jn 10:35 ESV) The order here is significant. The Father consecrated (i.e., set apart) the Son and *then* sent him into the world. Look closely. The Father is doing the consecrating; the Son is being consecrated; and this takes place before the Son is sent into the world at the Father's initiative.[35] This takes us back to when "the Word was with God" (Jn 1:1) and was the Father's agent in the creation of all things (Jn 1:3). The pattern is consistent. When Jesus recalls his preexistent life, the Father remains the Father, and the Son remains the Son with no apparent difference in authority roles, just as we see in father/son relationships of Jesus' day. "I am telling you," he says, "what I have seen in the Father's presence" (Jn 8:38).

Once a Son, Always a Son

Recall that Jesus assures his disciples, "[A] son is part of the family forever" (Jn 8:35 NLT). But does this mean the Son will always be in submission to his Father? Perhaps they will be equal in authority when Jesus completes his mission.

It doesn't seem so. In fact, Jesus indicates the exact opposite on at least two occasions. First, notice Jesus' famous words, "[T]he Father is greater than I" (Jn 14:28). It's often rightly pointed out that the word "greater" here does not mean the Father is superior by nature to the Son. Elsewhere in John, the same term for "greater" is used to speak of the superior role of Israel's forefathers.[36] Their role is superior, but not their race. Just as a general is greater than a captain and a captain is greater than a sergeant (but not superior as human beings), so a father is greater than his son. Jesus did not say, "The Father is *better* than I."

But let's get back to the question: Is Jesus referring only to his earthly situation? It appears Jesus speaks of his present *and future* relationship with the Father. Look up John 14:28 and read the entire verse. Note just prior to the "greater" statement Jesus says to his disciples, "If you loved me, you

---

35. Those who deny Jesus' personal preexistence in John sometimes object that coming or being sent "into the world" does not entail preexistence. With no implication of preexistence, Jesus speaks of a child born "into the world" (16:21) and sends his disciples "into the world" (17:18). While it is true the expression by itself does not necessitate preexistence, it is plain that some instances involving Jesus most certainly do—most notably 16:28, where his coming into the world is contrasted with his soon departure from it (cf. also 13:3).

36. Jn 4:12; 8:53; cf. also 13:16; 15:20. The Greek word translated "greater" in these instances is the comparative *meizōn*.

would rejoice that I am going to the Father. . ." The meaning seems to be that because Jesus is departing to the presence of one greater than he, his situation will dramatically improve, and if his disciples really cared about him, they would be glad for him. Jesus is joyously anticipating that soon he will be in the presence of his functional superior, the Father. But if Jesus is returning to someone with whom he will *then* be functionally equal, there is no point in mentioning the Father's greater position in the first place. In other words, the reason his disciples should be happy for Jesus is that he's going to one greater than he. Jesus anticipates not simply going to a better place, but to a greater person.

A second indication that the Son will always be submitted to the Father comes from Jesus' words to Mary Magdalene after his resurrection: "Go instead to my brothers and tell them, 'I am ascending to my Father and your Father, to my God and your God'" (Jn 20:17b). In this scene, Jesus' humiliating death is behind him; he has now been gloriously raised from the dead. And yet, Jesus assumes the Father/Son relationship is still in force and will apparently remain as such. Moreover, Jesus speaks of his relationship to God in the same terms of his disciples' relationship to God. He is the God and Father of both Jesus and his disciples, though Jesus' wording hints that it's not in the same exact sense. What's important here is that Jesus speaks in language that is characteristic of the new circumstances his death and resurrection have accomplished, where the disciples are considered the Son's siblings and God is the God and Father of both. Astonishing! Through his death and resurrection, Jesus has brought his followers into a child/Father relationship with God, and a sibling relationship with us! Just as revealing, the Son specifically speaks of himself in terms of being a devotee of *his* God. He will still have God as *his* God and Father, as will his disciples. Apparently, he will forever remain the Son just as his disciples will remain his siblings, and God will remain their God and Father.

To sum up this section, the pattern of the Son's full submission to his Father is evident before, during, and after the Son's mission to save the world. It extends backward before time as far as the eye can see and forward into the future in the same manner. Is it conceivable that some sort of agreement took place at a round table between the egalitarian members of the Trinity outside of time and space? If such an agreement took place, John apparently knows nothing of it, nor do any of the NT writers. After studying this subject for many years and rereading the Greek NT (Matthew through Revelation) numerous times, I have yet to find a single passage in which the Son is not either directly or indirectly in submission to the Father, even in texts in which the Son's full deity is most forcefully asserted. Believe me, I've looked! The only Son John (or any NT writer) knows is a Son fully submitted to his Father.

BUT ISN'T PATRIARCHY BAD?

In some circles, you'll never hear a positive word about *patriarchy*, the ancient social relationship in which the oldest male in the family is considered the leader. If you're a college student at a secular university or if you're into pop culture, you likely hear nothing but withering and disdainful criticism of it. Patriarchy is considered the root of all evil—a social institution with a long history of oppression and cruelty. The sooner our culture is completely cleansed of patriarchy, the better off we'll all be. Many biblical scholars believe the Bible and Christianity need to be rescued from patriarchy and all fixed hierarchies among humans. Others argue that Jesus' teachings, properly understood, undermine patriarchy and pave the way for a completely egalitarian community in which there are no permanent hierarchies of authority.

What should we make of this? Let's begin where just about everyone can agree: An untold amount of heartache, abuse, and oppression has been generated by men who have harshly and cruelly subjugated women and children throughout history. A tragic reality!

But I believe the Bible shows that this was never God's intention for humanity and that the battle of the genders is a negative consequence of humankind's fall into rebellion against God (Gen 3:16).[37] What is evil is not patriarchy itself, but patriarchy corrupted by human sinfulness. Yet my point here is not to argue for or against male headship, which has been hotly debated among many Christians and scholars for several decades. My point here is that whatever one's view on gender roles, we should recognize that the eternal patriarchy we observe in the Trinity is perfect, loving, and thoroughly good.[38]

"But can there ever be genuine equality" you ask, "when hierarchy is present in a relationship?" I believe this is a modern question that would not have occurred to the writers of Scripture. From their perspective, a person

37. Helpful resources on this point include Hurley, *Man and Woman*, esp. 20–114, 204–21; Block, "Marriage and Family," esp. 40–44.

38. One can hold an egalitarian view on gender roles while also embracing the eternal submission of the Son to the Father, as does evangelical scholar Craig Keener. See his "Subordination within the Trinity." Though one may argue the two topics are related, one's position on both subjects should be established on its own merits. It does not follow that if you hold to an egalitarian view of the Trinity, you logically must take an egalitarian view on gender roles (and vice versa).

could be a subordinate to someone in authority and still enjoy the highest form of love with that person. Note Jesus' words to his followers: "If you keep my commands, you will remain in my love, just as I have kept my Father's commands and remain in his love" (Jn 15:10). By submitting to Jesus' authority, we remain in his love. In fact, he says keeping his commands is a prerequisite for this. What's more, the same is true between Jesus and his Father. Jesus enjoys his Father's love by keeping his commands! For Jesus, submission is not a barrier but a necessity!

In short, we in the twenty-first century may think patriarchy (no matter how well practiced) is incompatible with equality, but Jesus and the writers of Scripture did not. Jesus' portrait of God as Father embodies all the best of ideal fatherhood with no negatives. Jesus pointed to human fathers as positive illustrations that mirrored God's characteristics.[39] This is not to minimize the abuses of patriarchy. Tragically, countless children have grown up without knowing a single example of a good and loving father. The point here is that from the viewpoint of Jesus and the biblical writers, good patriarchy can exist. In fact, between the Father and the Son, perfect patriarchy *does* exist.

SO WHAT?

We've learned something hugely important about God in this chapter. Though God the Father and God the Son are equals by nature, they have different roles, and not just during Jesus' earthly ministry but also in eternity. The Father is the leader, and the Son joyfully follows his Father's lead. As Father and Son, they do everything together within a relationship of perfect love and unity.

But what relevance does this have to our lives? First, it helps us understand how we are supposed to relate to God. Jesus says, "No one comes to the Father except through me" (Jn 14:6). Just as creation came *from* the Father *through* the Son, so we come *to* the Father *through* the Son. Jesus is the mediator who not only reveals God to us but also brings us into his presence.

Secondly, this discussion might help shed light on the question I raised at the beginning of this chapter: Will I always look up to my dad—even in heaven—just because he is my dad? Will the father/son relationship still be in force throughout eternity? Will your parents always be Mom and Dad to you? Will your kids always be your sons and daughters? This raises some huge, related questions we cannot delve into here, but my short answer is

39. E.g., Lk 11:11–13; 15:11–32.

that I think parent/child relationships will remain. Undoubtedly heaven will present us with many ginormous reversals among people who were once considered very important versus those who were supposedly not at all important. Jesus promised, "So the last will be first, and the first will be last" (Matt 20:16). Yet this doesn't mean that the natural order of parents and children, built into the human race at creation, will necessarily be erased.

But even if you differ with me on this, wouldn't you agree that the presence of perfect hierarchy among the Father and the Son (who are equal by nature) opens the door for the possibility of eternal role differences among us in eternity? Even if your answer to this question is no, wouldn't you agree, nonetheless, that in this life we can enjoy good and even loving relationships with persons in lower and higher positions at the workplace or in the family? Doesn't it also say that if we are placed in authority at, let's say, the workplace, we as Christ-followers should follow the perfect example of God the Father and lead with godly love, kindness, and no condescension?

QUESTIONS FOR DISCUSSION

1. What stood out to you most in this chapter? What points do you agree or disagree with and why?

2. Do you think it is possible to be truly equal and yet subordinate to someone at the same time?

3. What implications, if any, do the role relationships between the Father and the Son have for human relationships? What about the family? Why or why not?

A VERSE TO MEMORIZE

If you loved me, you would be glad that I am going to the Father, for the Father is greater than I. (Jn 14:28)

APPLY WHAT YOU'VE LEARNED

Quoting the fifth commandment, Paul says, "Honor your father and mother" (Eph 6:2). Do something tangible to honor your parents: either an encouraging visit, phone call, card, or email. If they are not still living, share a tribute to them, perhaps with your family or group. Share respectfully how authority worked in your relationship.

CHAPTER 7

Life on Steroids

Have you ever wondered how your life might have turned out if you had made different choices along the way? I've often pondered how different my life might have been if I had never become a Christ-follower. I was a teenager at the time and still had many big choices ahead of me, and so it's very hard to guess what my life would be like now if I had never followed Jesus. If you are a Christ-follower, try to imagine your life if Jesus had not rescued you.

Throughout my walk with Jesus, I've had the immense privilege of leading numerous people to saving faith in Christ and then experienced the thrill of watching their lives transform as they grew in their relationship with him. One friend of mine has made it a regular point to thank me profusely for leading him to the Lord and discipling him in Christ. I remind him, of course, that the credit goes not to me, but to the Lord. I was simply an instrument he used. But I must admit, it's so encouraging to witness my friend's heartfelt gratitude. He invariably recounts how much his marriage, family, and entire life have been dramatically turned around since becoming a Christ-follower. His life without Christ was existence, but now he has real life in Jesus. Needless to say, as a Christian and a pastor, I find this beyond gratifying. It's another reminder that Jesus Christ is indeed who he claimed to be and that he really does transform lives. What a thrill it is to have a part in leading a person from death to life and to see the impact that person makes on the lives of others. It's a glimpse of what Jesus meant when he said, "I have come that they may have life, and have it to the full" (Jn 10:10).

Life in Jesus is superior to just living! What's more, our mortal lives in Christ, good as they are, are only a shadow of what's to come when we'll be with the Lord in glory. Here we often suffer trials, disappointments, and heart-breaking loss. But in the new heaven and new earth, he has promised to wipe every tear away; we will know joy beyond our wildest imagination. Life in Christ begins here and now when you repent and trust in him as Lord and Savior, but the best is yet to come—life in the presence of the One who is infinite goodness itself. Nothing could be better! As David put it, "[Y]ou [Yahweh] will fill me with joy in your presence, with eternal pleasures at your right hand" (Ps 16:11). That will be the good life on steroids—not on drugs, but on Jesus!

In this chapter we will learn about this superior kind of life by observing in John's Gospel where it originates, what it involves, and how it gets from God to us. Have you ever wondered what it is that will make us so happy in heaven? What could be so satisfying, fulfilling, and joyous that you would never tire of it even after countless trillions of ages? If you're thinking of magnificent mansions or breathtaking landscapes or the exploration of all the galaxies, think again. Don't get me wrong. I look forward to all that stuff and much more. But it's all nothing compared to what we're learning about in this chapter. Hint: It's the same thing that keeps the Father, Son, and Holy Spirit infinitely joyful throughout eternity. What's more, it's also the key to understanding how Jesus is equal and yet submissive to his Father.

THE ESSENCE OF LIFE

The psychoanalyst and philosopher Erich Fromm famously wrote, "To die is poignantly bitter, but the idea of having to die without having lived is unbearable."[1] Likely Fromm had no idea how biblically correct he was. To live without knowing the meaning, purpose, and satisfaction of true love is to miss out on what life is all about. You may exist without it, and you may rightly call it a life, but in a very real sense, you are not truly living. Real life as God intended it is far more than mere existence.

This, I am convinced, is what Jesus meant when he said, "I have come that they may have life, and have it to the full" (Jn 10:10). Jesus himself is the embodiment of that life. As he famously said, "I am the way and the truth and the life" (Jn 14:6). Jesus does not merely *have* life, but *is* life itself. Before raising his friend Lazarus from the dead, Jesus said to the dead man's sister, "*I am* the resurrection and the life" (Jn 11:25; italics added). Again, Jesus *is* life itself. As for us, many years later John would write, "God has given us eternal life, and this life is in his Son. Whoever has the Son has life; whoever does not have the Son of God does not have life" (1 Jn 5:11–12). But what exactly is this life? How can Jesus actually *be* life? What does it mean?

1. Fromm, *Man for Himself*, 162.

The Meaning of Life

John's Gospel is uniquely equipped to answer this question.[2] The Greek word translated "life" in the passages quoted above is *zōē*.[3] It occurs thirty-six times in John—more than in any other book in the NT. In John it nearly always refers to eternal life,[4] even when the adjective "eternal" is not present[5] (as in the examples above).

When John's Jesus speaks of earthly, temporal, merely physical life, he uses the word *psychē* rather than *zōē*. Notice how Jesus contrasts the two words when he says, "The one who loves his life [*psychē*] will lose it, and the one who hates his life [*psychē*] in this world will keep it for eternal life [*zōē*]" (Jn 12:25 CSB). Notice that natural life [*psychē*] is characterized by "this world" in the here and now. This kind of life can be lost, says Jesus, and if you *hate* your life ("hate" is Jesus' shocking word to illustrate choosing him over the things of this world), you will experience the superior *zōē* life which lasts forever. Jesus isn't devaluing human life. Far from it! Jesus' mission to save us shows how much he cares about us. His point in this provocative text is to use colorful, hyperbolic language to illustrate how much better *zōē* is compared to *psychē*. To put Jesus' meaning another way, no matter how wonderful you think your *psychē* life is, you'll *hate* it compared to *zōē* life!

From this we learn that whatever this *zōē* is, it's much better than anything we can experience in this *psychē* life. Also, unlike mortal life, *zōē* lasts forever. What's more, it's not reducible to mere existence, because a person can have *psychē* without having *zōē*. In other words, you can live without true life! Notice carefully Jesus' words: "Very truly I tell you, unless you eat the flesh of the Son of Man and drink his blood, you have no life [*zōē*] in you" (Jn 6:53).[6] Obviously, Jesus didn't mean that the people listening to him did

2. For more, see Rheaume, "John's Jesus on Life Support."

3. For those who read NT Greek, you'll notice I use the lexical form of nouns, regardless of the case in a given text. This is to avoid confusion for those who don't read Greek. For the same reason, Greek verbs will also normally appear in their lexical forms, unless the circumstance requires otherwise.

4. The only time this word is used of natural life in John is when the verb form *zaō* occurs in 4:50–51, and 53, where Jesus restores a dying boy's life. But as some scholars have pointed out, this may not be a true exception because John is likely using the word in a double sense, as in the case of Lazarus (11:25–26), to point beyond the resuscitation of mortal life to Jesus' desire and ability to impart eternal life. See Brown, *Gospel According to John I–XII*, 191.

5. Sometimes *zōē* is used in John's writings by itself as an abbreviated expression for "eternal life [*zōē*]." But the two usages convey the same meaning (cf. Jn 3:36; 5:24; 1 Jn 1:2; 3:14–15; 5:11, 12–13).

6. Christians differ widely over what precisely Jesus means in Jn 6:53 by eating his flesh and drinking his blood. Many take it as a reference to the bread and wine (or the

not exist or weren't alive in any sense. They had physical life (*psychē*), of course, but not eternal life (*zōē*). The life of which Jesus speaks—the life he embodies—is not just living as most people live. It's a superior *quality* of life, not just an eternal *quantity* of mortal life. It is in every sense life to the full.

But what exactly is this eternal life we find in Jesus? Here's where it gets both exciting as well as profound. The closest thing we have to a definition of eternal life comes to us from Jesus as he prays to his Father. Please read it carefully: "Now this is eternal life [*zōē*]: that they know you, the only true God, and Jesus Christ, whom you have sent" (Jn 17:3). That's worth rereading. Note that the essence of eternal life is *knowing* God the Father and his Son Jesus Christ.

If this seems too simple or even a bit disappointing, I can relate. John 17:3 used to puzzle me because I really didn't understand it. In my ignorance I thought in terms of knowing a set of facts about God and Jesus that we need to believe in order to receive eternal life. "Yes, I realize that's hugely important," I thought. "It's where we begin to follow Jesus—knowing and believing that he is God's Son and that he died for our sins and arose from the dead. Yes, of course, that's crucial! But isn't eternal life a lot more than that? What about the ecstatic joy, perfected bodies, mansions, angels, the New Heaven and New Earth, and reuniting with departed loved ones—not to mention no more suffering or evil or death? Isn't Jesus massively understating it here when he says, 'This is eternal life. . .?'" Though I never admitted it to anyone, I thought eternal life sounded a bit ho-hum in John 17:3. And yet I couldn't have been more wrong!

Better than Sex!

Jesus' description of eternal life in John 17:3 is packed tight with profound meaning. It's vital to understand that when Jesus speaks here of knowing the Father and the Son, he means much more than simply apprehending some important facts. He's not talking about knowing as you and I know two plus two equals four or that December follows November or that George Washington was the first US president. It's knowledge of more than just raw facts. He's talking about knowing as a loving mother knows her child or a deeply committed husband and wife know each other. In other words, he's talking about a close, intimate relationship.

Eucharist) of the Lord's Supper (cf. Mk 14:22–14). Others see it as a vivid metaphor for believing in Jesus for eternal life (cf. Jn 6:35). The point I am making here does not depend on one's viewpoint on that topic.

The Greek verb translated "know" in John 17:3 is *ginōskō*. Like our English verb "to know," *ginōskō* can often mean comprehending an object externally, as in knowing facts. But in the Greek translation of the OT (the LXX), it often conveys the more Hebrew sense of experiencing something in a deeper way than merely knowing the facts. We see this, for example, when *ginōskō* is used as a euphemism for sexual union. In the LXX of Genesis 4:1, we read that "Adam *knew* [*ginōskō*, i.e., made love to] his wife Eve, and after becoming pregnant, she gave birth to her son Cain" (AT).[7] This is knowledge on a deeply personal, experiential, and intimate level. *Ginōskō* can also signify a *personal relationship*, with no sexual connotations, which goes beyond mere acquaintance. Notice how Jesus will speak to people at the last judgment who apparently knew a lot about him but never experienced a positive and personal relationship with him:

> Many will say to me on that day, "Lord, Lord, did we not prophesy in your name and in your name drive out demons and in your name perform many miracles?" Then I will tell them plainly, "I never *knew* [*ginōskō*] you. Away from me, you evildoers!" (Matt 7:22–23; italics added)

Obviously, Jesus isn't simply saying he never knew who these people were or that they never knew who he was. Clearly they knew he was the "Lord" and even performed miraculous deeds in his name. And he, in turn, knew a lot about them. He knew they were evildoers who evidently performed their good deeds with faulty motives. To know this, Jesus would have to be able to see into their hearts. In this sense he knew them well. But tragically, he never had a *relationship* with them nor did they with him, and this ends up being the deal-breaker. They knew about him but they weren't close to him. They weren't on the same page with him; they weren't even friends with him.

According to the prophet Jeremiah, knowing God in this close sense is the ultimate ingredient in life—the one experience a human being can legitimately brag about:

> Thus says the LORD: "Let not the wise man boast in his wisdom, let not the mighty man boast in his might, let not the rich man boast in his riches, but let him who boasts boast in this, that he understands and *knows* [LXX, *ginōskō*] me, that I am the LORD who practices steadfast love, justice, and righteousness in the earth. For in these things I delight, declares the LORD." (Jer 9:23–24 ESV; italics added)

7. See also LXX Gen 4:17; 1 Kgdms 1:19; Jdt 16:22. It's also used this way in Matt 1:25.

No matter what you may own or have achieved, knowing (*ginōskō*) God deeply and intimately is what life is all about.

When we come back to John 17:3, we have good reason to believe the *ginōskō* of which Jesus speaks is this deep, intimate, and experiential knowledge. Note how Jesus uses the word *ginōskō* in another key passage in John: "I am the good shepherd; I know [*ginōskō*] my sheep and my sheep know [*ginōskō*] me—just as the Father knows [*ginōskō*] me and I know [*ginōskō*] the Father—and I lay down my life for the sheep" (Jn 10:14–15). Jesus here speaks of his true disciples, his sheep, who listen to him and follow him and to whom he gives eternal life (10:27–28). He and the Father both hold them so securely that no one will ever be able to snatch them away, and Jesus is so devoted to them that he lays down his life for them (10:28–29). No bond can be any tighter or truer than this. And yet the word that Jesus uses to sum it up is *ginōskō*. When *ginōskō* is used in John of the eternal-life relationship between Jesus and his followers, this super tight and special bond is in view. And in case there's any doubt about the closeness and intimacy of this bond, note also that Jesus says this knowing (*ginōskō*) between him and his sheep is "just as the Father knows [*ginōskō*] me and I know [*ginōskō*] the Father" (10:15). Astounding! Recall our discussion in earlier chapters about Jesus' super close and loving relationship with his Father, and yet again Jesus sums that relationship up here with the word *ginōskō*.

What does all this mean? It means that when Jesus speaks of eternal life as knowing the Father and the Son, it's all about a *relationship* with God. This is the essence of eternal life, and it's what makes it better than anything imaginable. How so? All the good things we experience in this life are whiffs of the aroma of heaven—breathtaking sunsets, delicious food, loving relationships, etc. All good things come from God, the infinite source of all good.[8] We enjoy these things, but even at their best they never fully satisfy. What's worse is that often we idolize God's good gifts or twist and corrupt them into sinful pleasures. But even when we experience them at their very best, we can eventually get tired of them no matter how pleasurable, beautiful, and amazing. And even if we find, say, a lasting relationship with another human to be continually enriching, that person can never completely fulfill us or satisfy every need. But as C. S. Lewis brilliantly pointed out, these good gifts were never meant to satisfy or complete us, but only to point us to the ultimate source of all good—God himself.[9]

8. See Ps 145:9,16; Lk 6:35; Acts 14:17; Jas 1:17.
9. Lewis, *Mere Christianity*, 134–37.

God doesn't merely *have* goodness (as in the good things we know); God *is* goodness itself.[10] The best of mortal life is only the mouthwatering aroma from the kitchen, but heaven is the kitchen and God himself is the inexhaustible meal. It is literally impossible to get tired of him, because unlike everything else in our experience, he is infinite beauty, strength, joy, splendor, goodness, and love. Though I believe heaven is a real and tangible place,[11] what makes it special is not *where* it is but *who* it is. Heaven is more about a relationship than a location. All the beauty, wonder, and goodness we see only dimly reflected in God's earthly creations exist limitlessly in him.

At the end of the Bible, when John describes the new heaven and new earth, the climax of all the wonders of eternal life is boiled down to this: "They will see his face" (Rev 22:4a).[12] If you were to do nothing more for all eternity than simply stare at God's face, you would experience boundless, ecstatic joy and wonder forever without the tiniest trace of boredom. If God is the ultimate good (and he is!), there can be absolutely nothing better than knowing and enjoying him forever. That's what Jesus is talking about when he says in John 17:3 that eternal life is all about *knowing* God the Father and his Son.

GOD'S SON ON LIFE'S SUPPORT

All this background is vital for understanding the eternal relationship between the Father and the Son. Two fascinating statements of Jesus in John deserve our special attention here—texts in which Jesus says he receives life from the Father. Please read them carefully.

> For as the Father has life [*zōē*] in himself, so he has granted the Son also to have life [*zōē*] in himself. (Jn 5:26)

10. Pss 34:8; 100:5; 135:3; Jer 33:11; Mk 10:18; 1 Pet 2:3; 1 Jn 1:5.

11. In the final state (i.e., the new heaven and earth) the universe will be physically recreated (Isa 65:17; Rom 8:20–21; 2 Pet 3:7–13; Rev 21—22). The glorified bodies of believers will be tangible, just as Jesus' body was raised physically from the dead and glorified (Lk 24:36–43; Jn 5:28–29; 20:27; Rom 8:11, 23; Phil 3:20).

12. We may wonder if Revelation 22:4 speaks of seeing God the Father's face or the Son's. Interestingly, the previous sentence says, "The throne of God and the Lamb [a figurative title for Jesus in Revelation] will be in the city, and his servants will serve him" (22:3b). Note that both God (the Father) and the Lamb are seated on *one* throne! Do the "his"/"him" in 22:3 refer to the Father or the Son? Or might the singular pronouns somehow refer to both? The same intriguing question applies to the sentence, "They will see *his* face" (22:4a; italics added). Whose face—the Father's, the Son's, or both?

> Just as the living [*zaō*] Father sent me and *I live* [*zaō*][13] *because of the Father*, so the one who feeds on me will live [*zaō*] because of me. (Jn 6:57; italics added)

What does Jesus mean? As you might guess, these words have been pondered deeply throughout the centuries by biblical scholars and theologians. What does it mean for the Father to grant life to the Son? How does the Son live because of the Father? These are massively important questions. Let's explore various viewpoints.

The Son as the Source?

Some answer by saying that John 5:26 means the Father has made the Son to be the source of eternal life for humans. In other words, if you want eternal life, you must get it from the Son because God the Father has granted it to him to dispense it. Some English translations paraphrase Jesus' words to reflect this meaning: "The Father has life in himself, and he has granted that same life-giving power to his Son" (Jn 5:26 NLT). You might need to read that a couple times to spot the subtle shift in meaning. In this paraphrase it's not about the Son possessing life in himself but about having the power to give life. The difference may seem small but it's not.

What should we make of this explanation? On the one hand, John is certainly clear that the Son is the one to whom we must come in faith for eternal life, and in the immediate context, Jesus speaks of giving eternal life to people, just as the Father does (5:21, 26). But on the other hand, this is not what Jesus is talking about in 5:26. The text actually says the Father "has granted the Son also to have life in himself" with no mention of why the Father granted it or what the Son will do with it. It's all about life within Jesus himself. True, having this life is what makes Jesus the source of eternal life for others. But John 5:26 is simply talking about the Son himself. Furthermore, in John 6:57 Jesus clearly says, "I live because of the Father." As humans depend on the Son to live, so the Son depends on the Father to live. And so the source view doesn't do justice to the plain wording of the text.

The Son's Existence?

Some believe that John 5:26 and 6:57 speak of the Son's existence. The Son depends on the Father *eternally* for his existence.[14] Since the Son had no

---

13. *Zaō* is the corresponding verb form of the noun *zōē*.

14. On how this view can be understood consistently within Trinitarianism, see

beginning, this is an "eternal begetting" which has no beginning or end. For many this is the crux of what's called the doctrine of eternal generation.

But others insist these texts show the Son of God *began to exist* at a point in time and is therefore a creature, not the Almighty Creator.[15] If the Father granted the Son life, they argue, then he did not have life before the grant and therefore did not exist, just as a human son does not exist before he is conceived. Could this be decisive proof that the Son is not truly God but rather a creature that had a beginning?

Clearly not! First, there is good reason to question the premise that existence is the point of these two texts. We've already seen that *zōē* is not simply existence. It's a superior *kind* of existence which some living people have and others do not. When Jesus says to his enemies, "[Y]ou refuse to come to me to have life" (Jn 5:40), he doesn't mean they don't exist. Nor is he saying they'll begin to exist if they do come to him for life. The absence of eternal life is not nonexistence; it's the absence of knowing God. Secondly, John 5:26 and 6:57 cannot mean that the Father brought the Son into existence because John 1:3—as we learned in chapter 4—emphatically states that not a single thing (certainly not the Son himself!) came into being apart from the Logos's creative work. When John speaks of coming into existence, he uses the verb *ginomai* (1:3; 8:58),[16] not the verb *zaō* (Greek for "live"). If John wanted to state that the Father brought the Son into existence, his word usage pattern tells us he'd use *ginomai*, not *zaō* or *zōē*. The idea that receiving life means "coming into existence" is simply a nonstarter. As for the idea that the Son depends on the Father eternally for his existence, John 5:26 and 6:57 just don't seem to be saying this.

The Son's Humanity?

What then does it mean for the Son to receive his life from the Father? Some suggest it refers only to Jesus' spiritual life as a man, not to his eternal relationship with the Father.[17] For many years I thought this was the best option. As a true man, the Son depended upon the Father for everything—just as we are supposed to do. As the human mediator between humans and God, the human Jesus needed to receive life from the Father so that he could

---

Makin, "Philosophical Models of Eternal Generation," 243–59.

15. Dixon, "Arian Response," 32.

16. *Ginomai* is used to describe the bringing of all things into existence (1:3), the origins of John the Baptist (1:6), the beginning of Jesus' human nature (1:14), and the coming into existence of Abraham (8:58).

17. Belleville, "'Son' Christology," 73–74.

pass it along to us. In fact, Jesus insists his humanity is a key ingredient when he says,

> I am the living bread that came down from heaven. Whoever eats this bread will live forever. This bread is my flesh, which I will give for the life of the world. . . . [U]nless you eat the flesh of the Son of Man and drink his blood, you have no life in you. . . . For my flesh is real food and my blood is real drink. Whoever eats my flesh and drinks my blood remains in me, and I in them. Just as the living Father sent me and I live because of the Father, so the one who feeds on me will live because of me. (Jn 6:51, 53, 55–57)

Whatever he means by eating his flesh and drinking his blood (Christians differ on this), it certainly involves his humanity and his death as a man. And so, I used to think it made perfect sense for Jesus to say he, as the incarnate Son of God, received life from the Father so that he might become the human vessel that conveys eternal life to humans who come to him to receive it. Could this be what Jesus means when he speaks of receiving life in himself from the Father in John 5:26 and 6:57?

The humanity viewpoint gets a lot of things right, but it misses the mark at 5:26 and 6:57. It's certainly true that the Son needed to become human in order to suffer and die for our sins and rise bodily from the dead. The incarnation was God's plan to bring salvation to the world. The good news of salvation is that Jesus died for us, was buried, and raised to life (1 Cor 15:1–5). It is through his crucified flesh and spilled blood that we receive eternal life when we embrace him as Lord and Savior. And certainly as a man Jesus did indeed depend on his Father for the life he conveys to us when we receive him.

But what changed my mind about the humanity view is that Jesus seems to be talking about more than his human self in John 5:26 and 6:57. Sure, whatever's going on in these two verses was true during Jesus' earthly life, but is it restricted to that? I had an uneasy feeling it wasn't, but I couldn't put my finger on why.

Then one day, as I kept staring at the text and rereading it very carefully, I discovered the answer was right under my nose. The clincher for me is the little expression in 5:26 "in himself." The Father has "granted the Son to have *zōē in himself*" (AT). Jesus can't be referring simply to his human nature here; he's talking about his inner, deepest self—not restricted to his human body or soul—the self that was unembodied with the Father in the beginning (Jn 1:1–3). How do I know? First, notice Jesus says, "as the Father has life in himself, so he has granted the Son also to have life in himself."

The Son possesses life precisely the same way the Father does—"in himself."
Certainly the Father doesn't possess life in his humanity. He's not human,
but pure spirit (Jn 4:24)! Between the Father and Son, only Jesus possesses
both a human and divine nature, but here he speaks of what they share
in common. Jesus is speaking of his deepest interior self—the same self as
when he speaks of being in the Father's presence before coming into the
world as a man. The "in himself" has to be the same thing as the "I" when Jesus says, "*I* am telling you what *I* have seen in the Father's presence" (Jn 8:38;
italics added). Likewise, it's the same as the "I" when Jesus says, "the glory *I*
had with you [Father] before the world began" (Jn 17:5; italics added). The
"in himself" of 5:26 has to be the same as the "I" of "*I* am" in 8:58 where
Jesus in effect declares himself to be the eternal Yahweh. In short, Jesus cannot be talking about only his humanity in John 5:26 because he claims to
possess *zōē* innately within himself (within his "I"), just as the Father does.
He speaks of his eternal self. This is a death blow to the humanity view.

But where then does this leave us? If the humanity view doesn't work,
and if the other views we've discussed don't work either, what does Jesus
mean in John 5:26 and 6:57 when he says he received his life from the Father? Perhaps you've already figured it out by now.

How the Son Got a Life

The missing piece of the puzzle is the meaning of life (*zōē*) as found in John's
Gospel. Very simply, life is all about knowing God. As we learned earlier
in this chapter, *zōē* speaks of a deep and intimate relationship with the Father and the Son. The Jewish understanding in Jesus' day—informed by OT
Scripture—was that true and lasting life was sourced in God alone.[18] John's
Gospel develops and hones this truth by showing us that the fullest life is all
about knowing God through Jesus in a deep and intimate way.

The Son had life in himself not only during his earthly mission but also
when he preexisted with the Father. John tells us, "In him [the Logos] was
life [*zōē*], and that life [*zōē*] was the light of all mankind" (1:4). As noted
above, this refers to the ceaseless, perfect relationship the Son enjoyed in
the Father's presence—"in the bosom of the Father" (1:18; NKJV), as we
learned in chapter 3.

If this is the essence and meaning of *zōē*, then what does it really mean
for the Father to grant the Son to have life in himself (5:26)? The answer

18. God is the ultimate source of life. E.g., Gen 2:7, 9; 3:22, 24; Deut 30:6, 19–20;
32:39; Pss 21:4; 36:9; Prov 14:27; 16:22; 23:22; Wis 15:16–17; Philo *Creation* 135; Jos.
Asen. 12:1–2.

lies in the word translated "granted" in 5:26—the Greek verb *didōmi*. The
Father "has *granted* [*didōmi*] the Son also to have life in himself." *Didōmi*
is a common NT word that basically means "to give or grant." John likes
to use this word to mean *granting authorization*,[19] implying the authority
of the giver over the receiver, especially when the giver is God.[20] Note the
following examples:

> John answered, "A person cannot receive even one thing unless
> it is given [*didōmi*] him from heaven. (Jn 3:27 ESV)

> The Father loves the Son and has given [*didōmi*] all things into
> his hand. (Jn 3:35 ESV)

> Jesus, knowing that the Father had given [*didōmi*] all things into
> his hands, and that he had come from God and was going back
> to God . . . (Jn 13:3 ESV)

> . . . you [the Father] have given [*didōmi*] him [the Son] authority
> over all flesh, to give [*didōmi*] eternal life to all whom you have
> given [*didōmi*] him. (Jn 17:2 ESV)

> Jesus answered him [Pilate], "You would have no authority over
> me at all unless it had been given [*didōmi*] you from above.
> Therefore he who delivered me over to you has the greater sin."
> (Jn 19:11 ESV)

The first example (3:27) is noteworthy because it states a universal
principle: You can't receive a thing unless God so *grants* it—presupposing
total dependency on God—whether you recognize it or not. Likewise, in
John 19:11, Pilate may think he's in charge, but in reality his position of
power has been *given* to him from the Father. He's totally clueless as to how
dependent he is on God!

This idea of authority on the one hand and dependence on the other
seems to be what's going on with *didōmi* in John 5:26. In the very next verse,
in a similar construction, Jesus explicitly uses *didōmi* to speak of the authority the Father has delegated to him: "And he [the Father] has given [*didōmi*]
him authority to judge because he is the Son of Man" (Jn 5:27). The Father
is the ultimate authority, and the Son acknowledges this and depends totally
on him[21]—a theme strongly stressed in the context.[22] Similarly, in 5:26, the
Father "has granted (the privilege) of having life."[23] In other words, he has

19. See Loader, *Jesus in John's Gospel*, 59–61.

20. BDAG, 243.

21. Keener, *Gospel of John*, 1:654.

22. John 5:19, 22, 24, 30, 36–37, 43.

23. BDAG, 243.

bestowed on his Son this superlative relationship of intimate knowledge, and the Son has deferentially received it. As in all other matters, the Father leads and the Son follows.

How does this work outside of time? Here we are on ultra-holy ground. In eternity the Father extends his innate self-knowledge to his Son in a perfect bond of loving fellowship. The Father is the ultimate source of this *zōē* knowledge. What does it mean for the Father to have life in himself? This life is the perfect knowledge (experience) of his inexhaustible self and the reciprocal knowledge of his Son. It is the Father who takes the lead in conveying this loving communion to his Son, and the Son receives it in full dependence on the Father. Jesus speaks of this happening in the past in John 5:26 ("granted"), and from what we can deduce in John, this must refer to what we often call "eternity past."[24] In other words, the Father is the ultimate source of this full life (*zōē*) we've been learning about. The Father has always shared it with his Son, and the Son has always deferentially received it. Throughout all eternity the members of the Trinity[25] have enjoyed the perfect relationship of infinite love, goodness, and joy. And the Son has become human to bring us into this relationship.

HOW WE "GET A LIFE"

When I ponder and study the puzzles in Scripture long and carefully, I have often found that they eventually open up new vistas of profound discovery. Like finding a buried treasure after much backbreaking digging, the reward is worth the effort. When I set out to write my PhD dissertation on the topic of the Father and Son in John's Gospel, I was determined to penetrate the mystery discussed in the previous section: What does it mean for the Son to receive his life from the Father? I had no idea that probing this wonder would have radically awesome implications for us who follow him.

The big bonus in this study is finding that the same giving/dependency pattern which exists between the Father and the Son also exists between Jesus and his followers. The Son invites you to become God's child so you can enjoy this eternal life experience through trusting in (i.e., depending on) him for it. Look carefully at John's explanation of this: "Yet to all who did *receive* him [the Son], to those who *believed* in his name, he gave the

---

24. Similarly, Jesus speaks of eternity past in this way when he says, "Father . . . you *loved* me before the creation of the world." (Jn 17:24; italics added).

25. Though we are talking here about the Father and the Son, it should be noted briefly that the Holy Spirit too shares in this relationship. He is the giver of *zōē* (Jn 6:63; 2 Cor 3:6) and is in fellowship with the Father and the Son (2 Cor 13:14).

right to become *children of God*—children born not of natural descent, nor of human decision or a husband's will, but *born of God*." (Jn 1:12–13; italics added). This text tells us how a person becomes a child of God; it happens when you believe in (i.e., receive) Jesus. Believing in Jesus means more than simply accepting the truth about him. It's not just intellectual assent to the facts of who he is and what he did for you. In the Bible saving belief means to *depend* on Christ—to trust in (or entrust yourself to) him as Lord and Savior. Notice in John 1:13 that becoming God's child actually involves a supernatural birth. When you trust in Jesus, you are supernaturally born as a child of God.

The pattern may sound familiar to you. You become God's child in time and space the same way God's Son has always been God's Child in eternity. Just as the Son depends on the Father for life (throughout all eternity), so we depend on the Son for life so that we might be God's children forever. By depending on the Son for life, you become, in a very real sense, a sibling of God the Son, enjoying the life of God!

This opens up a whole new vista for understanding God's desire and intention for humans. God made humans in his image, which, as we learned earlier, means he is our Father and we his sons. God wanted us to experience unbroken fellowship with him, just as he experiences it within the Trinity. That fellowship, that perfect experiential knowledge of God, is what Scripture calls eternal life. But tragically, we humans fell into rebellion and ruined our relationship with him. The way to eternal life (i.e., fellowship with God) was blocked. To reconcile us, God sent his eternal Son to reveal to us the Father and provide redemption for the whole world through his death for our sins and his resurrection. The way into that perfect relationship entails rejecting our own corrupted life and embracing new life (*zōē*) in the Son (Jn 12:25–26). When we do so, we are reborn spiritually (Jn 3:3) and receive eternal life (Jn 3:16). In other words, the Father wants us to enjoy the same kind of relationship he has with his Son. He wants us to become part of the family! What could be better?

QUESTIONS FOR DISCUSSION

1. What was new to you in this chapter? How does the concept of eternal life discussed here differ from commonly held concepts of heaven?

2. How would you explain what you've learned about eternal life in this chapter to a person not familiar with the topic?

3. Have you found eternal life through depending on Jesus? If so, describe your relationship with God and how it came about.

A VERSE TO MEMORIZE

Now this is eternal life: that they know you, the only true God, and Jesus Christ, whom you have sent. (Jn 17:3)

APPLY WHAT YOU'VE LEARNED

Write your personal story about how you found new life in Jesus. Explain what your life was like before you trusted in Christ, how you heard the gospel message and accepted it, and how your life has changed since you became a Christ-follower. Keep the initial version short, say a page or two. While you're working on this, pray that you will take opportunities to share your story with non-Christians. You can post your story on social media or tell it to a friend. Writing it out helps you to think it through and to articulate it clearly.

CHAPTER 8

God's Big Secret

Recently I watched a Muslim cleric address the topic of Jesus' identity in front of a large crowd. A Christian man had stood up during the Q&A time to testify about the peace Jesus has given him. In answer to the man's testimony, the cleric asked him, "Do you believe Jesus is God?" When the Christian answered "yes," the cleric offered this challenge: "Show me a single verse in the Bible where Jesus claims unequivocally to be God! When did he ever say, 'I am God. Worship me!'? Show me that verse and I am ready to accept Christianity." I felt sorry for this dear Christian man. He had bravely stood up in front of a large Muslim audience to testify to the reality of Christ's peace within him, but when pressed, he was unable to articulate even a weak defense of Jesus' claim to be God. By the end of the conversation, the Muslim cleric had accused the Christian of worshiping a false god and experiencing a false peace. The audience erupted in thunderous applause.

If you had been in the position of that Christian man, what might you have said? When did Jesus himself ever claim to be God? Perhaps you've faced the same question from a Muslim you know or from a JW or a skeptic. If you're like me, you've wondered about this yourself.

In this chapter, we're asking why (even in John's Gospel) doesn't Jesus ever say, "I am God." True, others call him God, but why does he seem reluctant to say it himself? As we've noted before, Jesus claimed his true identity is crucial to salvation. He says, "[I]f you do not believe that I am he, you will indeed die in your sins" (Jn 8:24). But if Jesus really is God and believing this is essential, why didn't he simply say, "I am God. Worship me!"? You have to admit, it's a fair question. In this chapter we'll discover that the answer not

only helps us to understand Jesus' relationship to the Father better, but also
helps us in leading a person to follow Jesus.

WHAT'S THE PROBLEM?

At this point you might be wondering why I'm raising this question so far
into the book. Perhaps if you could talk to me now, you'd say, "Randy, haven't
you already amply demonstrated Jesus' full deity? Doesn't the first verse of
John explicitly say, 'the Word was God?'" My answer, of course, is yes. "And
doesn't this statement in John 1:1 assert that the Word is *actually* (i.e., ontologically) God—not just representing God but really and truly God?" Yes.
You've been paying attention! "And doesn't John 1:18 identify Jesus as God
the Son?" Yes. "Doesn't Thomas say to Jesus, 'My Lord and my God' (Jn
20:28)?" Yes. "Haven't we also learned that Yahweh appeared in bodily form
to people in OT and that John links these appearances to Jesus?" Yes again,
and the list could go on. "Okay Randy, then where's the problem?"

The problem is that something weird is going on! Doesn't it seem a bit
strange that the term "God" (Greek *theos*) is applied in John to the Father
about seventy-seven times but to the Son only three times (1:1, 18; 20:28)?
Why this imbalance if the Son is as truly God as the Father? If it's so important to believe Jesus is God, why isn't it stated ten times as often? And
something else is weird: Jesus' own reluctance on the matter seems puzzling,
does it not? Isn't Jesus himself the first and best person to ask about his
own identity? Even if John's Jesus leaves many strong hints about his true
identity, doesn't it seem strange he didn't just come out and say, "Let me
make this perfectly clear, just in case anyone hasn't gotten the memo yet: I
am God. You need to believe in me and worship me as God to be saved"?
That way no Muslim or JW could claim otherwise.[1]

THE SHY GOD

In chapter 2, we learned that Yahweh appeared numerous times to people in
the OT, often in bodily form. We found that God longs to interact directly

---

1. I am very much aware that as a rule mainstream NT scholars do not regard John's
Gospel to be a reliable historical account of Jesus' words and deeds. Also, many such
scholars see the earlier Gospels (Matthew, Mark, and Luke) as presenting a lower view
of Christ than John—a view which does not regard Jesus as God. In this book I am
taking John's witness of Jesus at face value. For a defense of the trustworthiness of John's
account, see Blomberg, *Historical Reliability of John's Gospel*. Also, for a defense of Jesus'
deity as presented in the other Gospels, see Hays, *Reading Backwards*.

with his people, despite the formidable obstacle of human frailty and sinful-ness. And yet, even when he does show up, often there's something quite mysterious going on. It seems that Yahweh is sometimes reluctant—at least at first—to reveal his identity.

God the Night Fighter

Sometimes when God appears to people his identity is revealed gradually. A good example is the ultra-weird story of Jacob wrestling with a man who turns out to be God.

> So Jacob was left alone, and a man wrestled with him till day-break. When the man saw that he could not overpower him, he touched the socket of Jacob's hip so that his hip was wrenched as he wrestled with the man. Then the man said, "Let me go, for it is daybreak." But Jacob replied, "I will not let you go unless you bless me." The man asked him, "What is your name?" "Jacob," he answered. Then the man said, "Your name will no longer be Jacob, but Israel, because you have struggled with God and with humans and have overcome." Jacob said, "Please tell me your name." But he replied, "Why do you ask my name?" Then he blessed him there. So Jacob called the place Peniel, saying, "It is because I saw God face to face, and yet my life was spared." (Gen 32:24–30)

This story bombards us with baffling oddities—far more than we have time to deal with properly here. What's important for our study is that this mysterious night wrestler enters the story described simply as "a man," and yet by the end Jacob is convinced he's God. How Jacob came to this conclu-sion is not entirely clear. How can a night stalker out of nowhere be God? And if he is God, why can't he even outwrestle Jacob? On the other hand, when the man wants to finish the fight, it only takes a touch to disable Jacob for life (Gen 32:31–32). Really weird! Somehow Jacob discerns this is no ordinary man. He begs the stranger to bless him, indicating Jacob recog-nizes him as his superior. He asks for the man's name, but the man refuses to reveal it, as though there is something special about it. Most telling of all, this mysterious wrestler renames Jacob, calling him "Israel," a name that likely means "he struggles with God."[2]

Imagine if someone you just met on the street picked a fight with you and then claimed the right to change your name! That would take a

2. NIV text note.

truckload of nerve, unless the person was way above your head on the authority scale. But it goes far beyond Jacob himself. As Genesis continues, it becomes clear that this new name, Israel, is not just for Jacob, but for the entire nation of God's people that will descend from him. Rather than conclude this wrestler dude is crazy, Jacob is certain he has seen God's face, and he's grateful he didn't lose his life during the experience.

The story boggles the mind. On the one hand, the text plainly states the stranger is a man, and apparently he's physically weaker than Jacob. Yet the text is equally clear that this man talks and acts with the authority of God himself. But the secret is not explicitly disclosed until the end of the story.

Touched by an Angel

As strange as this story sounds, it's not unique. Centuries later, the angel of Yahweh appears to a man named Gideon to commission him to lead Israel into battle. Three times the narrator plainly states it is Yahweh who is speaking to Gideon (Judg 6:14, 16, 18). But it's not until the end of the encounter that Gideon realizes his identity: "When Gideon realized that it was the angel of the LORD, he exclaimed, 'Alas, Sovereign LORD! I have seen the angel of the LORD face to face!'" (Judg 6:22). As with Jacob, Gideon doesn't figure it out until after the experience.

Another case is found a few chapters later when the angel of Yahweh appears to an unnamed woman to announce she will soon give birth. He also provides instructions for the child's upbringing. Though the woman is struck by his awesome appearance and suspects he may be an angel (Judg 13:6), neither she nor her husband Manoah (who also meets him) realizes he is God until his miraculous exit:

> Then Manoah took a young goat, together with the grain offering, and sacrificed it on a rock to the LORD. And the LORD did an amazing thing while Manoah and his wife watched: As the flame blazed up from the altar toward heaven, the angel of the LORD ascended in the flame. Seeing this, Manoah and his wife fell with their faces to the ground. When the angel of the LORD did not show himself again to Manoah and his wife, Manoah realized that it was the angel of the LORD. "We are doomed to die!" he said to his wife. "We have seen God!" (Judg 13:19–22)

Here again Yahweh's true identity is not revealed explicitly until after the appearance. (By the way, in case you're wondering, Manoah and his wife do not die from the encounter.) But oddly enough, similar to Jacob's encounter with the wrestler, when Manoah asks the angel of Yahweh for his name, he responds, "Why do you ask my name? It is beyond understanding" (Judg 13:18). Once again, he doesn't come right out and say, "I'm God," but he waits for Manoah and his wife to deduce it later on.

For reasons that are not always clear, God chooses in certain instances to reveal his identity slowly, especially in close encounters with people who may need to hear the message before knowing the identity of the messenger. In the cases of Jacob, Gideon, and Manoah and his wife, God was bringing big news that warranted a personal appearance, and yet apparently it was necessary to conceal his identity until after the news had been given.[3] Though big hints are dropped during each encounter, the puzzle's picture isn't plain until all the pieces are in place. Could the same be the case with Jesus?

God Makes a House Call

Were the Jews in Jesus' day expecting the Messiah to be God in human flesh? Though there were many different viewpoints floating around, a Yahweh-incarnate Messiah was not on the radar of most Jews when Jesus arrived on the scene.[4] Many Jews expected the Messiah to be a man (nothing more) whom God would use to bring about their liberation from oppression. It's one thing for God to make a temporary appearance as a man (as in some OT cases), but for him to become an actual flesh-and-blood earth-dwelling human who was born of a woman? That's a much different story. Pagan notions of multiple gods and gods who took on human form posed a threat to the Jewish belief in only one true God. We witness this in John when the

3. Also, in the OT we find a strong emphasis on Yahweh's oneness (Deut 6:4), as we learned in chapter 2. Though there are hints of plurality within God, Yahweh apparently wants to guard his people from any confusion with polytheism (i.e., the belief in [or worship of] many gods). Thus there is often a certain mystery and ambiguity about his OT appearances.

4. This is a hotly debated subject among specialists in the field. Many scholars (with wide variations among them) argue that certain entities in Jewish literature—such as principal angelic figures, God's personified attributes (wisdom, Spirit, etc.), or OT characters (Moses, Enoch, Jacob, etc.)—helped prepare the mindset of Jesus' early Jewish followers for a fully divine Messiah (e.g., Hurtado, *One God, One Lord*, 17–39, 93–124). Others scholars believe the pervasive Jewish monotheism in the first century constrained such notions, at least until the time of John's Gospel (e.g., Dunn, *Christology in the Making*) if not beyond (e.g., Harvey, *Jesus and the Constraints of History*, 154–73, 176–78). Other scholars have argued that a divine Messiah was anticipated among the Jews in Jesus' day (e.g., Boyarin, *Jewish Gospels*).

Jewish leaders interpret Jesus' claim to be God as a blasphemous violation of monotheism.[5]

But when we look at the OT Scriptures, we do find hints that God himself might show up on the scene one day as a true man after all. Isaiah, for instance, declares this startling prophecy about a descendent of King David:

> For to us a child is born,
> to us a son is given,
> and the government will be
> on his shoulders.
> And he will be called
> Wonderful Counselor,
> Mighty God,
> Everlasting Father, Prince of
> Peace.
> Of the greatness of his
> government and peace there will be no end.
> He will reign on David's
> throne
> and over his kingdom,
> establishing and upholding it
> with justice and
> righteousness
> from that time on and
> forever. (Isa 9:6–7)

The foretold child here is surely human; he's born as a son. But note also the title "Mighty God." Could someone less than Yahweh be addressed this way?[6] Then again, perhaps these are titles speaking *about* the God of this Davidic king, rather than describing the king himself.[7] The point is at least arguable.

Another instance is a psalm in which the Davidic king is hailed in unusually exalted terms: "Your throne, O God, will last / for ever and ever; / a scepter of justice will / be the scepter of your kingdom" (Ps 45:6). The psalm writer addresses the king as "God!"[8] This would seem to be an airtight affirmation of the Messiah as God himself. Then again, could the writer be addressing the king the same way Psalm 82 refers to the rulers as "gods" or

---

5. See Jn 5:18; 10:33; 19:7; cf. Mk 2:7.

6. See Brown, *Answering Jewish Objections to Jesus,* 2:44–47.

7. Berlin and Brettler, *Jewish Study Bible,* 802.

8. See Brown, *Answering Jewish Objections to Jesus,* 2:42–44.

as Pharaoh regarded Moses as "god" (Exod 7:1) as we observed in chapter 2? The point is arguable.

Another OT indication that Yahweh might show up in person among his people is found in his promise to decisively end Israel's return from exile.

> A voice of one calling:
> "In the wilderness prepare
>   the way for the LORD [Yahweh];
> make straight in the desert
>   a highway for our God." (Isa 40:3)

It's highly significant that this prophecy is quoted in all four of the NT Gospels in reference to John the Baptist[9] who is the "voice" preparing the way for Jesus, "the LORD" (i.e., Yahweh), "our God." The most obvious conclusion to draw is that Isaiah predicts the coming of Yahweh heralded by a messenger, and since the Gospel writers understand the messenger to be John the Baptist, Yahweh himself comes as Jesus. If so, this would constitute a powerful affirmation of Jesus' deity.

But perhaps you're wondering, "Do Isaiah and the Gospel writers really expect Yahweh to appear visibly to Israel? Isn't it more likely that a representative of Yahweh is meant?" It doesn't seem so. The "voice" in the prophecy is Yahweh's messenger, and so that position is already filled. By all indications Yahweh "our God." is expected to show up personally. Later in the same chapter, Isaiah doubles down on the point by insisting that Zion (i.e., Jerusalem) and the towns of Judah will actually see Yahweh himself.

> You who bring *good news* to
>   Zion,
>   go up on a high mountain.
> You who bring *good news* to
>   Jerusalem,
>   lift up your voice with a shout,
> lift it up, do not be afraid;
>   say to the towns of Judah,
>   "*Here is your God!*"
> See, the Sovereign *LORD* [Yahweh]
>   *comes* with power . . . (Isa 40:9–10; italics added)

Yahweh himself is coming and the people will behold him! Note that Isaiah calls this announcement "good news" which, tellingly, is the way Mark characterizes his account of Jesus (Mk 1:1). Also, Jesus characterized

---

9. Matt 3:3; Mk 1:3; Lk 3:4; Jn 1:23.

his basic messageas "good news" (i.e., "gospel").[10] The early Christians used the same term to characterize the salvation message of Jesus.[11] Taken at face value, it seems that the "good news" of which Isaiah speaks is that Yahweh himself is going to make a personal appearance and that Jesus is the embodiment of this news

But then again, perhaps the Isaiah prophecy is simply a poetic way (after all, it is poetry) of colorfully declaring that Yahweh will do something truly spectacular among his people when he finally and fully restores them. The point is a least arguable. On the other hand, looking back now on the OT—after Yahweh did indeed show up in Jesus—we can see many strong hints that God himself was somehow going to come among his people. Remember, Yahweh did show up several times in tangible form in the OT, as we learned in chapter 2. But exactly how or in what form he would come in the future was not clearly spelled out.

When God the Son finally visited planet Earth, he could have beamed himself down from heaven in full splendor for all to see and recognize him. Actually, he has promised to do something very much like that when he returns in power and great glory.[12] But when he came among us two thousand years ago, he chose to use the incognito approach. He was born in humble circumstances and grew up as a carpenter in an obscure Jewish village. By all outward appearances, to nearly everyone who knew him, he was quite ordinary. Like the wrestler who fought with Jacob, Jesus seemed at first to be simply a man.

God's Secret Identity

The Gospels—especially John—show us how Jesus slowly yet surely revealed his true identity to his followers. But before we turn to John, let's quickly examine a fascinating saying recorded (in slightly different forms) by both Matthew and Luke. Luke's version has Jesus putting it this way:

> All things have been committed to me by my Father. No one knows who the Son is except the Father, and no one knows who the Father is except the Son and those to whom the Son chooses to reveal him. (Lk 10:22; cf. Matt 11:27)

10. E.g., Matt 4:23; Mk 1:14–15; Lk 4:18.

11. E.g., Acts 5:42; Rom 1:16; 1 Cor 15:1–5. The Greek word for good news is often translated "gospel" in English.

12. E.g., Matt 24:30–31; Mk 14:62; 2 Thess 1:6–10. The OT prophet Zechariah speaks of Yahweh appearing on earth, having been "pierced" by his enemies (Zech 12:10). In the NT this is applied to Jesus at his return (Rev 1:7; cf. Jn 19:37).

Biblical scholars have long noted how this saying sounds strikingly similar to the way Jesus talks in John. Jesus here speaks of the utter uniqueness of the Father/Son relationship. By "the Son" Jesus means more than a purely human Messiah. The Father has placed everything (the whole universe?) in Jesus' hands. That's a mighty big bite for a mere man to chew and swallow! But the most intriguing detail is Jesus' insistence that no one really knows who he is or who the Father is. If Jesus were just speaking of his messiahship, we might expect him to say no one really knows who *he* is.[13] Yet he also says no one knows who the *Father* is! Jesus speaks here of much more than his identity as the Messiah. Look at it again. No one really knows who he is or who the Father is. It's a secret! Isn't the Father simply God and that's it? Once again (as we saw in chapter 7) the Greek word translated "know" here is *ginōskō*. Jesus is claiming exclusive, intimate knowledge of the Father and the Father of the Son. No one else anywhere is in this private club (except the Holy Spirit[14]). And according to Jesus, this secret knowledge is disclosed only by special revelation when he decides to do so. We might speculate and debate as to why God chose to reveal the Father's and Son's true identity gradually rather than immediately. But no one should miss the bare fact that this was the way God chose to handle it, and the task of revealing was placed in Jesus' hands.

Once again Yahweh was showing up on Earth—this time as a full flesh-and-blood human being. And just as in some of his previous appearances, he was not declaring from the housetops, "I am God. Worship me!" Jesus had a strategy in mind. But how did he go about revealing the true identity of the Father and the Son? Again, John provides us with the most help.

THE SON'S SLOW REVEAL

Did Jesus ever claim to be God? He certainly did, both indirectly and directly. But at least three factors keep many people from recognizing it. First, if you read the NT without understanding the Jewish and OT background of Jesus' culture, you can miss it. Secondly, if you fail to pick up the gradual way in which Jesus reveals his divine identity, you can miss it. Thirdly, there's more than one way to state the claim to be God; using the word "God" is only one.

---

13. Jesus usually spoke very discreetly about being the Messiah (e.g., Matt 16:20; Lk 22:67–68; Jn 10:24) due to the unwanted baggage this term often brought with it in his culture.

14. See Jn 16:14–15; 1 Cor 2:11.

"I am God!"

As we observed above, some people say, "If only Jesus had come right out and said, 'I am God,' he would have eliminated all doubt about his identity." But if you understand the OT background of the Gospels—especially John—Jesus says nearly these exact words.

Several times in John, Jesus applies the divine name Yahweh to himself by using the verbal expression "I am." Back in chapter 2 we discussed Jesus' declaration, "[B]efore Abraham was born, I am!" (Jn 8:58) The hostile Jerusalem crowd immediately picked up rocks to stone him to death for blasphemy, but Jesus escaped them (8:59). Later, back in Jerusalem, the crowd tells us why they believe Jesus deserves to be stoned:

> [Jesus said,] "I and the Father are one." Again his Jewish opponents picked up stones to stone him, but Jesus said to them, "I have shown you many good works from the Father. For which of these do you stone me?" "We are not stoning you for any good work," they replied, "but for blasphemy, because you, a mere man, claim to be God." (Jn 10:30–33)

Jesus' Jewish audience had no trouble recognizing his claim to be God. To them it was crystal clear. Notice the word "again" at the beginning of verse 31. This is now the second time they are attempting to stone Jesus to death; the first time was in 8:59 immediately after Jesus declared "I am." They clearly understood Jesus' usage of "I am" to refer to Yahweh's identification of himself in the OT. Recall Yahweh's words to Moses, "I AM WHO I AM.[15] This is what you are to say to the Israelites: 'I AM has sent me to you'" (Exod 3:14). As we learned in chapter 2, the name Yahweh means "he is"—referring to God as the eternal one who is always present. When Yahweh says "I am," he is speaking his own name in the first person.

This is huge! If Jesus' use of "I am" in John 8:58 alludes back to Yahweh's usage of it in the OT, then Jesus is in effect calling himself Yahweh. But can we be sure this is what Jesus is doing? Here's why I think we can. Recall that the Father has given his own name to his Son (Jn 17:11–12). This refers to God's personal name "Yahweh," not merely to the title or quasi-name, "God." But when did Jesus ever call himself Yahweh? This Hebrew word never appears in John, which is written in Greek. Jesus seems to heighten the mystery when he says to the Father, "I have revealed your name to the

---

15. You may wonder why some of the "I am" sayings are printed in uppercase letters and others are not. This is purely up to the English translators and editors, since biblical Hebrew has no upper and lower case distinction and in Greek the distinction did not develop until well after the NT era.

men you gave me out of the world. . . . I made known your name to them, and I will continue to make it known" (Jn 17:6, 26 NET©).[16] Again, when did Jesus ever reveal God's name (i.e., Yahweh) to his disciples? And if the Father gave his name to Jesus, when did Jesus ever use the name for himself? By far the best candidate is his usage of the "I am" expression.

Most English readers of John don't realize how Jesus uses the "I am" declaration in John and how it builds to a climax. Obviously the words "I am" by themselves do not constitute a claim to be Yahweh. We all use those words together constantly in daily conversation with no such meaning. The same was the case for people speaking Hebrew (the language of the OT) and Greek (the language of the NT).[17] It wasn't a magic formula. The key is the context and the way in which the expression is used. From the very first verse, John tells us directly "the Word was God." But as John unfolds his story of Jesus' ministry, he shows us how Jesus gradually revealed his Yahweh identity to his followers using his absolute "I am" sayings.

"I Am" in the OT

You can know the English Bible pretty well without realizing that Yahweh uses the "I am" expression numerous times in the OT. It's not just at the burning bush incident in Exodus 3:14–15. Yahweh also forcefully asserts his name with the Hebrew words 'ani hu—literally "I [am] he." The Jews of Jesus' day used this expression for the divine name Yahweh. In fact, Yahweh uses it numerous times in the OT to refer to himself, especially when he wants to declare emphatically that he and he alone is the one true God. What's so fascinating is that in the Greek of John's Gospel, the expression Jesus uses for "I am" is egō eimi—the exact equivalent to 'ani hu in numerous OT texts. John likely links this back to Exodus 3:14–15.[18]

16. Unfortunately, the NIV and NLT leave out the words "your name" (which occur in the Greek) in these verses. Instead they paraphrase the Greek to read, "I have revealed you. . ." (v. 6) and "I have made you known to them" (v 26; cf. NLT). The likely reasoning behind these renderings is the assumption that the "name" here signifies the character of the Father, not his actual name. But making a choice between God's character and his actual name is not necessary here because both can surely be signified in the same instance, as John's usage elsewhere would suggest. See Rheaume, *Exegetical and Theological Analysis*, 315–17.

17. For instance, the formerly blind man uses "I am" (egō eimi) to assert his identity in Jn 9:9.

18. See Rheaume, *Exegetical and Theological Analysis*, 292–98. On the absolute "I am" sayings in general, I have found the following works to be very helpful: Ball, *"I Am" in John's Gospel*; Bauckham, "Monotheism and Christology;" Harner, *"I Am" of the Fourth Gospel*; Lincoln, "Trials, Plots, and the Narrative;" Williams, *I Am He*; Williams,

Many of John's first readers were Jews and gentiles who knew only the Greek version of the OT. Now please stay with me here because this gets a little technical. A couple hundred years before Jesus' birth, the Hebrew OT was translated into Greek because many Jews and interested gentiles could not read Hebrew. We refer to that Greek translation of the Hebrew OT as the Septuagint (or LXX for short). When these readers read John 8:58, they would have immediately thought of OT passages in the LXX where Yahweh made the same declaration as Jesus makes in John 8:58. The following quotations of Yahweh are a few examples taken from an English translation of the Septuagint:

> See that I am [*egō eimi*], / and there is no god but me. (Deut 32:39 NETS)

> Be my witnesses; / I too am a witness, says the Lord God, / and the servant I have chosen / so that you may know and believe / and understand that I am [*egō eimi*]. / Before me there was no god, / nor shall there be after me. . . . I am [*egō eimi*], I am [*egō eimi*] / the one who blots out your acts of / lawlessness. . . (Isa 43:10, 25 NETS)

> Until your old age, I am [*egō eimi*], / and until you grow old, I am [*egō eimi*], / I bear with you; / I have made, and I will set free; / I will take up and save you. (Isa 46:4 NETS).

Another fascinating fact that few Bible English readers know is that when Jesus declared himself "I am" in John 8:58, the Jews in Jerusalem had just finished celebrating the Feast of Tabernacles. A regular part of the sacred liturgy of that celebration featured the repetition of these "I am he" (*'ani hu* or *egō eimi*) texts from Isaiah. And so when Jesus said "I am [he]" to the crowd, these words had been ringing in their ears over the past few days.[19] Jesus' declaration to be Yahweh was fairly hard to miss.

The "I Am" Learning Curve

In several instances in which John portrays Jesus using the "I am [he]"[20] expression, sometimes it can be taken as a simple identification. For instance, if you ask me, "Are you Randy Rheaume?" I will answer, "I am." Obviously,

---

"'I Am' or 'I Am He'?"; Young, "Study on the Relationship." For a dissenting viewpoint, see Loader, *Jesus in John's Gospel*, 347–54.

19. Stauffer, *Jesus and His Story*, 179, 189.

20. Strictly speaking, the pronoun "he" is not part of the expression *egō eimi* (in the LXX or John), even though many English translations insert it.

I'm not claiming to be Yahweh! But if you were well acquainted with the Greek OT (as John's readers were) and I said to you, "Before Abraham was born, *egō eimi*," you might call for the people in the white coats to take me away! Context is the key. In John, Jesus begins using this expression as a *simple* self-identification but then gradually inches forward toward a clear identification with Yahweh. With each successive usage, what Jesus is getting at becomes clearer.

To the Woman at the Well

Jesus' first usage of "I am" is very subtle and can be taken two ways. When the Samaritan woman at the well speaks of the Messiah, Jesus responds, "I Am [*egō eimi*]—the one who speaks with you" (Jn 4:26 CEB). In Greek, Jesus is stressing his identity, perhaps using more words than we might expect. Jesus could have simply said, "I am he," or "I am the Messiah." Why the extra words about the one speaking with her? This is a first alert that perhaps more is going on here than meets the eye.

When we probe the "I am" statements in Isaiah, however, we discover a startling resemblance. In the LXX of Isaiah, Yahweh says: "Therefore my people shall know my name in that day, because I myself am [*egō eimi*] the one who speaks" (Isa 52:6 NETS). In Isaiah, Yahweh is talking about making his identity known, and in John, Jesus is talking about making his identity known. Also, the Greek words translated "the one who speaks" are identical in both texts. Skillfully, Jesus seems to allude to the Isaiah text, hence the extra words. On one level he's identifying himself as the Messiah to the woman, and on another level as "the one who speaks" in Isaiah. Then again, the allusion is quite subtle. Unless the woman had a copy of the LXX opened to Isaiah 52, she would likely miss it. But this is only the first step in John's big reveal of Yahweh's name within the narrative.

To the Disciples in the Boat

The next incident is clearer but still a bit obscure. It occurs when Jesus is walking on the water to meet his terrified disciples in the boat: "When they had rowed about three or four miles, they saw Jesus approaching the boat, walking on the water; and they were frightened. But he said to them, 'It is I [*egō eimi*]; don't be afraid'" (Jn 6:19-20). Most English translations paraphrase Jesus' words here. Literally he says, "I am; don't be afraid" (AT). Could Jesus simply be identifying himself to his panicked disciples, as in, "It's me, guys! Don't freak out!"? Absolutely. Undoubtedly this is the way the disciples first understood his words. But in John, Jesus has a way of wording things so they can have two meanings, what we often call a double entendre.[21] Upon further reflection, his deeper meaning becomes clear.

Many NT scholars believe that this "I am" saying (also in Matthew and Mark where the walking on water incident is recorded) alludes to various OT passages that speak of Yahweh himself.[22] For instance, speaking of God, Job says, "He alone stretches out the heavens and treads on the waves of the sea" (Job 9:8). In another OT text, Yahweh says, "When you pass through the waters, I will be with you" (Isa 43:2). Perhaps most telling is to compare Yahweh's words in Isaiah to what Jesus says on the water to his disciples: "Do not be afraid, for I am with you" (Isa 43:5); "I am; don't be afraid" (Jn 6:20 AT). The two sound very similar. Is Jesus claiming to be Yahweh or are we reading too much into his words here? If we only had this incident, we couldn't be certain. But as the pattern continues to develop, Jesus' real meaning only gets clearer.

To the Crowd in Jerusalem

Up until now Jesus' usage of "I am" has been ambiguous and needed to be pondered to see its connection to Yahweh's self-identification in the OT. But these statements have not been made in a vacuum. Jesus has been accused of making himself equal with God by calling God "his own Father" and by claiming he works alongside of the Father on the Sabbath (Jn 5:18). This outraged his enemies enough to seek his death. But in John 8, the situation rapidly heats to a boil because Jesus audaciously applies the divine name to himself. Three times Jesus uses the "I am" expression in such a way that the crowd grows more and more suspicious and angry until finally they try to stone him.[23]

In the first instance, Jesus says, "That is why I said that you will die in your sins; for unless you believe that I AM [*egō eimi*] who I claim to be, you will die in your sins" (Jn 8:24 NLT). This is a stunning statement to be sure, even apart from the reference to the divine name. "You will die condemned for your sins" says Jesus, "unless you embrace my true identity. It's a matter of eternal life or death!" Staggering! Yet like the earlier usages,

21. A classic example is John 3:3, where the Greek word often translated "again" (*anōthen*) can also mean "from above." Since both meanings fit the context so well, this is likely a deliberate play on words. Cf. Carson, *Gospel According to John*, 189.

22. See Rheaume, *Exegetical and Theological Analysis*, 66–68, 306–8.

23. See Motyer, *"Your Father the Devil?,"* 158–59. Jesus also uses the "I am" expression to declare his divine identity in John 13:19 and quite dramatically in 18:5–6 and 8. But space limitations compel me to mention them here only in passing.

Jesus' "I am" here could be a simple self-identifier. But the crowd rightly suspects Jesus may mean more than this. Notice their question in the very next verse: "'Who are you?' they asked. 'Just what I have been telling you from the beginning' Jesus replied" (Jn 8:25). Obviously they know who he is on one level: Jesus of Nazareth. They want to know who he is *claiming* to be. Jesus' answer likely refers back to his FST (which we discussed in chapter 5) found in John 5, where he claimed to be both equal to his Father and yet subordinate to him as his Son. What's more, by the words "from the beginning" John may also want us, his readers, to flash back mentally to John 1:1 where "In the beginning. . . the Word was God." In any case, Jesus' first use of "I am" here raises more than a few eyebrows.

Before we look at Jesus' second "I am" in John 8, I'd like to skip down to the third usage in a text we've already discussed a bit: John 8:58. (We'll come back to the second usage in a moment.) Before Jesus makes his bold declaration in 8:58, the crowd is getting increasingly alarmed at what they suspect he may be saying, and they demand clarification. Yet the crowd's anger continues to escalate as Jesus accuses them of spiritual illegitimacy and compares himself favorably to their great forefather Abraham. Finally, the enraged crowd presses him in 8:53 to state his identity unequivocally: "Who are you making yourself out to be" (AT)? The answer they demand finally comes in verse 58 and confirms their worst suspicions, prompting them to attempt to stone him for blasphemy (8:59). As one scholar puts it, here "the overtone of the divine name is unmistakable, and so . . . requires all previous occurrences of the expression to be re-read"[24] in its light. Thus John's readers are brought along the same learning path as the Jews in the text, leading to the climactic declaration in 8:58. But obviously the story in John 8 does not have a happy outcome. Jesus' claim is roundly rejected as blasphemy and he is nearly stoned to death. Yet something big is coming that will clear away the doubt.

Jesus' Big Reveal

This leads us back to Jesus' second usage of "I am" in John 8. It's one of the most important of all. Jesus says, "When you lift up the Son of Man, then you will realize that I AM [*egō eimi*], and that I do nothing on my own, but I say only what the Father taught me" (Jn 8:28 NAB). Even though Jesus seems to be claiming Yahweh's name, he insists he's a fully subordinate Son—as we've seen all along. Again, though Jesus is Yahweh, he is not the Father. Just as

24. Ibid., 159.

in John 1:1 Jesus shares God's nature and identity but is distinct from the Father. Jesus is Yahweh but he's not all there is to Yahweh.[25]

But what's new in this text is that Jesus unveils the timing of his big reveal: "[w]hen you lift up the Son of Man." What does that mean? On the surface, being lifted up refers to Jesus' crucifixion—when he will be nailed and hoisted up on the cross. John later tells us this is what Jesus means, and in that case even the crowd gets it (Jn 12:32–34). But John's Jesus has more in mind than simply his crucifixion. The lifting up of Jesus is the salvation event that will "draw all people" to him (12:32), bring eternal life to those who believe (3:14–15), and will also reveal his true identity (8:28). Most likely Jesus is using another double entendre. On one level "lift up" surely refers to his crucifixion where he will give his life for the sins of the world. But on another level it will fulfill Isaiah's ancient prophecy of the Suffering Servant who will both die a horrible death and then be exalted to the place which only God can occupy. Take a close look at this incredible prediction:

> See, my servant will act
>   wisely;
>   he will be *raised* and *lifted
>   up* and *highly exalted.*
> Just as there were many who
>   were appalled at him—
>   his appearance was so
>   disfigured beyond that
>   of any human being
>   and his form marred beyond
>   human likeness—
> so he will sprinkle many
>   nations,
>   and kings will shut their
>   mouths because of him.
> For what they were not told,
>   they will see,
>   and what they have not heard,
>   they will understand. (Isa 52:13–15; italics added)

25. Some scholars believe Jesus' use of the absolute "I am" sayings is a claim to be Yahweh's agent endowed with the name and powers of God, rather than a claim to be Yahweh himself. In their view, a claim to be Yahweh would be tantamount to declaring himself to be God the Father, which of course Jesus did not do. But, as I have argued elsewhere, the view I defend here fits the evidence much better. See Rheaume, *Exegetical and Theological Analysis*, 310–17.

This stunning text deserves far more attention than I can afford to give it here.[26] Isaiah wrote this prophecy many hundreds of years before Jesus' birth, and yet he and the NT writers clearly believed it spoke of him. When Jesus speaks of being "lifted up," he's alluding to this "servant" who is "lifted up." The wording Isaiah uses here he applies only to Yahweh elsewhere.[27] And yet this servant has been horribly disfigured, and later we are told he is killed (Isa 53:8–9). On the other hand, the servant is so highly exalted that many nations (even kings!) are startled and awestruck by him. Later in the prophecy, Isaiah tells us the servant's violent death will constitute an offering for our sins (53:4–10) and that he will be restored to life (53:10–11). John's Jesus applies this prophecy to himself. He is the servant who will be both lifted up to die and lifted up to be glorified. And in John 8:28, Jesus says when this has happened, people will finally understand his true identity.[28] That's when the big reveal comes!

JESUS AS LORD

After Jesus rises from the dead, his true identity is not only understandable but also believable to his disciples, and eventually to all who believe in him in the way the NT prescribes. When Jesus is fully lifted up, God reveals him as Yahweh and calls on us to believe in him as such.

Polling Jesus' Disciples

What did Jesus' disciples make of his "I am" sayings during his ministry? We are not told, and so we can only speculate. But when we look back over Jesus' ministry, we find several clues as to what they thought of Jesus.

Early in Jesus' ministry, Nathaniel called him the Son of God, the king of Israel (Jn 1:49). Sounds right on! But then again, he had only just met Jesus and he might have been speaking more out of exuberance than careful thought. Some time later, Peter (Jesus' lead disciple) spoke for the Twelve when he said, "We have come to believe and to know that you are the Holy One of God" (Jn 6:69). But what did Peter mean by this? The disciples came to see him as the Messiah during his ministry, but their understanding of what Jesus' messiahship would entail was muddled with many

26. For an excellent treatment of how Isa 52:13—53:12 is fulfilled in Jesus—in answer to Jewish objections—see Brown, *Answering Jewish Objections to Jesus,* 3:40–86.

27. Compare Isaiah 6:1 and 57:15 with 52:13.

28. Note also that Jesus predicted his resurrection would be the definitive sign of the truthfulness of his claims (Jn 2:18–22; Matt 12:38–40).

misunderstandings at the time.[29] One of the most startling declarations of faith comes from a disciple named Martha just before Jesus raises her brother Lazarus from the dead: "I believe," she says to him, "that you are the Messiah, the Son of God, who is to come into the world" (Jn 11:27). Outstanding! But did she mean "Son of God" as only the Davidic king, a strictly human Messiah, or did she mean it in the unique God-the-Son sense John has been telling us about since he declared it in the prologue of his Gospel (1:14, 18)? Martha probably didn't understand it in the full sense at this point. How could she? The night before Jesus died his disciples said they believed he came from God (Jn 16:30). But what exactly did they understand by this? We're not told. And the same goes for his "I am" sayings. Perhaps they were puzzled by them, wondering if his enemies, due to their hatred of him, had interpreted his claims in the most negative light possible. "Maybe he meant something other than claiming to be Yahweh," they may have thought. We can only speculate.

Clear as the "I am" sayings are, there's just enough ambiguity about them to make certainty elusive. I believe Jesus intended it this way as part of his strategy. What we do know is that Jesus' resurrection was about to make things clear.

Putting Two and Two Together

John structures his book as only a superb literary artist can do. He begins by boldly declaring, "the Word was God" (1:1). But then, equally surprising, the Word takes on genuine humanity and lives on earth as a man (1:14). Throughout the book we readers know who Jesus is, but John shows us how Jesus gradually revealed his identity to his disciples as his ministry unfolded. In Jerusalem his claim that God was "his own Father" with whom he closely worked, even on the Sabbath, shockingly implied that he was the "Son of God" like no other in a way that made him equal with God (5:16–18). Jesus also used the somewhat obscure yet highly audacious "I am" sayings on a learning curve that increasingly infuriated his enemies and likely left his disciples scratching their heads.

But when Jesus was arrested and then put to death on the cross—a horribly shameful and excruciatingly torturous way to die—the disciples' faith in Jesus must have been shaken to the core. Under pressure, Peter denies three times that he even knows Jesus (Jn 18). Three days later, the first report of Jesus' empty tomb leaves them bewildered (Jn 20:9). That evening they are cowering behind locked doors afraid of the Jewish leaders

29. Matt 16:15–23; Mk 8:27–33; Lk 9:18–22.

(Jn 20:19). Then Jesus appears to them and convinces them he's been raised from the dead (20:9–23).

Here's where the artist in John shines brightest while still reporting the facts as they actually happened. Throughout John's Gospel we the readers have known from the first chapter that Jesus is God (1:1) and that he became flesh (1:14) to give his life for the world (1:29). John's purpose in writing the book is to convince his readers of this so they will believe it and have eternal life (20:30–31). And so John provides a narrative that gradually reveals this to us, his readers. The opposite of belief is doubt, and so—in case there are any doubts—at the end of the book, John focusses on a stubborn doubter named Thomas. Yes, this is the infamous doubting Thomas! For him the light bulb finally comes on when he sees the risen Jesus. The doubter becomes a believer! It's the climax of John's Gospel:

> Now Thomas (also known as Didymus), one of the Twelve, was not with the disciples when Jesus came. So the other disciples told him, "We have seen the Lord!" But he said to them, "Unless I see the nail marks in his hands and put my finger where the nails were, and put my hand into his side, I will not believe." A week later his disciples were in the house again, and Thomas was with them. Though the doors were locked, Jesus came and stood among them and said, "Peace be with you!" Then he said to Thomas, "Put your finger here; see my hands. Reach out your hand and put it into my side. Stop doubting and believe." Thomas said to him, "My Lord and my God!" Then Jesus told him, "Because you have seen me, you have believed; blessed are those who have not seen and yet have believed." (Jn 20:24–29)

After everything Thomas has seen and heard during his time with Jesus, the living proof is now literally standing right in front of him. Thomas puts two and two together and declares Jesus to be Yahweh God. Thomas' confession of faith in 20:28 is perhaps the clearest affirmation of Jesus' deity found anywhere in the NT. John concludes where he began. John 1:1 and 20:28 are the front and back covers of his book. And just as Jesus predicted in 8:28, now that he has been lifted up, his "I am" identity is crystal clear. The Father gave his name to Jesus (17:11–12), and Jesus revealed it to his disciples (17:6, 26). But only after Jesus is "lifted up" can they really accept it (8:28).

To call Jesus Lord in the full sense is to call him Yahweh God. The Greek word used to translate the Hebrew name Yahweh is *kyrios*. This word has a wide range of meaning. It can mean "sir" or "master" or—as I've noted—it can be used for the divine name "Yahweh." In the latter case,

English translations render *kyrios* "Lord" (with a capital L). When a NT writer quotes from the OT, the Greek word *kyrios* is used for the Hebrew Yahweh. Because of this, when we read the NT, we English readers need to determine from the context if the writer means "lord" in one of the lower senses, or "Lord" as in "Yahweh." As we will see in the next chapter, Thomas's confession, "My Lord and my God," is appropriate only for Yahweh. And it was the reality of Jesus' bodily resurrection from the dead that spawned this faith in the former doubter's heart.

JESUS COMES OUT!

When the Son rises on that first Resurrection Sunday, the sun also rises on his true identity. In the wake of Jesus' exaltation, the Father declares his Son to be both Yahweh and Messiah.[30] Though Jesus was always the Son of God, his unique sonship is declared powerfully by his resurrection.[31] John and several other writers of the NT use "Lord" (*kyrios*) in the highest sense for Jesus.[32]

When this is understood, we see that Jesus' deity is declared far more often than just the handful of times he's called "God."[33] In the OT, "God" was the title/name that emphasizes his transcendence, but Yahweh, on the other hand, stresses his interaction with his people.[34] And so in the NT it's appropriate that the unseen Father would typically be called "God," and the Son—who came among us as a man—would typically be called "Lord" (in the exalted sense). Both "God" and "Lord" are applied to the Father and the Son, but their distinctive roles play a part in what they're called most often. "God" is the title of deity used most often for the Father, and "Lord" (i.e., Yahweh) is the title of deity used most often for the Son. If Jesus had declared, "I am God," he would too easily be misunderstood to mean, "I am God the Father." The NT writers keep the persons distinguished by typically calling the Father "God" and the Son "Lord" (= Yahweh).

But in the Gospels Jesus' divine identity is revealed gradually. Several NT writers—like John—imply that Jesus' divine identity is fully known as

30. Acts 2:36; Phil 2:9–11.

31. Matt 28:19; Acts 13:32–33; Rom 1:3–4.

32. E.g., Matt 3:3; Mk 1:3; Lk 3:4; Jn 1:23; Rom 10:9, 12–13; 1 Cor 2:8; 8:6; Eph 1:2; Phil 2:9–11; Heb 1:10; Jas 2:1; Rev 19:16. See Bauckham, *Jesus and the God of Israel*, 219–21 and esp. Capes, *Divine Christ*.

33. In addition to John 1:1, 18; 20:28, Jesus is very likely called "God" in Rom 9:5; Titus 2:13; Heb 1:8; 2 Pet 1:1; and possibly in Acts 20:28; 1 Jn 5:20. See Harris, *Jesus as God*.

34. See Rheaume, *Exegetical and Theological Analysis*, 331–35.

the result of his resurrection and ascension. The Son has always been God, but when he came to earth, his identity was gradually disclosed until his resurrection let the cat out of the bag!

QUESTIONS FOR DISCUSSION

1. Has anyone ever challenged you, "If Jesus was really God, why didn't he ever say, 'I am God. Worship me!'?" If not, have you ever wondered this yourself? Now that you have read this chapter, how would you answer?

2. What do you think a person needs to understand and believe in order to be saved? How do you think John 8:24 figures in to John's view on this issue?

3. Why do you think Jesus revealed his identity slowly rather than immediately? What other great truths in Scripture are revealed gradually?

A VERSE TO MEMORIZE

When you lift up the Son of Man, then you will realize that I AM, and that I do nothing on my own, but I say only what the Father taught me. (Jn 8:28 NAB)

APPLY WHAT YOU'VE LEARNED

In your discussion group, do a role-play between a Christian in a respectful dialogue with a Muslim or JW who asks, "When did Jesus ever claim to be God?" How might each side answer the other? How can a Christ-follower share the truth plainly and yet respectfully and persuasively?

CHAPTER 9

Earthquake of the Soul

Have you ever experienced an event so impactful that it completely changed your outlook on life—an experience that prompted a 180-degree turn in your thinking, behavior, and lifestyle? Think of people who've experienced firsthand a catastrophe like 9/11, the horrors of a Nazi death camp, a harrowing war experience, or a maniacal school shooting. That could do it. To affect a person deeply and permanently, it often takes something traumatic. But sometimes the impact comes from a positive experience, such as a life rescue or a highly influential person who turns your world around. I've seen it happen. I call it an earthquake of the soul,[1] a shaking so deep and powerful that everything beneath and above the surface is in some way altered as a result.

The most powerful earthquake of the soul ever took place within Jesus' followers in the wake of his resurrection from the dead. In this chapter we'll witness the aftershocks of that quake in them and, God willing, in us.

PERSONAL EARTHQUAKES

I experienced an inner earthquake when I became a Christ-follower. The very night I gave my life to Jesus I told my brother Ron, "I will never again see the world the same way. Everything has changed." No experience before or since has shaped me more. It was a personal earthquake, and the aftershocks have

---

1. For my metaphor "earthquake of the soul," I'm indebted to psychiatrist Dr. John White's book *Changing on the Inside*. White helpfully describes genuine repentance as an "inner earthquake," and I have adapted and used the figure in my pastoral ministry for many years.

continued for decades. My life and eternity did a one-eighty. And since that night many years ago, I've also witnessed countless others experience that awesome earthquake of the soul. Unlike typical earthquakes, this shaking is always positive. People consumed with hatred begin to love. Entrenched values, addictions, and immoral behavior patterns undergo deep structural change.

Yes, we Christ-followers still have problems, as all humans do. We're far from perfect. It's an ongoing transformation within us that occurs both in baby steps and in spurts as the aftershocks continue throughout our lives.

But from the moment a person embraces Jesus, a major quake rocks the soul, bringing inevitable change. When you truly repent and trust in Jesus as Lord and Savior, a new life begins. As Jesus put it, you cross over from death to life (Jn 5:24). Your worldview, values, habits, interests, goals, and lifestyle are upended. It dramatically alters not just your life, but your eternity as well! It's the full life we learned about in chapter 7.

EASTER EARTHQUAKE

For the early followers of Jesus, his resurrection produced within them an earthquake of the soul, and the aftershocks of that quake have multiplied exponentially throughout the centuries all over the world. The epicenter of that earthquake is the risen Jesus. For those first followers (and for all who've followed him since), he became the center of their universe.

Think of it! All of Jesus' first followers were Jews who believed in only one God. They grew up reciting the words of the Shema twice every day: "Hear, O Israel: The LORD our God, the LORD is one" (Deut 6:4). The first of the Ten Commandments—about having no other gods before Yahweh[2]—was as familiar to them as your street address is to you. For them this was not merely truth; it was sacred truth that shaped and defined their identity as Jews. And yet in the earliest writings of the Christian movement, we find Jesus hailed as Yahweh along with God the Father.

Suppose you are a Jew living in Jerusalem during the early days of the Christian movement. You've heard from eyewitnesses about Messiah Jesus and his resurrection, and now you want to become a follower. So you ask one of the apostles, "What must I do to be saved?" It is then explained to you that you must call upon Jesus as Yahweh to save you. To seal your new allegiance to Jesus, you will call on him just before you are dunked under water in a ritual called baptism.[3]

2. Exod 20:2–3; Deut 5:6–7.

3. Matt 28:19; Acts 2:21, 38, 41; 16:30–33; 22:16; Rom 6:3–4; Gal 3:26–27; Col

This is precisely what the early writings of the Christian movement prescribe and describe. In his letter to the assembly of Christ-followers in Rome, the apostle Paul says, "If you declare with your mouth, 'Jesus is Lord,' and believe in your heart that God raised him from the dead, you will be saved" (Rom 10:9). When Paul says "Jesus is Lord" in this text, "Lord" (*kyrios*) clearly means "Yahweh," as his usage a few verses later confirms (10:12–13). For the early Christians the risen Yahweh Jesus was at the epicenter of salvation. Somehow the strict monotheism of Jesus' original followers had undergone a dramatic expansion from the inside which now included him within the identity of the one true God. How did this happen? What could cause such a seismic shift in these early Jewish followers and the many who embraced their teachings?

This question has become the intense object of scholarly study for over two centuries. Many theories have been suggested.[4] For a long time, the prevailing view among scholars was that the idea of a divine Jesus evolved in the first and second centuries as Christianity spread among non-Jews who thought in terms of many gods and the human offspring of gods. Though he was a Jew, the apostle Paul brought many gentile notions into Christianity to help broaden its ranks. These non-Jewish ideas, so the theory goes, infiltrated the faith and brought about the deification of Jesus, who had never dreamed of claiming he was God nor had his earliest followers claimed this for him. But this construction of early Christianity has been increasingly discredited. In recent decades, as the Jewishness of Jesus (and Paul) has been better understood and appreciated, it has become progressively clearer that the exalted view of Jesus (or "high Christology" as scholars call it) was the earliest view of Jesus.[5]

Jesus' resurrection was a pivotal moment—the earthquake felt round the world! As the apostle Paul says, "[H]e was shown to be the Son of God when he was raised from the dead by the power of the Holy Spirit. He is Jesus Christ our Lord" (Rom 1:3 NLT). Paul speaks here of Jesus' sonship not only as a human Messiah, but as the Father's unique Son. According to the early witness of Jesus' followers, after his resurrection Jesus ascended into heaven where he was seated at the right hand of the Father. The same man the Jewish leaders had trashed has now been thoroughly vindicated by God!

2:11–12; etc.

4. See Wright, *Jesus and the Victory of God*, 3–124. Also very helpful is Spence, *Christology*.

5. See e.g., Bauckham, *Jesus and the God of Israel*; Capes, *Divine Christ*.

Earthquake for Eternity

The reverberations of that first Easter earthquake will be heard for all eternity. After exalting Jesus, God the Father now calls on the entire universe to declare his Son to be Yahweh:

> Therefore God exalted him to
>   the highest place
>   and gave him the name
>   that is above every
>   name,
>   that at the name of Jesus every
>   knee should bow,
>   in heaven and on earth and
>   under the earth,
>   and every tongue
>   acknowledge that Jesus
>   Christ is Lord,
>   to the glory of God the
>   Father. (Phil 2:9–11)

This passage is hugely significant. Many Bible readers mistakenly think the "name above every name" is the name "Jesus." But remember, Paul (who wrote this passage) was raised as a strict Jew—and a Pharisee at that! To such a person there could be only one "name above every name"—the sacred name of God, Yahweh—which for those writing in Greek (like Paul) was rendered "Lord" (*kyrios*). The name that now *belongs to* Jesus, before which every knee should bow (in the whole universe) and tongue confess, is Lord (*kyrios* = Yahweh).[6] When he says, "Jesus Christ is Lord," he means Yahweh. Paul is paraphrasing a text from Isaiah about Yahweh which the apostle applies directly to the exalted Jesus: "By myself I have sworn, my mouth has uttered in all integrity a word that will not be revoked: Before me every knee will bow; by me every tongue will swear. They will say of me, 'In the LORD alone are deliverance and strength'" (Isa 45:23–24). In Isaiah, every knee bows and tongue swears to Yahweh, but in Philippians 2, Paul says this is fulfilled in Jesus. He will be declared Yahweh by all!

What's more, many scholars believe Philippians 2:6–11 was originally a hymn used by the early Christ-followers in their worship meetings.[7] (They determine this by the style and rhythm of the passage.) This hymn

6. See Bauckham, *Jesus and the God of Israel*, 199–200, 209.

7. See Gordley, *New Testament Christological Hymns*, 79–110; Porter, "Creeds and Hymns," esp. 235.

begins with Christ in his prehuman state "in the form of God" (Phil 2:6 ESV), but then he humbles himself by becoming a man and finally dies the shameful death of the cross. In response to this unparalleled sacrifice, God exalts Christ so that the whole universe will confess Jesus as Yahweh. Paul is quoting this hymn to make his larger point that like Jesus, we Christians should humble ourselves to serve others and leave the exalting to God. If this text was indeed a hymn (as biblical scholars commonly think), it shows all the more how early and widespread was the view that Jesus is Yahweh. It was so widely accepted that the early Christians were singing about it their congregations! Paul has no need to argue the point. Apparently no Christ-follower he knows of would disagree. Paul can safely use the hymn to make his practical point about Christ's supreme example of humility. And yet, as we've seen all along in our study of John, Jesus is God, but he's also in full submission to his Father. Jesus is hailed in the hymn as Yahweh "to the glory of God the Father" (Phil 2:11).

As we saw in chapter 8, this brings us back to what Jesus predicted in John 8:28. As a result of his being "lifted up" (in his cruel death and glorious exaltation), all people will acknowledge Jesus is the "I Am." When Thomas confessed to Jesus, "My Lord and my God" (Jn 20:28), he was only the first of many. The aftershocks of that first Easter earthquake are still felt today. Have you experienced that awesome earthquake of the soul? If not, why not turn to him now in repentance and faith as your Lord and Savior?

Only One God?

You may be thinking, "Wait a minute, Randy. You've been saying Jesus is Yahweh along with God the Father. Now you're telling me the early Christians even sang hymns declaring this! What's more, the entire universe—all creation—will one day acknowledge Jesus is Yahweh to the Father's glory. It sounds to me more like two Gods than one. How can you claim with a straight face the early followers of Jesus were truly monotheists when they plainly worshiped more than one person as God?" Fair question! And as you might expect by now, I'm going to tell you the answer is ultimately found in the Gospel of John. But first we need to take a short detour.

The Incredible Expanding Shema

Imagine discovering an important fact about yourself that you never knew before, such as, you were adopted but were never told until now. Or in your infancy you were separated from a twin sibling who's still living. Or though you and your family have always celebrated your heritage from nationality X, a DNA test now reveals you're descended from nationality Y. Stop to imagine it for a moment. You're still the same person you were just before you discovered this momentous news, but now you will rethink your whole life in light of what you never knew before. It will take some getting used to, won't it?

It's hard to imagine something more deeply ingrained in the mind of a faithful, first-century Jew like the apostle Paul than the Shema (which we discussed in chapter 2). Like his family and friends, Paul grew up reciting the Shema at least twice a day since he first learned to talk. It begins, "Hear, O Israel: The LORD our God, the LORD is one" (Deut 6:4). If you were raised reciting the Pledge of Allegiance or the "Our Father," you can somewhat relate. To the ancient Jews (and religious Jews today), what could be more sacred than the Shema? This was God's holiest holy word, the central creed of Jewish heritage and faith. Think of how the most patriotic American you know honors the flag, and you have a dim comparison.

But now try imagining something else. What would it take for a faithful Jew like Paul—trained as a Pharisee under one of the greatest rabbis of his day[8]—to modify the Shema? Yes, to tweak it a bit so that it speaks of two persons as Yahweh God instead of just one! Unthinkable! Any Jew would consider it an unimaginable desecration of the vilest kind! To make such an alteration could only come about as the result of defiant apostasy *or* a dramatic earthquake of the soul prompted by none other than Yahweh himself. In Paul's case, it was the latter.

One of the most breathtaking passages in all of Paul's writings is his modified version of the Shema, which he recaps as he teaches the Corinthian church about food offered to idols:

> So then, about eating food sacrificed to idols: We know that "An idol is nothing at all in the world" and that "There is no God but one." For even if there are so-called gods, whether in heaven or on earth (as indeed there are many "gods" and many "lords"), yet for us there is but one God, the Father, from whom all things came and for whom we live; and there is but one Lord, Jesus Christ, through whom all things came and through whom we live. (1 Cor 8:4–6)

This text gives us a unique glimpse into the early Christian view of monotheism, God the Father, and Jesus Christ. To get a firm grip on it, we

---

8. Acts 22:3; Gal 1:14; Phil 3:4–6.

would need to devote far more space than we can afford to give it here.[9] I can only highlight a few crucial points.

First, this passage is found in a letter from Paul we call 1 Corinthians, written to a church in Greece around AD 55. It is among the early NT writings, composed likely before any of our four Gospels. Second, Paul is addressing a question the Corinthian Christians had about eating food that had been offered to pagan idols. Is it okay for a Christian to eat such food or not? Some thought the practice was scandalous, but others were saying, "Since idols are not real gods, where's the harm?" Paul's answer involves reminding his readers about the distinction between the one true God and what Paul calls "so-called gods," i.e., "gods" in name only. (Recall what we learned about this in chapter 2.)

To do this, Paul rehearses what NT scholars say is a modified version of the Shema. First, Paul alludes to the Shema when he says, "There is no God but one" (8:5). Both Jews and non-Jewish Christians would immediately say "Amen!" Paul is definitely a monotheist. But in verse 6 he gives us a distinctly Christian view of monotheism. Note how Paul uses both titles of deity found in the Shema—"God" (Greek *theos*; Hebrew *elohim*) and "Lord" (Greek *kyrios*; Hebrew Yahweh)—but astoundingly he assigns them to two distinct persons: the Father and Jesus. Paul here divides the key words of the Shema between God the Father and the Lord Jesus. The Father is the "one God," and Jesus is the "one Yahweh!" And yet, we know from verse 5 that Paul is still a die-hard monotheist. Somehow the identity of the one God is encapsulated in both the Father and Jesus. Notice too that both divine persons had a role in creating the universe—just as we've seen in John. The Creator is both the Father and the Son.

This is utterly amazing—one of the strongest affirmations of Jesus' deity found anywhere in the Bible! What's so extra incredible about this text is that obviously Paul is not teaching the Corinthians anything new about the Shema. In fact, the topic under discussion isn't primarily the Shema but food offered to idols. He brings up the Shema—knowing they all agree on this—to apply its truth to the food issue they've asked him about. In other words, Paul is referring to established Christian teaching, not some new, innovative way of speaking about Jesus. Paul cites it as a bedrock principle of his argument.

---

9. For more on the reformulated Shema in 1 Cor 8:6, see Bauckham, *Jesus and the God of Israel*, 97–104, 210–18; Fletcher-Louis, *Jesus Monotheism*, 9–10, 17, 32–55; Wright, *Paul and the Faithfulness of God*, 2:661–70. For a dissenting viewpoint, see McGrath, *Only True God*, 38–54. Though McGrath acknowledges Paul is paraphrasing the Shema, he does not think he includes Jesus within God's nature.

Astounding! By AD 55 (only about twenty years since Jesus' resurrection), the Lord Jesus shares the identity of the one true God within the Shema, and this was considered noncontroversial, established Christian teaching. According to Paul, there is only one true God—but the one true God exists as "God" (the Father) and "Lord"/"Yahweh" (the Son). Clearly Paul—a faithful Jew raised on the Shema and the Ten Commandments—has experienced an earthquake of the soul!

Calling on Jesus' Name

Once we recognize this phenomenon, similar Jesus-as-Yahweh references begin to jump out to us from the pages of the NT. For instance, notice Paul's greeting to the Corinthians back at the beginning of his letter: "To the church of God in Corinth, to those sanctified in Christ Jesus and called to be his holy people, together with all those everywhere who *call on the name of our Lord Jesus Christ*—their Lord and ours" (1 Cor 1:2; italics added). The words "call on the name of our Lord Jesus" are striking. The expression "call on the name" is used in the OT of pagans worshiping and praying to a false god.[10] For God's people, however, it is used only for calling on the name of Yahweh.[11] But in this passage, Paul uses that exact expression with the Lord Jesus in the place of Yahweh.[12] What's more, the scope of Paul's letter extends beyond the Corinthian congregation to all people ("all those everywhere") who call on Jesus. Once again, the assumption is that the universal practice of all Christians of whom Paul is aware is to call on Jesus (i.e., worship him and pray to him) as Yahweh. In fact, Paul's wording indicates this particular activity distinguishes a Christian from everyone else. A Christian, Paul assumes, is a person who calls on the name of (i.e., prays to and worships) the Lord Jesus as Yahweh.[13]

Jesus' resurrection was the earthquake which shook his early followers to embrace this seismic shift in their view of God. But, of course, just because a man is resurrected doesn't mean he's Yahweh in human form. Where would Jesus' early followers get such an idea? It seems his claim to share

10. 1 Kgs 18:24-25

11. Gen 4:26; 1 Kgs 18:24-25; 2 Kgs 5:11; Ps 116:13, 17; Joel 2:32; Zeph 3:9.

12. Cf. Capes, *Divine Christ*, 71-73, 116.

13. NT evidence would suggest praying to Jesus was typical among NT believers (Jn 14:14; Acts 7:59-60; 9:14; 22:16; 1 Cor 16:22; 2 Cor 12:8-9; Rev 22:20). Evidence that the Son was worshiped by the early Christians is found in the Philippians hymn (2:5-11), Revelation (5:8-10), and in some Gospel texts (e.g., Matt 28:9-10, 17; Lk 24:52). Also, the angels are commanded by God to worship the Son (Heb 1:6). For a book-length treatment, see Hurtado, *How on Earth Did Jesus Become a God?*

the identity of Yahweh with the Father must have come during his earthly ministry *before* his resurrection, just as we've seen it did. His resurrection did not *create* this claim; it *clarified* and *confirmed* the claim. But if so, did Jesus' early followers get the radical notion to include him within the Shema from Jesus, as well? To answer that question we need to end our brief detour and return to our study of John.

Jesus and the Father are One

Shortly after I became a Christ-follower, two JWs visited my home. It didn't take long for our friendly discussion to move to the topic of Jesus' identity. Since I was a newbie Christian, my knowledge of Scripture was very limited. I hadn't even finished reading through the Bible for the first time. But I knew one verse I was certain proved Jesus is God, and so I quoted it to my guests. "Didn't Jesus say, 'I and the Father are one' (Jn 10:30)?" "Yes," they answered confidently. "But this doesn't prove Jesus was God. Notice that later, when praying to the Father for his disciples, Jesus says, 'that they may be one as we are one.'[14] Obviously," said my JW friends, "Jesus didn't mean he and the Father were one person, any more than all his followers are one person. Jesus is talking about *oneness of purpose*. Just as he and the Father are united in purpose, so he prays for his disciples to be unified the same way."

I had to admit their explanation made sense to me. How could I deny the comparison to the disciples? With my one-verse arsenal for Jesus' deity obliterated, I was stumped. Though I later found many convincing proofs elsewhere that Jesus is God, I was convinced for many years afterward that John 10:30 was not one of them.

The Wonder of "One"

But I now believe that John 10:30 is more than just a proof text for Jesus' deity; it's also an allusion to the words of the Shema—"the LORD our God, the LORD is one" (Deut 6:4). Notice the crowd's instant reaction to Jesus' words:

> "I and the Father are one." Again his Jewish opponents picked up stones to stone him. . . . "We are . . . stoning you . . . for blasphemy, because you, a mere man, claim to be God." (Jn 10:30–31, 33)

14. Jn 17:11, 22; cf. also v. 21.

Obviously, Jesus' original hearers understood "I and the Father are one" as a blasphemous infringement on Yahweh's oneness worthy of death.

To them Jesus wasn't just talking about oneness of purpose but some sort of parity with the Father. Surely even his enemies would agree that unity with God is good and desirable. If this is all Jesus meant, why pick up the stones? On the other hand, you may be thinking, perhaps his enemies totally misconstrued Jesus' words. (When we studied this passage back in chapter 5, we saw they at least partially mischaracterized Jesus' claim here.) Perhaps my JW friends were correct in saying (along with many NT scholars on this point) that Jesus was only claiming unity of purpose with the Father, but the antagonistic crowd twisted his meaning. Could this be right?

Here's what convinced me it was far more than that. When I examined this text in depth during my PhD studies, I discovered that the Jews of Jesus' day sometimes compared God's perfect oneness to various things, such as the one temple in Jerusalem, one holy city, one Mosaic law, one altar, and especially one chosen people, the Jews.[15] Obviously these Jewish writers didn't believe Israel could ever be one as perfectly as God is one. No way! For them God's oneness was the ideal model that Israel should always strive to obtain. That struck a cord for me. Jesus compares his oneness with the Father to the oneness he prays to see happen among his followers (Jn 17:11, 22). Jesus is making the same sort of comparison. He and the Father's oneness is Yahweh's perfect oneness as found in the Shema. And, as his followers, we are to be imitators of God (cf. Eph 5:1).

Secondly, the oneness Jesus speaks of between him and the Father is a closeness and intimacy beyond human understanding. Notice how Jesus describes it in these texts:

> . . . that you may know and understand that the Father is in me, and I in the Father. (Jn 10:38)

> Don't you believe that I am in the Father, and that the Father is in me? The words I say to you I do not speak on my own authority. Rather, it is the Father, living in me, who is doing his work. Believe me when I say that I am in the Father and the Father is in me; or at least believe on the evidence of the works themselves. (Jn 14:10–11)

15. I am especially indebted to Richard Bauckham for this insight in *Jesus and the God of Israel*, 104–6, whose argument I follow here. See *2 Bar.* 48:23–24; Josephus *Ant.* 5.112; Philo *Spec. Laws* 1.52; 4.159; *Virt.* 7.35. See also Rheaume, *Exegetical and Theological Analysis*, 134–39.

Do you find it hard to get your head around Jesus' meaning here? Join the club! The tightness of bond Jesus describes here between him and the Father boggles the mind.

Here's an illustration which helps me: Picture a regular-size envelope that says "Father" on it. Put that envelope inside of a slightly larger envelope labeled "Son." That illustrates John 10:38; the Father is in the Son. But then take that two-in-one envelope and place it in a third slightly larger envelope labeled "Father." This illustrates John 14:10–11; the Father is in the Son and the Son is in the Father, all in *one* package. Why did Jesus speak like this? It was his way of communicating the profound oneness he and the Father share.

But Jesus then applies God's oneness to us. Using the same expression, Jesus says he desires this same tight-knit relationship with his followers: "When I am raised to life again, you will know that I am in my Father, and you are in me, and I am in you" (Jn 14:20 NLT). Astonishing! Jesus wants our relationship with him to be like his is with the Father! To return to our envelope illustration, *you* are an envelope within the Son envelope, which, in turn, is within the Father envelope. It's breathtaking! You are part of the relationship package, together with the Father and the Son. Remember this when you talk with him and read the Scriptures. Remember this when you feel lonely or forgotten. He wants to be super tight with you. Pursue and develop this relationship. You'll find it's as limitless as the sky.

What's more, he wants all his followers to aspire to close, loving relationships patterned after the relationship between the Father and the Son (17:21, 23). Jesus speaks of his followers as profoundly unified in "one flock" 10:16). Imagine what Christian marriages, families, and churches would be like if we were this tight with one another! It's the perfect ideal we should all aspire and strive to achieve, even though we'll never see it fully in this mortal life. Even in our glorified state, our finite unity could never equal God's infinite oneness. In John, the pattern is that human things are sometimes comparable to divine things but only on a smaller and inferior scale.[16]

But we must remember that when Jesus says "I and the Father are one," he certainly does not mean they are one person.[17] If he meant that, he would have used the masculine form of the Greek word "one" (*heis*), rather than the neuter form (*hen*). On the other hand, the word "one" in the Shema doesn't necessitate that Yahweh is absolutely one, i.e., a singular person.

16. Jn 3:6, 12; 4:13–14; 10:35–37; 13:34. Paul also points to God's oneness as the perfect model for unity among believers (Eph 4:3–6).

17. Recall from our discussion in chapter 1 that Trinitarians do not teach God is one person who shows himself three different ways—as in the Oneness view. The Trinity teaching is that God exists eternally in three distinct persons.

Both the Hebrew word "one" (*'echad*) in Deuteronomy 6:4 and the Greek word (*hen*) in John 10:30 can refer to a compound oneness involving a plurality of persons, such as the "*one* flesh" relationship of marriage consists of two persons.[18] This doesn't mean the Shema teaches God is a plurality of persons, but it does allow for it.

Finally, when Jesus says he and the Father are one, it reminds us that "[e]ach is essential to the identity of other."[19] The Father is a Father because of the Son, and the Son is a Son because of the Father. Without one, there would not be the other. This refers to not simply *who* they are but *what* they are—the kind of Father/Son relationship John has been describing since his opening prologue (1:1–18). Both the Father and the Son are God *by nature*, not simply by title or function. They are of *one* nature—i.e., of the same kind or species. That's what John has been showing us about Jesus and the Father all along, and that's why I think John 10:30 is an allusion to Yahweh's oneness in the Shema. The enraged crowd that wanted to stone Jesus was right about the gist of his claim. Their problem was they didn't believe him.

The Epicenter

But Paul and the other followers of Jesus believed him. I'm convinced the expanded Shema we find in Paul and the similar declarations of Jesus' deity in the NT ultimately go back to Jesus himself. And nowhere do we find this more clearly than in John. Jesus made extraordinary claims that enraged his enemies and baffled his followers. But when he arose bodily from the dead, his disciples understood and embraced his claims. This was the earthquake that shook the world and will echo in eternity.

But what now? If Jesus belongs with God the Father in the core confession of our faith, then how should we relate to him? To whom do we pray? Jesus or the Father or both? How does it work? And where does Jesus fit into our worship? Once again, John shows us the way.

IN THE WAKE OF THE QUAKE

After the Easter earthquake, the ground beneath the feet of Jesus' followers shifted dramatically. And even though John's Gospel ends shortly after

18. Gen 2:24; Matt 19:5–6. Cf. also Gen 11:6; 34:16, 22; 2 Sam 7:23; Ezek 37:22; Jn 10:16; 11:52; 1 Cor 12:12; Eph 5:31. For further discussion see Brown, *Answering Jewish Objections to Jesus*, 2:4–7.

19. Bauckham, *Jesus and the God of Israel*, 106.

Jesus' resurrection, the newly revealed solid ground provides a firm foundation for what we need to believe and how to worship and pray.

Thomas: Portrait of a True Believer

One of the earliest aftershocks of the Easter earthquake took place about a week following Jesus' resurrection. It's the story of the "Doubting Thomas" we learned about in chapter 8. John places this episode as the climactic event of his Gospel. When Thomas says to Jesus, "My Lord and my God," it becomes the matching bookend on the opposite end of the shelf from John 1:1. Jesus is declared "God" by the narrator at the beginning and then "my Lord and my God" by a doubter-turned-believer at the end. Next John ties it all together by succinctly stating the purpose of the book (20:29–31). Chapter 21 is an epilogue. For John, Thomas's confession sums up in one event everything to which the book has been pointing since 1:1.

First, notice how Jesus responds to Thomas's confession: "Jesus told him, 'Because you have seen me, you have believed; blessed are those who have not seen and yet have believed'" (Jn 20:29). Yes, Jesus mildly rebukes Thomas for demanding tangible proof beyond the testimony of his close friends. But don't miss the larger point—Thomas *did* end up believing! And what exactly did he believe? He believed in Jesus as his Lord and his God. This is huge!

Since John 1, the Gospel has been showing us readers why we should believe in Jesus. The Greek word translated "believe" (*pisteuō*) is used nearly one hundred times in John. We hear the constant drumbeat in nearly every chapter reminding us that we need to believe in Jesus to have eternal life. The Thomas story is the grand finale—a guy who says he won't believe believes! Immediately, on the heels of Thomas's declaration, John sums up his purpose for writing his book: "Jesus performed many other signs in the presence of his disciples, which are not recorded in this book. But these are written that you may believe that Jesus is the Messiah, the Son of God, and that by believing you may have life in his name" (Jn 20:30–31).

Thomas's confession is the event that prompts John's summary and conclusion. Notice how the confession is linked to the summation. To believe that Jesus is the Messiah, the Son of God, entails confessing him as your Lord and your God—just as Thomas did. The terms "Messiah" and "Son of God" must be understood in light of the whole book and especially Thomas's confession. Throughout his Gospel, John has defined for us what sort of Messiah Jesus is. Yes, he's a flesh-and-blood, real man, but not merely a man. Yes, he is a king, but not merely an earthly king. Jesus is the sort of

Messiah who is God in the flesh and gave his life and arose from the dead to save us. His body still bears the nail marks in his hands and the spear wound in his side. John has also defined for us what it means for Jesus to be the Son of God—a key theme throughout his Gospel. He's not the same as any of the "sons of God" that foreshadowed him in the OT or in the Jewish literature of the day. Jesus is the eternal, one and only (or only begotten) Son who shares the very nature of God with his Father. Finally, notice John says, ". . . by believing you may have life in *his name*" (20:31; italics added). What is Jesus' name? Is it the name "Jesus" or "Lord" (= Yahweh) or "I Am?" John never spells it out for us precisely, but based on what we learned in this chapter and chapter 8, it at least has to include the understanding that Jesus is Yahweh revealed in the flesh. All this comes together in Thomas's confession, "My Lord and my God." This is what John means when he directs a person to believe in Jesus for eternal life.

Dear Reader, have you ever come to the point in your life when you crossed over from death to life? The whole Gospel of John was written to usher you gently to take that awesome step of faith. It involves rejecting your sins and turning to Jesus—who died for you and rose from the dead—as your Lord and your God. Trust in him with your whole being today and begin to live the new life he has for you. And once you do so, John's Gospel will also show how you can grow and develop in your new life in Jesus.

Thomas: Portrait of a Jesus-Worshiper

A major part of following Jesus is worshiping him. The closer we examine the Thomas episode, the more extraordinary it looks. First, Thomas's confession "My Lord and my God" does more than simply identify Jesus as the true God revealed in the OT.[20] It moves beyond a statement of fact to a declaration of worship. Notice Thomas does far more than state Jesus is Lord and God. He breaks new ground here. He says to Jesus, "*my* Lord and *my* God" (italics added). That's not just identification; that's worship. To exclaim to someone that he is *your* Lord and *your* God is a form of worship.

If Jesus were anyone less than Yahweh himself, he should have harshly rebuked Thomas for breaking the first commandment, where Yahweh says, "You must not have any other god but me" (Exod 20:3 NLT). Notice the instant rebuke the apostle Peter and an angel give when they smell the slightest whiff of worship directed towards them:

---

20. Thomas's confession is strikingly similar to the words spoken to Yahweh in Psalm 35:23, "my God and my Lord" (ESV).

> As Peter entered the house, Cornelius met him and fell at his
> feet in reverence. But Peter made him get up. "Stand up," he said,
> "I am only a man myself." (Acts 10:25)

> I, John, am the one who heard and saw these things. And when
> I had heard and seen them, I fell down to worship at the feet of
> the angel who had been showing them to me. But he said to me,
> "Don't do that! I am a fellow servant with you and with your
> fellow prophets and with all who keep the words of this scroll.
> Worship God!" (Rev 22:8–9)

Only God is to be worshiped, period! If Jesus were less than the true
God, he should have reacted similarly. But instead he affirms Thomas's belief is correct (Jn 20:29).

Around the time John wrote his Gospel, the Roman Emperor Domi-
tian styled himself as "our Lord God."[21] Knowing this, John's readers would
find Thomas's confession especially relevant to their situation. We can imagine them saying to one another, "The emperor demands to be addressed
as Lord and God, but we reserve that for Jesus!" Are you in the habit of
worshiping Jesus? Allow me to suggest that you take a moment right now to
tell him sincerely and adoringly that he is your Lord and God.

Objection!

But some argue that Thomas's confession falls short of declaring Jesus to be
the true God. One approach claims Thomas was actually speaking to God
the Father, not to Jesus. Others say Thomas was voicing an overenthusiastic
exclamation, as in, "Oh my God!" But neither idea fits the text. Notice that
verse 28 plainly says, "Thomas said *to him*, "My Lord . . . !" (italics added).
Thomas was addressing Jesus directly with words of belief and worship.

More seriously, others argue that since Jesus is the perfect representation of Yahweh, Thomas can address Jesus as God's stand-in representative.[22] In biblical times, the messenger of the king was to be treated as the
king himself. So perhaps Thomas was treating Jesus (Yahweh's messenger)
as Yahweh, even though he was not *actually* Yahweh. After all, didn't Jesus
say, "Anyone who has seen me has seen the Father" (Jn 14:9)?

But this view doesn't work either. Recall our study of Yahweh's agents
back in chapter 2. Yes, they speak *for* Yahweh but never *as* Yahweh in the

---

21. The ancient Roman historian Suetonius records this in *Dom.* 13.

22. Rich, "Contextual Key to John 20:28," 589–601; Buzzard and Hunting, *Doctrine of the Trinity*, 291–93; Harvey, *Jesus and the Constraints of History*, 172.

first person (unless it's a quote), nor are they worshiped *as* Yahweh[23]—as is Jesus in John. Certain things Yahweh reserves only for himself. The king's messenger may represent the king, but does that mean he sleeps with the queen? Not on your life! If Jesus were not Yahweh himself, receiving worship as he does in John 20:28–29 would be the equivalent of the king's messenger sleeping with the queen!

In Jesus' Name

When I teach about the Trinity, I am often asked, "If the one God is three persons, to whom should I direct my prayers?" If you've wondered about this, you're certainly not alone. Since we have not yet discussed the Holy Spirit, let's begin with only the Father and the Son.

When Jesus taught his disciples to pray, he instructed them to address God the Father. His own practice of addressing God in this personal and intimate manner likely raised some eyebrows.[24] Jesus' model prayer for us begins with the words, "Our Father in heaven. . ." (Matt 6:9). In addressing God this way in his own prayers, Jesus led by example,[25] and we find the early Christians followed suit.[26] Here we discover the most basic truth about prayer: On the authority of Jesus' teaching, we come by faith to God as to a loving Father, who cares more about us than the most adoring human parent ever could.

For illustration purposes, let's paint a word picture of how prayer as Jesus taught it should look. When you pray, picture yourself entering a quiet room with a comfortable chair near a cozy fireplace with a crackling fire. This is where you will meet with your heavenly Father. Jesus himself painted a similar word picture when he advised, "But when you pray, go into your room, close the door and pray to your Father, who is unseen" (Matt 6:6). The person you address in prayer is your loving heavenly Father.

But where is God the Son in this room? Here's where John's portrait of Jesus again becomes very helpful. Remember, as we learned in chapter 7, believing in Jesus' name is what gave you the right to be a child of God: "Yet to all who did receive him, to those who believed in *his name*, he gave the right to become *children* of God" (Jn 1:12; italics added). Once again, notice the words "his name." Becoming a child of the Father takes place through

23. The only exception is the angel of Yahweh, who actually *is* Yahweh.

24. See Thompson, *Promise of the Father*, 21–34.

25. In the Gospels Jesus addresses the Father in prayer numerous times. E.g., Matt 11:25–26; Mk 14:36; Lk 10:21; 23:34, 46; Jn 11:41; 12:28; 17:1, 5, 11, 21, 24, 25.

26. E.g., Rom 8:15; Gal 4:6; Eph 1:17; 3:14; Col 1:3.

believing in Jesus as God in the flesh. What's more, Jesus' name is also the key that gets us into the prayer room with the Father. Jesus repeatedly tells his disciples to ask the Father "in my name."[27]

Picture yourself outside God's house where there's a long line of people expecting to enter. Many are turned away because they don't know Jesus (Matt 7:21–23), but when you arrive on the premises, you go straight to the doorkeeper—Jesus—and call on his name, since you know him as your Lord and your God. You are given instant access. But that's not all. Jesus not only gets you in to meet with the Father, he also accompanies you in the room during the meeting. During your prayer session with the Father, Jesus sits at your side as part of the conversation.

What goes on in that room? Notice how Jesus puts it: "If anyone loves me, he will keep my word, and my Father will love him, and we will come to him and make our home with him" (Jn 14:23 ESV). Jesus is not speaking here of a corporate experience. The Greek pronouns are singular. This is a personal experience between the individual believer, God the Father, and Jesus. The Greek word translated "home" (*monē*) here is rendered "rooms" (plural) in 14:2. Whether we call it a room or a home, the idea is of a permanent dwelling place where you, the Father, and Jesus meet together. And in John 14:23, the meeting place isn't just a place you go to visit; the meeting place is within you. You become the home! This warm, intimate setting is what Jesus pictures for us when we experience God's company.

Note the links in the chain of this experience. First, out of love for the Son, you keep Jesus' word. (Jesus doesn't mention it here, but our love for him is first prompted by God's love for us.[28]) Jesus says the next link is the Father will love you. Since we know he already loves you, this must speak of your experience of his love, as you begin to realize and enter into it. It's similar to today's expression to "love on" someone. The person getting "loved on" is *experiencing* love that's already there. But we experience God's love in a deeper way when we, out of love, obey Jesus' words. That's his promise. What's happening in biblical terms is that you are experiencing fellowship with God. Later John echoed the truth of John 14:23 when he said, "[O]ur fellowship is with the Father and with his Son, Jesus Christ" (1 Jn 1:3). The whole Christian life—including prayer—is all about this fellowship.

As for prayer in particular, while you might typically address the Father, you may certainly also talk to the Son. As Jesus says: "And *I* will do whatever you ask in my name, so that the Father may be glorified in the Son. You may ask *me* for anything in my name, and *I* will do it" (Jn 14:13–14;

27. Jn 14:13–14; 15:16; 16:23, 24, 26.
28. Jn 3:16; 1 Jn 4:19.

italics added). Notice the pronouns "me" and "I." Jesus expects to be included in your prayers. He's in the room with you and the Father, and he's part of the fellowship experience. On the other hand, try not to mix up the persons of the Trinity in your prayers. For instance, don't thank the Father for dying for your sins (a common mistake); the Son did that. Thank the Father for sending the Son and the Son for dying for you.

QUESTIONS FOR DISCUSSION

1. Have you ever experienced an earthquake of the soul of any kind? How about the kind described in this chapter? How have you been affected?

2. What's the most important thing you learned in this chapter? How might you explain it to a Christian friend? What remains unclear to you?

3. Can you relate to experiencing God's love more so when you, out of love, obey Jesus' word? What's the difference between this and the legalistic practice of obeying God to *obtain* his love?

A VERSE TO MEMORIZE

Thomas said to him, "My Lord and my God!" (Jn 20:28)

APPLY WHAT YOU'VE LEARNED

Find the lyrics of a worship song or hymn you really like that addresses or speaks of Jesus, and bring it to your discussion group to read or (if you have the courage) sing. Tell them why you like it. Does it bring the Father and the Holy Spirit into the lyrics or does it focus only on Jesus? How are worship songs and hymns we sing today similar or different to the hymn in Philippians 2:5–11?

CHAPTER 10

Enter the Holy Spirit

Have you ever seen the movie *To Kill a Mockingbird*? I remember how that film (based on the book by Harper Lee) impacted me as a young boy the first time I watched it. All through the story, the two kids, Jem and Scout, ponder the neighborhood gossip about the mysterious Arthur "Boo" Radley—a crazed maniac who lives in a broken-down, scary-looking house on their street. Over the course of the story you discover Boo Radley has been secretly watching the kids with a creepy fascination. Your impression of Boo is anything but positive. But that's exactly what you're supposed to think, because the story is all about illustrating the terrible consequences that can result from knee-jerk judgments—prejudices—about people who are different from you. In the surprise finish of the film (spoiler alert!), Boo Radley's watchful eye and courage end up saving the lives of the two children from an embittered stalker. In the end, Boo Radley is a silent hero who's been badly misjudged.

Something similar (though usually less sinister) often happens to the Holy Spirit when people read the Scriptures. Though he shows up on the first and last pages of the Bible and in hundreds of places in between, the Spirit is mostly in the background. Unlike the Son, no Bible book is devoted to telling his story, and even when his work is highlighted, the spotlight is quickly shifted to the Father or the Son. The unintended consequence is that sometimes the Holy Spirit is badly misunderstood or neglected in the beliefs and lives of many.

This book is mainly about the Son's relationship to the Father as portrayed in John. But my work here would not be complete without at least devoting one chapter to the Holy Spirit's role in the relationship.[1] Really, the topic deserves its own book to do it justice.[2] In this chapter, we'll have to settle for a very brief overview of the Spirit's person and work, especially concerning how he relates to the Father and the Son in John's Gospel and why this is important for us. But first, we need to deal with some background issues, both personal and scriptural.

WHAT'S YOUR STORY?

Depending on your background, the topic of the Holy Spirit might raise excitement or a red flag. If you grew up active in a Pentecostal or charismatic church, your experience and viewpoint are likely much different from a person raised in, say, a Baptist or Bible church setting. Or if you have little or no religious background, the topic may seem mysterious, weird, or a disjointed jumble of ideas.

The purpose of this chapter is not to compare various views within Christian circles, but to survey the biblical evidence, especially in John, in order to see how the Spirit relates to the Father and the Son and how this knowledge should affect our lives as Christ-followers. We'll learn truths that are basic to a biblical understanding of the Spirit. And so whatever your background experience—whether good, bad, or indifferent—try to see the topic with fresh eyes and an open heart.

PROGRESSIVE REVELATION

A good murder mystery movie usually has a surprise ending that compels you to reexamine the whole story in a new light. I've always enjoyed the classic Sherlock Holmes films. By the end of an episode, assumptions you made about the characters or circumstances may have to be revised in light of what you discover when the culprit is revealed. You then realize that what you thought were incidental details at first were tell-tale clues that all fit together when you see the fuller picture.

Though the Bible is certainly not a murder mystery, the comparison helps illustrate the grand story of God's progressive revelation of himself in Scripture. When we look back at the OT from the NT perspective, we can see there are clues and hints pointing all along in the direction of the NT

1. I cover this topic in a more technical manner in Rheaume, *Exegetical and Theological Analysis*, 342–62.

2. For a book-length treatment of the Holy Spirit in John, see Burge, *Anointed Community*.

picture. We definitely want to let the OT authors speak for themselves and avoid reading later ideas back into their writings. But, on the other hand, a close look at details of the OT text often exposes the foundations of later-revealed truths.

The Son from Behind the Clouds

In recent chapters we've observed that the Son's divine identity was revealed gradually throughout the history of God's people. Only with the NT perspective of Jesus as Yahweh in human flesh can we see he was there all along in the OT. He existed eternally with the Father (Jn 1:1), but in Genesis 1 we detect him only in retrospect as God's voice speaking creation into existence (cf. Jn 1:3). The strange OT appearances of Yahweh (which began in the Garden of Eden) seem to contrast (or even contradict) sharply with the uncompromising fact that God cannot be seen by humans.

As a thought experiment, try limiting your knowledge of God to only what had been revealed in OT times. Should you take literally the OT prophecies about Yahweh one day showing up among his people? If so, how will he do this? The basic facts were announced, but the details were sketchy. When Yahweh finally shows up in the person of Jesus, he's wrapped in human flesh. He arrives incognito! To virtually everyone, Jesus seemed at first like an ordinary man.[3] Even John the Baptist—the man God appointed to introduce Jesus to Israel—had no idea who he was until God told him (Jn 1:31, 33), and even then it was a partial revelation (cf. Matt 11:2–3).

But Jesus' resurrection was the pivot point. Though he dropped many big hints and made audacious claims during his ministry, Jesus also foretold that his true identity would not be comprehended until after he was lifted up in death and in glory (Jn 8:28). In fact, he insisted his true identity could not be understood and accepted apart from a direct revelation from God.[4] After his resurrection, his disciples finally got the memo (Jn 20:28–31), and eventually all of creation will declare Jesus is Yahweh to the glory of God the Father (Phil 2:9–11). In his infinite wisdom, God chose to reveal Jesus' divine identity progressively.

3. A fact noted in all four Gospels: Matt 13:54–57; Mk 6:1–3; Lk 4:22; Jn 1:26.
4. Lk 10:22; Jn 14:20–21.

The Breath of God

As with the Son, the identity of the Holy Spirit is revealed progressively. Just as, in light of NT revelation, the Son shows up in Genesis 1 as God's voice, the Spirit shows up as God's breath or wind in the same chapter.

> In the beginning God created the heavens and the earth. Now the earth was formless and empty, darkness was over the surface of the deep, and the Spirit of God was hovering over the waters. And God said, "Let there be light," and there was light. (Gen 1:1–3)

The Hebrew word translated "Spirit" here is *rûaḥ*. It frequently means "breath" or "wind" in the OT. In fact, some scholars believe it's better to translate verse 2 to read, "a wind from God swept over the face of the waters" (NRSV). Scholars who take this view believe that translating *rûaḥ* as "Spirit" (especially with a capital S!) risks reading a NT understanding back into this text.[5] They have a point.

Back when Genesis was written (many centuries before the birth of Jesus), *rûaḥ* was understood to be God's creative power and presence—his mighty wind, not a distinct person.[6] God's *rûaḥ* (his breath or spirit) was his life force that was active in the creation of the cosmos and all living things. Notice that Yahweh's *rûaḥ* works with his Word in creating the universe: "By the word of the LORD the/ heavens were made,/ their starry host by the/ breath [*rûaḥ*] of his mouth" (Ps 33:6). Fascinating! Yahweh's word and breath together created the cosmos! His *rûaḥ* was also responsible for creating people. Elihu says, "The Spirit of God has/ made me;/ the breath of the Almighty/ gives me life" (Job 33:4). Elihu is alluding back to the creation of the first human: "Then the LORD God formed a man from the dust of the ground and breathed into his nostrils the breath of life, and the man became a living being" (Gen 2:7).

Breathing in and out is what keeps you alive. If you stop breathing, you stop living. In the OT mindset, breathing in and out is directly associated with the life (or breath) Yahweh imparts to you. The psalm writer adds that Yahweh's *rûaḥ* also creates and sustains nonhuman creatures: "When you send your Spirit,/ they are created,/ and you renew the face of/ the ground" (Ps 104:30). Like the wind that blows in the trees and the breath that animates all living creatures, *rûaḥ* is invisible yet powerful. And so if you are a Jew in Jesus' day, God's *rûaḥ* is the invisible animating power and presence

---

5. Cf. Waltke and Yu, *Old Testament Theology*, 182, 213.

6. See *HALOT*, 2:1200.

that created the universe, gives life, and sustains all things. It's God's very breath!

May Much More than the Force be with You

But it's important to emphasize that God's *rûaḥ* is not just an impersonal force.[7] Several factors lead to this conclusion. First, the OT speaks of spirits (*rûaḥ*) that were angels or wicked spirits[8] (what would later be called demons). These beings are unembodied but possess consciousness, intellect, and free choice. In other words, unlike inanimate things like wind or breath, there exist "spirit" entities that are both personal and invisible to humans.

Second, the human *rûaḥ* can refer to attitudes or emotions or a person's will.[9] Or sometimes human *rûaḥ* refers to a person's inner self. For example, Elisha says to his servant, "Was not my spirit with you when the man got down from his chariot to meet you" (2 Kgs 5:26)? Elisha was not physically present when this event took place, but he says his "spirit" (*rûaḥ*) was somehow conscious of it, as though he was actually there in unembodied form. This presupposes that *rûaḥ* is not simply the breath in Elijah's lungs or his impersonal life force (like electricity), but an entity with attributes of personhood—what we might call his *mind* or *self*.

Third, we find that God's *rûaḥ* has personal attributes as well. In the OT, God's *rûaḥ* instructs people. The Levites say to Yahweh, "You gave your good Spirit to instruct them [God's people]" (Neh 9:20). This is before the days when an impersonal computer or TV could teach you. In the ancient world, teaching someone would most naturally presuppose personhood. Also, Yahweh's *rûaḥ* can be rebelled against (Ps 106:33), again presupposing personhood. Significantly, notice that God's *rûaḥ* can be grieved: "Yet they rebelled/ and *grieved his Holy Spirit*./ So he turned and became/ their enemy /and he himself fought/ against them" (Isa 63:10; italics added). An inanimate force cannot grieve; grieving definitely presupposes personhood.

A fifth indication of personhood is speaking. David says, "The Spirit of the LORD spoke/ through me;/ his word was on my tongue" (2 Sam 23:2).

All these traits of personhood point to God's consciousness, mind, or self—not simply his impersonal power. God's *rûaḥ* is his personal presence which exists everywhere. David says to Yahweh,

---

7. For a fuller treatment of this topic, see the excellent discussion in Brown, *Answering Jewish Objections to Jesus*, 2:52–59.

8. E.g., 1 Sam 16:15; 1 Kgs 22:21–23.

9. E.g., Exod 6:9; Job 7:11; Ps 34:18; Prov 18:14.

Where can I go from *your*
  Spirit [*rûaḥ*]?
Where can I flee from your
  presence?
If I go up to the heavens, *you*
  are there;
  if I make my bed in the
    depths, *you* are
    there.
If I rise on the wings of the
  dawn,
  if I settle on the far side of
    the sea,
even there *your hand* will
  guide me,
  your right hand will hold
    me fast. (Ps 139:7–10; italics added)

Notice the italicized words. Observe that "your Spirit" is parallel to "your presence." Yahweh's Spirit is his invisible, personal presence everywhere in creation. Then in verse 8, David uses the pronoun "you" twice as he marvels over the Spirit's omnipresence throughout the universe. In verse 10, David switches the metaphor to "your hand" and "your right hand" to describe Yahweh's personal activity of guiding and protecting him.

Often in the OT, Yahweh's *rûaḥ* is said to come upon someone to empower the person to perform an office or task requiring supernatural ability.[10] Thus the Holy Spirit is God's personal and powerful presence which is conscious and active everywhere in creation, especially in people chosen to serve him through supernatural deeds.

But is the Holy Spirit just another way of speaking about God himself or is the Spirit a distinct person within the identity of Yahweh? On the one hand, God can send his *rûaḥ* to perform deeds (Ps 104:30) and give[11] or take away[12] his *rûaḥ*. This would seem to suggest a distinction between Yahweh and his *rûaḥ*. On the other hand, this is by no means a decisive indication of distinct personhood. If we only had the OT revelation, we might easily conclude the Spirit is an aspect of God, similar to his wisdom. Yahweh's wisdom is often personified in OT poetry as a woman who was by his side

---

10. E.g., Num 11:26; Judg 14:6; 1 Sam 10:10; 16:13; 2 Chr 24:20; Isa 61:1.

11. E.g., Num 11:26, 29; Judg 3:10; 11:29; 1 Sam 10:6; 16:13; Neh 9:20.

12. 1 Sam 16:14; Ps 51:11.

at creation[13] and speaks and instructs people on his behalf.[14] But "Lady Wisdom" is a poetic device, not an actual person separate from Yahweh. Wisdom is one of Yahweh's attributes; personifying it is a colorful way of illustrating its cleverness, beauty, and value. Certainly God is not dependent on a separate, created entity for his wisdom! Yahweh is infinitely wise by his very nature. Might the Spirit likewise simply be a way to speak of God's presence without implying a person distinct from Yahweh? As we will see, the NT provides the answer.

Finally, Yahweh predicted the day when his Spirit would be poured out abundantly upon his people in an unprecedented manner, supernaturally remaking them to be pure[15] and enabling them to serve him with new and powerful abilities.[16] When John the Baptist arrived—hundreds of years after these prophecies—he foretold that the one coming after him would bestow this unparalleled blessing of the promised Holy Spirit.[17] In the OT, only Yahweh confers the Holy Spirit,[18] and yet in the NT it happens through Jesus—only in a much greater way than ever before.

In this brief and piecemeal survey of the Spirit in the OT, we've seen that he is present and active with Yahweh from the dawn of creation and throughout OT history. Like wind, God's *rûaḥ* is invisible yet powerful. Like breath, God's *rûaḥ* gives and sustains life. God's *rûaḥ* is his personal, omnipresent mind or self that empowers his people for service and will be poured out one day upon them in an unprecedented way. But as to his distinct personhood, this awaited the NT revelation.

THE HOLY SPIRIT IN THE NT

Was the man a raving lunatic? Some people thought so. His style of dress, diet, place of residence, and hellfire-and-brimstone preaching definitely ruffled lots of feathers and raised more than a few eyebrows. But John the Baptist was anything but crazy. Recall, as we saw in chapter 8, John was God's messenger sent to the Jews to prepare the way for Yahweh's appearance among his people.

But how would Yahweh show up? This is how John the Baptist was told it would work: An unidentified man would come to him for baptism

13. Prov 3:19; 8:22–31.

14. E.g., Prov 1:20–33; 8:1–21, 32–36; 9:1–6.

15. Isa 32:15; Ezek 36:25–27; 37:14; 39:29.

16. Joel 2:28–29; cf. Num 11:29.

17. Found in all four Gospel accounts: Matt 3:11; Mk 1:8; Lk 3:16; Jn 1:33.

18. E.g., Num 11:25; Joel 2:28–29.

and would be recognized when the Holy Spirit comes on him in the form of a dove and remains on him (Jn 1:32–34). He's the one! This man is the one who will impart the Spirit (as only Yahweh can) to others in fulfillment of the awesome promises spoken centuries earlier by the OT prophets. Here's how Mark recorded that golden moment:

> At that time Jesus came from Nazareth in Galilee and was baptized by John in the Jordan. Just as Jesus was coming up out of the water, he saw heaven being torn open and the Spirit descending on him like a dove. And a voice came from heaven: "You are my Son, whom I love; with you I am well pleased." (Mk 1:9–11)

This scene sets the stage for the NT revelation of the person and work of the Holy Spirit. Note that the Son is baptized, the Father speaks, and the Holy Spirit descends. This trio of persons shows up regularly throughout the NT.

The indications of the Holy Spirit's personhood intensify in the NT. We see the traits of personhood attributed to the Holy Spirit—not simply in poetic literature (as with wisdom), but in historical narratives and letters of instruction. Intellect is attributed to the Spirit; he is said to have a mind (Rom 8:27) and the capacity to make decisions (Acts 15:28). The Holy Spirit has feelings. He can be insulted (Heb 10:29) and grieved (Eph 4:30). He expresses love (Rom 15:30) and makes choices (1 Cor 12:11). The Spirit is not just an impersonal force or the power of God. The Holy Spirit is a person. Notice that he speaks,[19] teaches (Jn 14:26), testifies (Jn 15:26), hears (Jn 16:13), and even applies the first-person pronoun "I" to himself.[20]

Sometimes people who deny the Spirit's personhood note that the Greek word translated "Spirit" (*pneuma*) in the NT is neuter. But this doesn't disprove personhood. Angels[21] and demons[22] are "spirits" (*pneuma*), yet they are clearly personal beings. Also, the Greek word for "child" (*teknon*) is neuter, but children are persons. Some object by saying, "The Holy Spirit is said to be 'poured out' on people (Joel 2:28–29). How can a person be poured out?" But David (foreshadowing Jesus' death) uses this metaphor of himself (Ps 22:14). It does not deny personhood.

When you combine the NT evidence with the OT data, the case for the Holy Spirit's personhood is substantial and compelling. As we learned

---

19. Jn 16:13; Acts 10:19; 13:2; 1 Tim 4:1; Rev 2:7, 11, 17, 29; 3:6, 13, 22. He also does so in the OT (Ezek 2:2–3; 3:24; 11:5).

20. Acts 10:20; 13:2.

21. Heb 1:7, 14.

22. E.g., Mk 3:11; Acts 8:7; Rev 16:14.

earlier, the Holy Spirit is said to do what only God himself can do—create the universe and give life. In the NT, the Spirit is also called "God" (Acts 5:3–4) and "the Lord" (2 Cor 3:17[23])—two major titles of deity in the Bible.

But perhaps you're wondering, "Could the Holy Spirit be just another term for God's self rather than a person distinct from the Father and the Son?" Before we turn our focus back to John, we need to briefly address NT evidence for the triunity of God.

ONE GOD IN THREE PERSONS

In one of my early encounters with JWs, they correctly pointed out to me that the word "Trinity" never appears in the Bible. "If God is a Trinity," they asked, "why doesn't God or any writer of Scripture ever use the word?" This, of course, is an excellent question.

The word "Trinity" was coined long after the NT era as a one-word term (meaning "triunity") to capture what the Bible teaches about God's oneness and threeness. Let's say the writers of Scripture told us 2 + 3, but did not complete the equation. Would not = 5 be a warranted and even biblical deduction?[24] The word "Bible" never occurs in the Bible either, nor is there a list (or a table of contents) within Scripture that tells us which books to include. The deduction—based on the evidence within Scripture and the practice of God's people—took place after all the books were written. Likewise, the word "Trinity" is a good term to sum up what the Bible teaches. God is revealed as one being, and yet the Father, Son, and Holy Spirit are three distinct persons who are each clearly identified in the Bible as God. The word "Trinity" simply encapsulates the deduction of the biblical evidence.[25]

23. Some believe this text refers to the spirit of the Lord Jesus rather than the Holy Spirit. But see Fee, *God's Empowering Presence*, 311–13.

24. I am indebted to Fred Sanders, who mined this illustration from the works of fourth-century theologian Gregory of Nazianzus. "Fred Sanders: The Triune God," On Script. http://onscript.study/podcast/fred-sanders-the-triune-god/ (accessed March 5, 2018).

25. Many excellent books have been written on the Trinity. On the biblical evidence, see White, *Forgotten Trinity*, and Wainwright, *Trinity in the New Testament*. For dealing with some of the theological issues of the Trinity, see Sanders, *Triune God* and the volume of essays in Ware and Stare, *One God in Three Persons*. On the practical implications of the Trinity, see Reeves, *Delighting in the Trinity*.

One Name, Three Persons

One such instance is given to us by none other than the risen Jesus himself at a gathering in Galilee with his disciples. The importance of these words cannot be overemphasized:

> Then Jesus came to them and said, "All authority in heaven and on earth has been given to me. Therefore go and make disciples of all nations, baptizing them in the name of the Father and of the Son and of the Holy Spirit, and teaching them to obey everything I have commanded you. And surely I am with you always, to the very end of the age." (Matt 28:18–20)

These are the final words of Matthew's Gospel. At the beginning of Matthew, Jesus was called "Immanuel," which Matthew rightly says means, "God with us" (1:23). But now at the end of the Gospel, Matthew puts the corresponding back cover on his book with Jesus' words, "I am with you always." Similar to John, Matthew stresses Jesus' divine presence at both the beginning and the end of his Gospel. And once again, God expresses his desire and his promise to be with us, and this desire is fulfilled in Jesus.

Equally significant in this text is the formula Jesus gives us for baptism. Though Christian denominations differ on the meaning and method of baptism, it is by all accounts an initiation rite signifying a person as a Christ-follower. Here's where converts go public, declare their new faith,[26] and become part of the family of believers. We might compare it to the oath of office taken by a public official before beginning to serve. Jesus sums up that declaration of faith as taking place "in the name of the Father and of the Son and of the Holy Spirit." Notice Jesus does not say "in the names," plural, but "in the name," singular. Jesus places these three persons under the umbrella of the one name of God.[27] According to Jesus, Yahweh *is* the Father, Son, and Holy Spirit. In NT times, converts to Jesus were baptized when they first believed. And here Jesus directs that at the gateway to the Christian life you declare allegiance to God as Father, Son, and Holy Spirit. The person baptized is now under the authority of the one God in three persons. Also, notice that the three persons are distinct. The Spirit here cannot simply be another word for God's self or mind; that would make no sense in this context. This passage is of immense importance because it shows that

26. In the case of those who practice infant baptism, typically the parents or godparents declare faith on behalf of or in anticipation of the child consciously doing so when old enough.

27. Carson, "Matthew," 668–69.

the whole Christian life is to be characterized as commitment to one God in three persons.

Triunity in the NT

The three persons of the Trinity are mentioned together at key junctures of Jesus' life and ministry. When he is conceived in the womb, the angel includes the three persons in the announcement to Mary (Lk 1:35). We have already seen that the three persons are mentioned together at Jesus' baptism. Actually, Jesus' whole ministry involved the activity of all three persons.[28] The writer of Hebrews involves the three persons in Jesus' atoning death for our sins (Heb 9:14), and Paul speaks of the three in relation to Jesus' resurrection.[29] A careful reading of the NT also reveals a hefty number of triadic passages—texts in which the three persons of God are mentioned together, often in their respective roles in the work of redemption.[30] One such text reads, "May the grace of the Lord Jesus Christ, and the love of God, and the fellowship of the Holy Spirit be with you all" (2 Cor 13:14). In this closing blessing to the believers in Corinth, Paul highlights the distinctive role of each of the three persons of the Trinity performs in the life of a Christ-follower.

Though the cumulative case for the Trinity is strong, you still may be wondering why the Holy Spirit's distinct personhood and role are revealed so slowly. Why does it take the gradual accumulation of evidence throughout both testaments of the Bible for the full picture of the Trinity to immerge? While I don't believe God gives us a full answer to this question, the best place to turn is back to John's Gospel.

WHY SO SHY?

At first it might appear that the Gospel of John is not a promising place to make a case for including the Holy Spirit within God's identity. Unlike the

---

28. Matt 12:28; Lk 4:17–19; 10:21; Jn 3:34; Acts 10:38.

29. Rom 1:1–4; cf. 8:11.

30. The most striking in Paul's letters are 2 Cor 13:14; 1 Cor 12:4–6; cf. Eph 4:4–6. A Trinitarian unfolding of salvation has been observed in Rom 5:1–8; 2 Cor 3:1—4:6; Gal 4:4–6; Eph 1:3–14; and more subtly in 1 Thess 1:4–5; 2 Thess 2:13; 1 Cor 1:4–7; 2:4–5, 12; 6:11, 19–20; 2 Cor 1:21–22; Gal 3:1–5; Rom 8:3–4, 15–17; Phil 3:3; cf. Col 3:16; Eph 1:17; 2:18, 20–22. See Fee, *God's Empowering Presence*, 839–42. Other triadic texts include Acts 20:28; 1 Pet 1:2; 4:14; Jude 20–21; Rev 1:4–5. See Wainwright, *Trinity in the New Testament*, 243–45.

Son, John (or Jesus) never calls the Spirit "God," "Lord," "I am," or any other familiar title of deity.[31] We don't find any statement comparable to John 1:1 where we're told "and the Spirit was God," nor does anyone worship the Spirit as, "my Lord and my God," as Thomas did with Jesus. Unlike the Son, John never speaks of the Spirit as the object of belief, worship, or prayer. Unlike the Father and Son, no domestic relational title (such as mother, brother, sister, cousin, etc.) is attributed to the Spirit to show he's part of the divine family. When Jesus speaks of himself and the Father in his allusion to the Shema (10:30), the Spirit appears nowhere in the context. Perhaps the silence is most deafening in the prologue (1:1–18) where the Son's deity is emphasized but the Spirit is nowhere to be found. Nor is the Spirit mentioned in Jesus' prayer to the Father in John 17 where their oneness is highlighted. If John understands the one true God to be triune, why this silence?

The Spirit Follows the Son

The key to unlocking this enigma is to compare the unveiling of the Son's identity to that of the Holy Spirit. Before coming into the world, the Son's distinct identity was unknown to any human. John tells us at the beginning that the Son required a PR agent (John the Baptist) to announce his identity and presence (1:6–8). Yet even so, his own creation rejected him because it "did not recognize him" (1:10). "He's among you right now," John the Baptist told inquirers, "but you don't recognize him" (paraphrase of 1:26). Yet even the baptist himself did not recognize Jesus for who he was until his identity was supernaturally revealed to him (1:31, 33). Until the Son's debut on the world's stage, God's revelation was primarily mediated through Moses' law, and then afterward "grace and truth came through Jesus Christ" (1:17). Granted, many didn't recognize Jesus due to the self-imposed blindness of human evil,[32] but the Baptist's ignorance and the comparison with Moses' law show that it was *also* due to God's gradual unfolding revelation of himself in the story of salvation. And even after the Son arrives on the scene, he still deflects glory away from himself. Jesus repeatedly states he didn't come to glorify himself but the Father.[33] Only when the timing is right—through

---

31. Jesus' words "God is spirit" (Jn 4:24) do not speak directly of the Holy Spirit but God's nature as a nonphysical being.

32. Jn 1:5; 3:19–21.

33. Jn 7:18; 8:50; 12:28; 17:4.

being lifted up to die and be exalted (8:28)—does the Son seek to be glorified by the Father.[34]

The Holy Spirit follows the same deferred disclosure pattern. The Spirit will do nothing to upstage Jesus. The Son's work on earth must first be completed before the Spirit steps onto the stage from behind the scenes. Look carefully at what Jesus says and then how John follows up with his own commentary:

> On the last and greatest day of the festival, Jesus stood and said in a loud voice, "Let anyone who is thirsty come to me and drink. Whoever believes in me, as Scripture has said, rivers of living water will flow from within them." By this he meant the Spirit, whom those who believed in him were later to receive. Up to that time the Spirit had not been given, since Jesus had not yet been glorified. (Jn 7:37–39)

Notice Jesus loudly makes his announcement about the Spirit in a public forum on the biggest day of the Festival of Tabernacles.[35] Believing in him will result in receiving the Holy Spirit, as John the Baptist had foretold (Jn 1:33). And yet Jesus doesn't come right out and say he's referring to the Holy Spirit, but uses the figure of "rivers of living waters." Thankfully, John explains Jesus' remarks. Jesus was speaking of the Spirit, but receiving the Spirit required that Jesus first be glorified. The Spirit's presence is powerful but not showy; the world "neither sees nor knows" him (14:17). As Jesus would later say, "But very truly I tell you, it is for your good that I am going away. Unless I go away, the Advocate [the Spirit] will not come to you; but if I go, I will send him to you" (Jn 16:7).

The Spirit Points to Jesus

Eventually—several weeks after Jesus' resurrection and ascension into heaven—the Holy Spirit makes his grand entrance at the Jewish Festival of Pentecost, as recorded in Acts 2. God's mighty wind blows, tongues of fire appear over the disciples, and they receive the supernatural ability to speak in languages they never studied (Acts 2:1–4). What's happened? The exalted Jesus himself has "poured out" the gift of the Spirit on his followers (Acts 2:33), marking a new era in God's plan of redemption. This is the flowing of living waters Jesus promised back in John 7:37–39. Yet even when the Spirit

34. Jn 8:54; 17:1, 24.

35. The festival referred to in this passage is identified as Tabernacles in John 7:2.

steps on stage, he still turns the spotlight onto Jesus, as we see from Peter's sermon that day (Acts 2:14–37).

Just as Jesus did not come to glorify himself but the Father, so the Holy Spirit does not come to call attention to himself but to the Son. His role is not to speak for himself but to speak for the Son. As Jesus says, "He will not speak on his own; he will speak only what he hears, and he will tell you what is yet to come. He will glorify me because it is from me that he will receive what he will make known to you" (Jn 16:13–14). Does this sound familiar? Jesus did the same thing with respect to the Father. He didn't speak on his own but only what the Father told him.[36] He didn't glorify himself but only the Father.[37] The Spirit follows the same pattern with the Son. Unlike Luke's noisily celebrated arrival of the Spirit at Pentecost (Acts 2), the Spirit in John is given behind locked doors to a small gathering of disciples via the barely audible breath of Jesus (20:22).[38]

A grand strategy is behind the Spirit's slow reveal. Just as the Son's identity was gradually divulged, so was the Spirit's. In his infinite wisdom, God decided to reveal the Trinity gradually as he unfolded his plan of salvation. But what exactly is the Holy Spirit's role in relation to the Father and Son and to us?

THE SPIRIT IN JESUS' FAREWELL ADDRESS

The night before Jesus died he shared supper with his disciples. Only John records Jesus' lengthy parting words to them, often called his Farewell Address (or FA for short). In this setting and during their walk later to the Garden of Gethsemane, Jesus shared his most intimate yet weighty words. Since John devotes five chapters to this talk (Jn 13–17), it's safe to assume he regarded it as hugely important. Up till now, most of what's been said about the Holy Spirit focused on Jesus rather than on his relationship to us.

One exception was when Jesus told Nicodemus a person must be born of the Spirit in order to enter God's kingdom (3:5–6, 8). You must believe in Jesus to become God's child (1:12–13). That's your part. God's part is your supernatural birth whereby the Holy Spirit procreates you with new life.[39] Jesus calls it being born again (3:3). It's totally a God thing. The Spirit

36. Jn 7:17; 12:49–50.

37. Jn 8:54; 12:28; 17:4.

38. It is often observed by commentators that Jesus' action here alludes back to God's breathing the breath of life into Adam (Gen 2:7). If so, John again casts Jesus in the role of Yahweh.

39. The imagery Jesus uses of water and spirit (Jn 3:5) likely alludes to the Spirit's

makes you into a child of God when you believe. Have you experienced this new birth? It takes only a simple step of sincere faith in Jesus, and yet it will transform you forever.

Another mention of the Spirit's work in us before the FA is the text in John 7:37–39 (which we looked at above) where Jesus promised the Spirit would flow from within every believer like a rushing river, quenching our deep, inner thirst. Water is necessary to sustain life, and the Spirit is the one who supplies you with spiritual H_2O in ample quantities.

And so, by the time you get to the FA, you've learned two crucial facts about the Spirit's role regarding your relationship to God: 1) you become a child of God when the Spirit gives you new life, and 2) he sustains your new life with a never-ending flow of spiritual refreshment. Are you experiencing this living river within you? Do you sense his presence sustaining you? It's your birthright as God's child. To learn more we must now turn to the FA itself.

New Role, New Title

What's the Holy Spirit's name? Other than "Yahweh" and "God"—which the Father and Son also share—the Holy Spirit does not have a personal name that applies only to him. Actually, neither does the Father ("Father" is a title). Only the Son has a personal name ("Jesus") that applies to him but not to the other two members of the Trinity.

In the FA, however, Jesus bestows a new and important title on the Spirit. It's the word "Paraclete," and Jesus uses it four times for the Holy Spirit.[40] If you've read John numerous times and yet you don't recognize this term, don't assume you dozed off during your reading. Paraclete is an untranslated form of the Greek word *paraklētos*. English translations of the Bible differ on how it should be rendered into our language. Some translate it "Advocate,"[41] conveying the idea of an attorney who defends and speaks for you at court. Others prefer "Counselor" (CSB), suggesting encouragement with perhaps a legal connotation. Other English translations use the more general word "Helper,"[42] which conveys the idea of assistance yet doesn't narrow it down to a legal understanding. Other translations include "Comforter" (KVJ), "Companion" (CEB), and "Friend" (NIrV).

---

purifying and renewing work as described by the prophet Ezekiel (Ezek 36:25–27; cf. Isa 44:3).

40. Jn 14:16, 26; 15:26; 16:7.

41. NET©, NAB, NLT, NRSV, and NIV (not capitalized in 14:16).

42. ESV, NASB, NKJV, and *GOD'S WORD* (not capitalized).

As you might have guessed by now, scholars haven't reached a consensus on the precise meaning of the term. It's possible that several shades of meaning—as represented in the various translations—come together in this word. If the Spirit is our Advocate, he's the sort who helps, comforts, and never leaves us (Jn 14:16–17). That's why I prefer to simply leave it untranslated as "Paraclete." My working definition for the Paraclete is *the Jesus-like, divine person who carries on God's kingdom advance after Jesus' physical departure*.

Two Paracletes

The Paraclete is so much like Jesus in so many ways that some scholars have concluded that he's actually the nonphysical Jesus, only under a different title. But while they're astonishingly similar, Jesus indicates the Paraclete is a distinct person. Notice carefully how Jesus introduces him in the FA:

> And I will ask the Father, and he will give you another Counselor [Paraclete] to be with you forever. He is the Spirit of truth. The world is unable to receive him because it doesn't see him or know him. But you do know him, because he remains with you and will be in you. (Jn 14:16–17; CSB)

Let's camp on this passage for a moment to make a few observations. Notice first that Jesus calls the Spirit "another" Paraclete. Who is the *other* Paraclete? According to John, the other Paraclete is Jesus. In his first letter John writes, "My dear children, I write this to you so that you will not sin. But if anybody does sin, we have an advocate [Paraclete] with the Father—Jesus Christ, the Righteous One" (1 Jn 2:1). And so there are actually two paracletes—Jesus and the Holy Spirit. They share the title because their roles are similar in many ways, but they're also two distinct persons. The word translated "another" (*allos*) in John 14:16 indicates they are different (i.e., not the same person) yet similar.

Second, notice both the Father and the Son have a part in conveying the Spirit to us. The Son asks the Father, and the Father sends the Spirit. Once again the three members of the Trinity work together.

Third, notice that hugely important word "forever." Once the Spirit is given to you, he's with you permanently! In the OT, God's Spirit would come and go from people,[43] but not in the new era. After Jesus rises from the dead and gives the Spirit, he's with us to stay!

---

43. E.g., 1 Sam 10:10; 16:13, 14; Ps 51:11

Fourth, notice the Spirit is received only by Christ-followers, not the world. Jesus calls him "the Spirit of truth," and, unfortunately, since the world rejects the truth of Jesus, it cannot receive or know the Spirit. If you've ever wondered why your unbelieving relatives and friends just can't seem to understand your faith, it's because they don't have the Spirit to enlighten their understanding. It's not just an intellectual issue; it's primarily a spiritual issue. Fortunately, as we share the truth and love of Jesus with them, the Spirit works to convince them of their plight and bring them to faith in Jesus.[44]

Fifth and finally, notice the present and future distinction Jesus makes when he says, "He remains with you and will be in you." In the new era—post Easter—the Spirit will not only be "with" Jesus' followers, but "in" them. In other words, he's not just visiting; he's come to take up permanent residence *within* you. This is deeply personal and intimate. Paul calls this the "fellowship of the Holy Spirit" (2 Cor 13:14). He's within you so you and he can do life together! The Spirit comes to live within us—just as the Father and the Son do (Jn 14:23). Once again, the three members of the Trinity work cooperatively together for us, with us, and also in us.

But what does the FA reveal that is unique about the Spirit's work? It would appear the Paraclete is the member of the Trinity who most directly communicates with you inwardly. Though the Father and Son make their home with you (14:23), the Spirit within you guides you into all truth (16:13), teaches you all things (14:26), and causes you to remember Jesus' words (14:26). This involves very personal interaction as the Spirit inwardly communicates with your spirit. In other words, though the Spirit is perhaps the least-talked-about member of the Trinity, he is the one who deals most directly and personally with you to nurture your relationship with God. He's the one who speaks to your heart, warns you, prompts you, guides and teaches you. Elsewhere in the NT, we're told, among other things, he's the one who gives you inner assurance that you're God's child,[45] helps you to pray,[46] gifts you with special abilities for service (1 Cor 12), and empowers you to convey the message of God's forgiveness in Christ.[47]

If we return to our analogy of the meeting room with the Father and the Son, the Son has given you access to the room and is seated beside you as you speak with the Father and him. But the Spirit is there too, inside of you,

---

44. Jn 16:7–11. The Son and the Father are also vitally involved in bringing unbelievers to faith (Jn 1:9; 6:44, 65; 12:32).

45. Rom 8:14–16, 26; 1 Jn 3:24.

46. Rom 8:26; Gal 4:6.

47. Jn 20:21–23; Acts 1:8.

prompting and helping you with what to say. Perhaps now would be a good time to pause and thank the Spirit for all he does for you.

Follow the Leader

Throughout this book we've seen that though the Father and Son are equal by nature, the Son always follows the Father's lead—not just during his earthly life, but in eternity too. This pattern continues with the Spirit. Just as the Son submits to the Father, the Holy Spirit summits to both the Father and the Son. To illustrate how the Spirit follows the lead of the Son just as the Son follows the lead of the Father, look carefully at the following chart produced by Gary Burge.[48]

The Paraclete		Christ
14:16	given by the Father	3:16
14:16–17	with, in, by the disciple	3:22; 13:33; 14:20
14:17	not received by the world	1:11; 5:53; (12:48)
14:17	not known by the world (only believers know him)	16:3; 8:19; 10:14
14:7	not seen by the world (only believers see him)	14:19; 16:16–17
14:26	sent by the Father	cf. chs. 5, 7, 8, 12
14:26	teaches	7:14–15; 8:20; 18:19
15:26; 16:7, 13	he comes (from the Father into the world)	5:43; 16:28; 18:37
15:26	gives testimony	5:31ff.; 8:13ff; 7:7
16:8	convicts the world	(cf. 3:19–20; 9:41; 15:22)
16:13	speaks not of self but of what is heard	7:17; 8:26ff.; 14:10
16:14	glorifies the Sender (Jesus/Father)	12:28; 17:1, 4
16:13ff	reveals, discloses, proclaims	4:25 (16:25)
16:13	leads into the fullness of truth	18:37; 14:6
15:26	is the Spirit of Truth; Jesus is	14:6
14:17; 16:13	the Truth	
14:16 (etc.)	a Paraclete	(14:16) 1 John 2:1

As Burge's chart shows, the Spirit/Paraclete regularly fills the role of deference and submission toward the Son that the Son fills toward the Father. In the FA, Jesus speaks about the post-Easter setting, and so we can't limit these roles to the Spirit's relationship to Jesus during only his earthly career.[49] Especially noteworthy is that just as the Father sent the Son, the Son sends the Paraclete (14:16); just as Jesus glorified the Father rather than

---

48. Burge, *Anointed Community*, 141.

49. E.g., Jn 14:25–26; 16:7, 12–13; cf. 7:39.

himself,[50] so also the Paraclete glorifies Jesus rather than himself (16:14). Jesus did not speak in his own authority but in the Father's name and authority.[51] Likewise, the Paraclete speaks not in his own authority but in the Son's name and authority.[52] In regard to these activities, the roles of Jesus and the Spirit are not portrayed as reciprocal or interchangeable. Finally, it is significant that the Father is viewed as the ultimate leader of the Trinity, for though the Son, as the Father's agent, sends the Paraclete, the Father sends him as well and is his ultimate source.[53] Just as the Father gives all things to the Son,[54] so the Spirit takes what belongs to the Son and gives it to the disciples (16:14–15).

DEPICTING THE TRINITY

In drawing this book to a close, I thought it would be helpful to include two diagrams that have been very useful to me in understanding the Trinity as presented in Scripture. The first can be found in countless forms on the internet. I have no idea of who originally came up with it; I have seen it throughout my Christian life from many different sources. It's popular because it's so helpful.

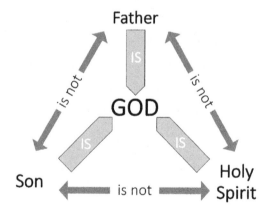

---

50. Jn 8:54; 17:1, 4, 22, 24.

51. Jn 5:43; 7:16–17; 8:26, 28; 12:49–50; 14:10.

52. Jn 14:26; 16:13–15.

53. Jn 14:16, 26; 15:26.

54. Jn 3:35; 13:3; 16:14; 17:2.

As you can see, there is only one God, and yet there are three distinct persons who exist as God. All three persons are God, but each is distinct from the others.

The next diagram[55] illustrates the equality and submission within the Trinity. Each of the three persons is equal to the others (by nature), but there is an order of position (or role) in which the Son submits to the Father and the Spirit submits to both the Father and the Son.

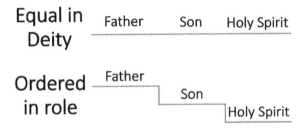

TYING IT ALL TOGETHER

As we wrap up this book, we have covered a lot of ground in the past ten chapters. We've learned about God's oneness, the OT appearances of Yahweh, the Son's deity and preexistence as portrayed in John, the meaning of Jesus' sonship in John, the meaning of life (*zōē*) as found in John, the Christian reformulation of the Shema in Paul and in John, and the person and role of the Holy Spirit. We've also learned about how the three persons relate to one another in the Trinity. All of this is important for understanding what Scripture and John in particular teach us about God. I hope you will ponder, discuss, and pass along what you've learned in this book.

But this book is intended to do more than just inform you about these important truths. I want to underscore here the main takeaways for your life and relationship with God. First, John emphasizes that the mission of salvation is to convey God's life to you so you can know the Father as Jesus knows him. Essentially, the whole drama of redemption is aimed at bringing you and me into the intimate relationship the members of the Trinity share with one another. Of course, this doesn't mean we'll somehow become God or add to the Trinity. But God does want us to finitely enjoy forever what the three members enjoy infinitely.

---

55. I do not know the ultimate source of this diagram. I first learned it from Dr. Gary Habermas when I was his undergraduate student in 1979 at William Tyndale College. He too was passing it along from someone who had showed it to him.

When God became man in Jesus, he joined himself forever to genuine humanity so he could experience our life and we could experience his. His death and bodily resurrection assure us he will fully redeem us as humans. Salvation is not about divesting ourselves of humanity and physicality, but becoming what God has always wanted for us. From the opening chapters of the Bible, God showed his desire to live among us. The barrier of sin became an ominous obstacle between God and mankind that only he could overcome. But Jesus has bridged that divide. He came to us since we could not come to him.

If you have never crossed over from the death of sin into the life Jesus died to impart, surrender yourself to him today in faith. He loves you, died for your sins, and arose bodily from the dead. He came to give you life to the full. If you already know the Lord, pursue the relationship with him that this book shows he desires to have with you.

QUESTIONS FOR DISCUSSION

1. What was your understanding and experience of the Holy Spirit growing up? Before you became a Christ-follower? How has this chapter affected your understanding?

2. What do think about the way God gradually revealed himself throughout the course of biblical history? Is a person required to know more about God to be saved now than in OT times? Did your understanding of God come gradually or in big leaps?

3. How often do you think of the Holy Spirit's role in your everyday life? As you look back on your life, can you see how he affected you, even though you weren't aware of him?

VERSES TO MEMORIZE

And I will ask the Father, and he will give you another Counselor to be with you forever. He is the Spirit of truth. The world is unable to receive him because it doesn't see him or know him. But you do know him, because he remains with you and will be in you. (Jn 14:16–17 CSB)

APPLY WHAT YOU'VE LEARNED

Share your experience with your group or a friend of when you were born again. Or share your experience of the rivers of living waters flowing from within you. If these experiences are unknown to you, talk about it with God and a Christian friend or pastor.

Bibliography

Akala, Adesola. "Sonship, Sending, and Subordination in the Gospel of John." In *Trinity without Hierarchy: Reclaiming Nicene Orthodoxy in Evangelical Theology*, edited by Michael F. Bird and Scott Harrower, 23–37. Grand Rapids: Kregel Academic, 2019.

Anderson, Paul N. *The Christology of the Fourth Gospel*. WUNT 2/78. Tubingen: Mohr Siebeck, 1996.

Ball, David Mark. *"I Am" in John's Gospel: Literary Function, Background, and Theological Implications*. JSNTSS 124. Sheffield: Sheffield Academic, 1996.

Balla, Peter. *The Child-Parent Relationship in the New Testament and its Environment*. WUNT 155.Tübingen: Mohr Siebeck, 2003.

Barker, Margaret. *The Great Angel: A Study of Israel's Second God*. Louisville: Westminster/John Knox, 1992.

Barrett, C. K. "'The Father is Greater than I' (John 14:28): Subordinationist Christology in the New Testament." In *Essays on John*, 19–36. London: SPCK, 1982.

Bauckham, Richard. *Jesus and the Eyewitnesses: The Gospels as Eyewitness Testimony*. 2nd ed. Grand Rapids: Eerdmans, 2017.

———. *Jesus and the God of Israel: God Crucified and Other Studies on the New Testament's Christology of Divine Identity*. Grand Rapids: Eerdmans, 2008.

———. "Monotheism and Christology in the Gospel of John." In *Contours of Christology in the New Testament*, edited by Richard Longenecker, 148–66. Grand Rapids: Eerdmans, 2005.

———. *The Testimony of the Beloved Disciple: Narrative, History, and Theology in the Gospel of John*. Grand Rapids: Baker Academic, 2007.

Bauer, W., et al. *A Greek-English Lexicon of the New Testament and Other Early Christian Literature*. 3rd ed. Chicago: University of Chicago Press, 2000.

Beale, G.K., and D.A. Carson, eds. *Commentary on the New Testament use of the Old Testament*. Grand Rapids: Baker Academic, 2007.

Belleville, Linda L. "'Son' Christology in the New Testament." In *The New Evangelical Subordinationism? Perspectives on the Equality of God the Father and God the Son*, edited by Dennis W. Jowers and H. Wayne House, 59–81. Eugene, OR: Wipf and Stock, 2012.

Berlin, Adelle, and Marc Zvi Brettler, eds. *The Jewish Study Bible*. New York: Oxford University Press, 2004.

Bernard, David K. *Essentials of Oneness Theology*. Hazelwood, MO: Word Aflame, 1985.

Bird, Michael F. "Preface: Theologians of a Lesser Son." In *Trinity without Hierarchy: Reclaiming Nicene Orthodoxy in Evangelical Theology*, edited by Michael F. Bird and Scott Harrower, 23–37. Grand Rapids: Kregel Academic, 2019.

Blass, F., et al. *A Greek Grammar of the New Testament and Other Early Christian Literature*. Chicago: University of Chicago Press, 1961.

Block, Daniel I. "Marriage and Family in Ancient Israel." In *Marriage and Family in the Biblical World*, edited by Ken M. Campbell, 33–102. Downers Grove, IL: Inter Varsity, 2003.

Blomberg, Craig L. *The Historical Reliability of John's Gospel: Issues & Commentary*. Downers Grove, IL: IVP, 2001.

Bock, Darrell L. "Jesus as Blasphemer." In *Who Do My Opponents Say I am? An Investigation of the Accusations against Jesus*, edited by Scot McKnight and Joseph B. Modic, 76–94. LNTS 327. London: T. & T. Clark, 2008.

Boettner, Loraine. *Studies in Theology*. Philadelphia: Presbyterian and Reformed, 1947.

Boyarin, Daniel. *The Jewish Gospels: The Story of the Jewish Christ*. New York: New Press, 2012.

Brown, Michael L. *Answering Jewish Objections to Jesus, Vol. 2: Theological Objections*. Grand Rapids: Baker, 2000.

———. *Answering Jewish Objections to Jesus, Vol. 3: Theological Objections*. Grand Rapids: Baker, 2003.

Brown, Raymond E. *The Community of the Beloved Disciple*. New York: Paulist, 1979.

———. *The Death of the Messiah*. 2 vols. New York: Doubleday, 1994.

———. *The Gospel According to John I-XII*. Anchor Bible 29A. Garden City, NY: Doubleday, 1966.

———. *An Introduction to the Gospel of John*, edited by Francis J. Moloney. New York: Doubleday, 2003.

Burge, Gary M. *The Anointed Community: The Holy Spirit in the Johannine Tradition*. Grand Rapids: Eerdmans, 1987.

Buzzard, Anthony F., and Charles F. Hunting. *The Doctrine of the Trinity: Christianity's Self-inflicted Wound*. Lanham, MD: International Scholars, 1998.

Capes, David B. *The Divine Christ: Paul, the Lord Jesus, and the Scriptures of Israel*. Grand Rapids: Baker Academic, 2018.

Carson, D. A. *The Gospel According to John*. Grand Rapids: Eerdmans, 1991.

———. *Jesus the Son of God*. Wheaton, IL: Crossway, 2012.

———. "Matthew." In *The Expositor's Bible Commentary*. Vol. 9. Revised ed. Edited by Tremper Longman III and David E. Garland, 23–670. Grand Rapids: Zondervan, 2010.

Carson, D. A., and Douglas Moo. *An Introduction to the New Testament*. 2nd ed. Grand Rapids: Zondervan, 2005.

Charlesworth, James H. "The Johannine Community and Its Jewish Background." *Studies in Philosophy and Theology* 38.1 (2013) 46–51.

Charlesworth, James H. ed. *The Old Testament Pseudepigrapha*. 2 vols. New York: Doubleday, 1983, 1985.

Culpepper, R. Alan. *John, the Son of Zebedee: The Life of a Legend*. Minneapolis: Fortress, 2000.

Dixon, Danny André. "An Arian Response to a Trinitarian View." In *The Son of God: Three Views on the Identity of Jesus*, edited by Charles Lee Irons et al., 23–33. Eugene, OR: Wipf and Stock, 2015.

————. "An Arian View: Jesus, the Life-Given Son of God." In *The Son of God: Three Views on the Identity of Jesus*, edited by Charles Lee Irons et al., 65–83. Eugene, OR: Wipf and Stock, 2015.

Dodd, C. H. *The Interpretation of the Fourth Gospel*. Cambridge: Cambridge University Press, 1953.

Dunn, James D. G. *Christology in the Making: A New Testament Inquiry into the Origins of the Doctrine of the Incarnation*. 2nd ed. London: SCM, 1989.

————. *Did the First Christians Worship Jesus? The New Testament Evidence*. Louisville: Westminster John Knox, 2010.

Durham, John I. *Exodus*. WBC 3. Waco, TX: Word, 1987.

Erickson, Millard J. *Who's Tampering with the Trinity? An Assessment of the Subordination Debate*. Grand Rapids: Kregel, 2009.

Fee, Gordon D. *God's Empowering Presence: The Holy Spirit in the Letters of Paul*. Peabody, MA: Hendrickson, 1994.

Fletcher-Louis, Crispin. *Jesus Monotheism, Vol. 1. Christological Origins: The Emerging Consensus and Beyond*. Eugene, OR: Cascade, 2015.

Fredriksen, Paula. "Mandatory Retirement: Ideas in the Study of Christian Origins Whose Time has Come to Go." In *Israel's God and Rebecca's Children: Christology and Community in Early Judaism and Christianity: Essays in Honor of Larry W. Hurtado and Alan F. Segal*, edited by David B. Capes et al., 25–38. Waco, TX: Baylor, 2007.

Fromm, Erich. *Man for Himself: An Inquiry into the Psychology of Ethics*. New York: Henry Holt, 1947.

Gieschen, Charles A. *Angelomorphic Christology: Antecedents and Early Evidence*. Leiden: Brill, 1998.

Giles, Kevin. *The Eternal Generation of the Son: Maintaining Orthodoxy in Trinitarian Theology*. Downers Grove, IL: IVP, 2012.

————. *Jesus and the Father: Modern Evangelicals Reinvent the Doctrine of the Trinity*. Grand Rapids: Zondervan, 2006.

Goldsworthy, Graeme. *The Son of God and the New Creation*. Wheaton, IL: Crossway, 2015.

Gordley, Matthew E. *New Testament Christological Hymns: Exploring Texts, Contexts, and Significance*. Downers Grove, IL: InterVarsity, 2018.

Grabbe, Lester L. *Judaic Religion in the Second Temple Period: Belief and Practice from Exile to Yavneh*. London: Routledge, 2000.

Greene, John T. *The Role of the Messenger and Message in the Ancient Near East*. Brown Judaic Studies 169. Atlanta: Scholars, 1989.

Gruenler, Royce Gordon. *The Trinity in the Gospel of John: A Thematic Commentary on the Fourth Gospel*. Grand Rapids: Baker, 1986.

Hamerton-Kelly, Robert. *Preexistence, Wisdom, and the Son of Man: A Study of the Idea of Preexistence in the New Testament*. SNTSMS 21. London: Cambridge, 1973.

Harner, Philip B. *The "I Am" of the Fourth Gospel: A Study in Johannine Usage and Thought*. FBBS 26. Philadelphia: Fortress, 1970.

————. "Qualitative Anarthrous Predicate Nouns: Mark 15:39 and John 1:1." *Journal of Biblical Literature* 92 (1973) 75–87.

Harris, Murray J. *Exegetical Guide to the Greek New Testament: John*. Nashville: B&H Academic, 2015.

————. *Jesus as God: The New Testament Use of Theos in Reference to Jesus.* Grand Rapids: Baker, 1992.

Harvey, A. E. *Jesus and the Constraints of History.* Philadelphia: Westminster, 1982.

Hays, Richard B. *Reading Backwards: Figural Christology and the Fourfold Gospel Witness.* Waco, TX: Baylor University Press, 2014.

Heiser, Michael S. *The Unseen Realm: Recovering the Supernatural Worldview of the Bible.* Bellingham, WA: Lexham, 2015.

Hengel, Martin. *The Four Gospels and the One Gospel of Jesus Christ.* Harrisburg, PA: Trinity Press International, 2000.

Hill, Wesley. *Paul and the Trinity: Persons, Relations, and the Pauline Letters.* Grand Rapids: Eerdmans, 2015.

Hurley, James B. *Man and Woman in Biblical Perspective.* Grand Rapids: Zondervan, 1981.

Hurtado, Larry W. *How on Earth Did Jesus Become a God? Historical Questions about Earliest Devotion to Jesus.* Grand Rapids: Eerdmans, 2005.

————. *One God, One Lord: Early Christian Devotion and Ancient Jewish Monotheism.* 2nd ed. Edinburgh: T. & T. Clark, 1998.

Irons, Charles Lee. "A Lexical Defense of the Johannine 'Only Begotten.'" In *Retrieving Eternal Generation,* edited by Fred Sanders and Scott R. Swain, 98–116. Grand Rapids: Zondervan, 2017.

Josephus, Flavius. *The New Complete Works of Josephus.* Translated by William Whiston. Rev. ed. Grand Rapids: Kregel, 1999.

Jowers, Dennis W., and H. Wayne House, eds. *The New Evangelical Subordinationism? Perspectives on the Equality of God the Father and God the Son.* Eugene, OR: Wipf and Stock, 2012.

Keener, Craig S. *The Gospel of John: A Commentary.* 2 vols. Peabody, MA: Hendrickson, 2003.

————. "Subordination within the Trinity: John 5:18 and 1 Cor 15:28." In *The New Evangelical Subordinationism? Perspectives on the Equality of God the Father and God the Son,* edited by Dennis W. Jowers and H. Wayne House, 39–58. Eugene, OR: Wipf and Stock, 2012.

Klink, Edward W., III. *The Sheep of the Fold: The Audience and Origin of the Gospel of John.* SNTSMS 141. Cambridge: Cambridge University Press, 2007.

Koehler, Ludwig, and Walter Baumgartner. *The Hebrew and Aramaic Lexicon of the Old Testament.* Study Edition. Translated and edited by M. E. J. Richardson. 2 vols. Leiden: Brill, 2001.

Lewis, C. S. *Mere Christianity.* New York: HarperCollins, 1952.

Lincoln, Andrew T. "Trials, Plots and the Narrative of the Fourth Gospel." *Journal for the Study of the New Testament* 56 (1994) 3–30.

Loader, William. *Jesus in John's Gospel: Structure and Issues in Johannine Christology.* Grand Rapids: Eerdmans, 2017.

Makin, Mark. "Philosophical Models of Eternal Generation." In *Retrieving Eternal Generation,* edited by Fred Sanders and Scott R. Swain, 98–116. Grand Rapids: Zondervan, 2017.

Martyn, J. L. *History and Theology in the Fourth Gospel.* 3rd ed. Louisville: Westminster, 2003.

Matthews, Victor H. "Marriage and Family in the Ancient Near East." In *Marriage and Family in the Biblical World,* edited by Ken M. Campbell, 1–32. Downers Grove, IL: Inter Varsity, 2003.

McGrath, James F. *The Only True God: Early Christian Monotheism in its Jewish Context.* Chicago: University of Illinois Press, 2009.

McHugh, John F. *John 1–4.* International Critical Commentary. London: T. & T. Clark, 2009.

Meier, Samuel A. *The Messenger in the Ancient Semitic World.* Harvard Semitic Monographs 45. Atlanta: Scholars, 1988.

Moody, Dale. "God's Only Son: The Translation of John 3:16 in the Revised Standard Version." *Journal of Biblical Literature* 72 (1953) 213–19.

Motyer, Stephen. *"Your Father the Devil?" A New Approach to John and "The Jews."* Carlisle, UK: Paternoster, 1994.

Neusner, Jacob. *A Rabbi Talks with Jesus.* 2nd ed. Montreal: McGill-Queen's University Press, 2000.

Neusner, Jacob, trans. *The Mishnah: A New Translation.* New York: Yale University Press, 1988.

Neyrey, Jerome H. *The Gospel of John.* The New Cambridge Bible Commentary. New York: Cambridge University Press, 2007.

Norris, David S. *I AM: A Oneness Pentecostal Theology.* Hazelwood, MO: WAP Academic, 2009.

Ovey, Michael J. *Your Will be Done: Exploring Eternal Subordination, Divine Monarchy and Divine Humility.* London: Latimer Trust, 2016.

Philo. *The Works of Philo.* Translated by C. D. Yonge. Peabody, MA: Hendrickson, 1993.

Pitre, Brant. *The Case for Jesus: The Biblical and Historical Evidence for Christ.* New York: Image, 2014.

Porter, Wendy J. "Creeds and Hymns." In *Dictionary of New Testament Background,* edited by Craig A. Evans and Stanley Porter, 231–38. Downers Grove, IL: InterVarsity, 2000.

Reeder, Caryn A. "Family." In *Dictionary of Jesus and the Gospels,* edited by Joel B. Green et al., 262–65. Downers Grove, IL: InterVarsity, 2013.

Reeves, Michael. *Delighting in the Trinity: An Introduction to the Christian Faith.* Downers Grove, IL: IVP Academic, 2012.

Rheaume, Randy. *An Exegetical and Theological Analysis of the Son's Relationship to the Father in John's Gospel: God's Equal and Subordinate.* Lewiston, NY: Edwin Mellen, 2015.

———."John's Jesus on Life Support: His Filial Relationship in John 5:26 and 6:57." *Trinity Journal* 33 NS (2012) 49–75.

Rich, Mark J. "The Contextual Key to John 20:28: Unlocking the Meaning of Thomas' Confession." In *Divine Truth or Human Tradition: A Reconsideration of the Orthodox Doctrine of the Trinity in Light of the Hebrew and Christian Scriptures,* edited by Patrick Navas, 589–601. Bloomington, IN: AuthorHouse, 2011.

Robertson, A. T. *A Grammar of the Greek New Testament in the Light of Historical Research.* Nashville: Broadman, 1934.

Robinson, John A. T. *The Priority of John,* edited by J. F. Coakley. Oak Park, IL: Meyer-Stone, 1985.

Ronning, John. *The Jewish Targums and John's Logos Theology.* Peabody, MA: Hendrickson, 2010.

Sanders, Fred. *The Triune God.* New Studies in Dogmatics. Grand Rapids: Zondervan, 2016.

Schäfer, Peter. *The Jewish Jesus: How Judaism and Christianity Shaped Each Other*. Princeton: Princeton University Press, 2012.

Segal, Alan F. *Two Powers in Heaven: Early Rabbinic Reports about Christianity and Gnosticism*. Studies in Judaism in Late Antiquity 25. Leiden: Brill, 1977.

Sidebottom, E. M. *The Christ of the Fourth Gospel: In the Light of First-Century Thought*. London: SPCK, 1961.

Smith, Dustin R. "A Socinian View: Jesus, the Human Son of God." In *The Son of God: Three Views on the Identity of Jesus.*, edited by Charles Lee Irons et al., 127–79. Eugene, OR: Wipf and Stock, 2015.

Spence, Alan. *Christology: A Guide for the Perplexed*. New York: T. & T. Clark, 2008.

Stafford, Greg. *Jehovah's Witnesses Defended to Scholars and Critics*. 3rd ed. Murrieta, CA: Elihu, 2009.

Stauffer, Ethelbert. *Jesus and His Story*. Translated by Richard and Clara Winston. New York: Knopf, 1959.

Suetonius. *The Twelve Caesars*. Translated by Robert Graves. London: Penguin, 2007.

Thompson, Marianne Meye. *The God of the Gospel of John*. Grand Rapids: Eerdmans, 2001.

———. *The Promise of the Father: Jesus and God in the New Testament*. Louisville: Westminster/John Knox, 2000.

Wainwright, Arthur W. *The Trinity in the New Testament*. London: SPCK, 1962.

Wallace, Daniel B. *Greek Grammar Beyond the Basics*. Grand Rapids: Zondervan, 1996.

Waltke, Bruce K., and Charles Yu. *An Old Testament Theology: An Exegetical, Canonical and Thematic Approach*. Grand Rapids: Zondervan, 2007.

Ware, Bruce A., and John Stare, eds. *One God in Three Persons: Unity of Essence, Distinction of Persons, Implications for Life*. Wheaton IL: Crossway, 2015.

Warfield, Benjamin Breckinridge. "The Biblical Doctrine of the Trinity." In *Biblical and Theological Studies*, edited by Samuel G. Craig, 22–59. Philadelphia: Presbyterian and Reformed, 1968.

Wenham, Gordon J. *Genesis 1–15*. WBC 1. Waco, TX: Word, 1987.

White, James R. *The Forgotten Trinity: Recovering the Heart of Christian Belief*. Minneapolis: Bethany, 1998.

White, John. *Changing on the Inside*. Ann Arbor, MI: Servant, 1991.

Williams, Catrin H. *I Am He: The Interpretation of "Ani Hu" in Jewish and Early Christian Literature*. Tübingen: Mohr-Siebeck, 2000.

———. "'I Am' or 'I Am He'? Self Declaratory Pronouncements in the Fourth Gospel and Rabbinic Tradition." In *Jesus in the Johannine Tradition*, edited by Robert T. Fortna and Tom Thatcher, 343–52. Louisville: Westminster, 2001.

Wink, Walter. *The Engaging Powers: Discernment and Resistance in a World of Domination*. Minneapolis: Augsburg Fortress, 1992.

Witherington, Ben, III. *John's Wisdom: A Commentary on the Fourth Gospel*. Philadelphia: Westminster, 1995.

Wright, N. T. *Jesus and the Victory of God*. Christian Origins and the Question of God 2. Minneapolis: Fortress, 1996.

———. *Paul and the Faithfulness of God*. 2 vols. Christian Origins and the Question of God 4. Minneapolis: Fortress, 2013.

Yancey, Philip. *The Jesus I Never Knew*. Grand Rapids: Zondervan, 1995.

Young, F. W. "A Study on the Relationship of Isaiah to the Fourth Gospel." *Zeitschrift fu* 46.3–4 (1953) 215–33.

Subject Index

Made in the USA
Monee, IL
09 February 2021